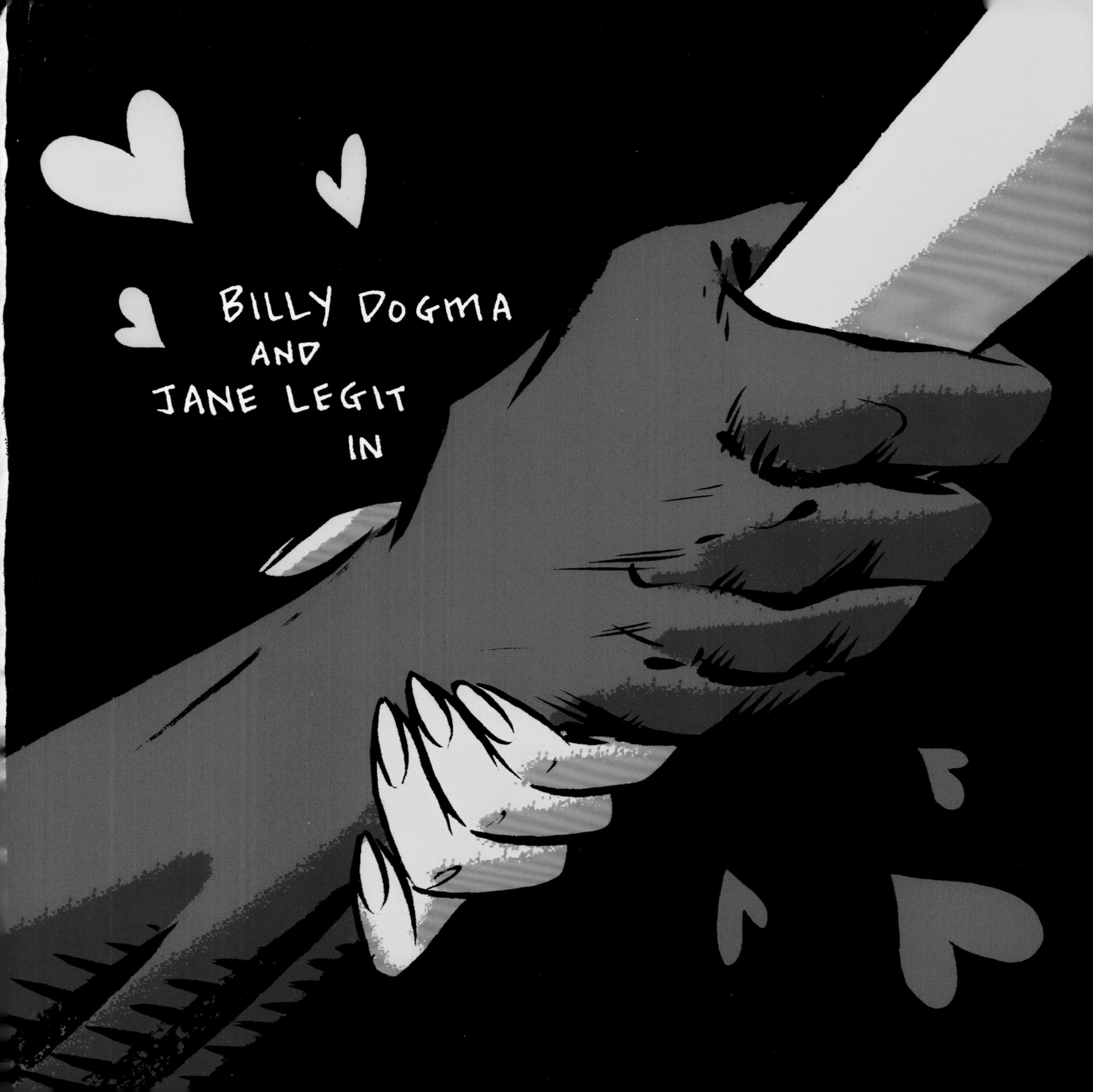
BILLY DOGMA
AND
JANE LEGIT
IN

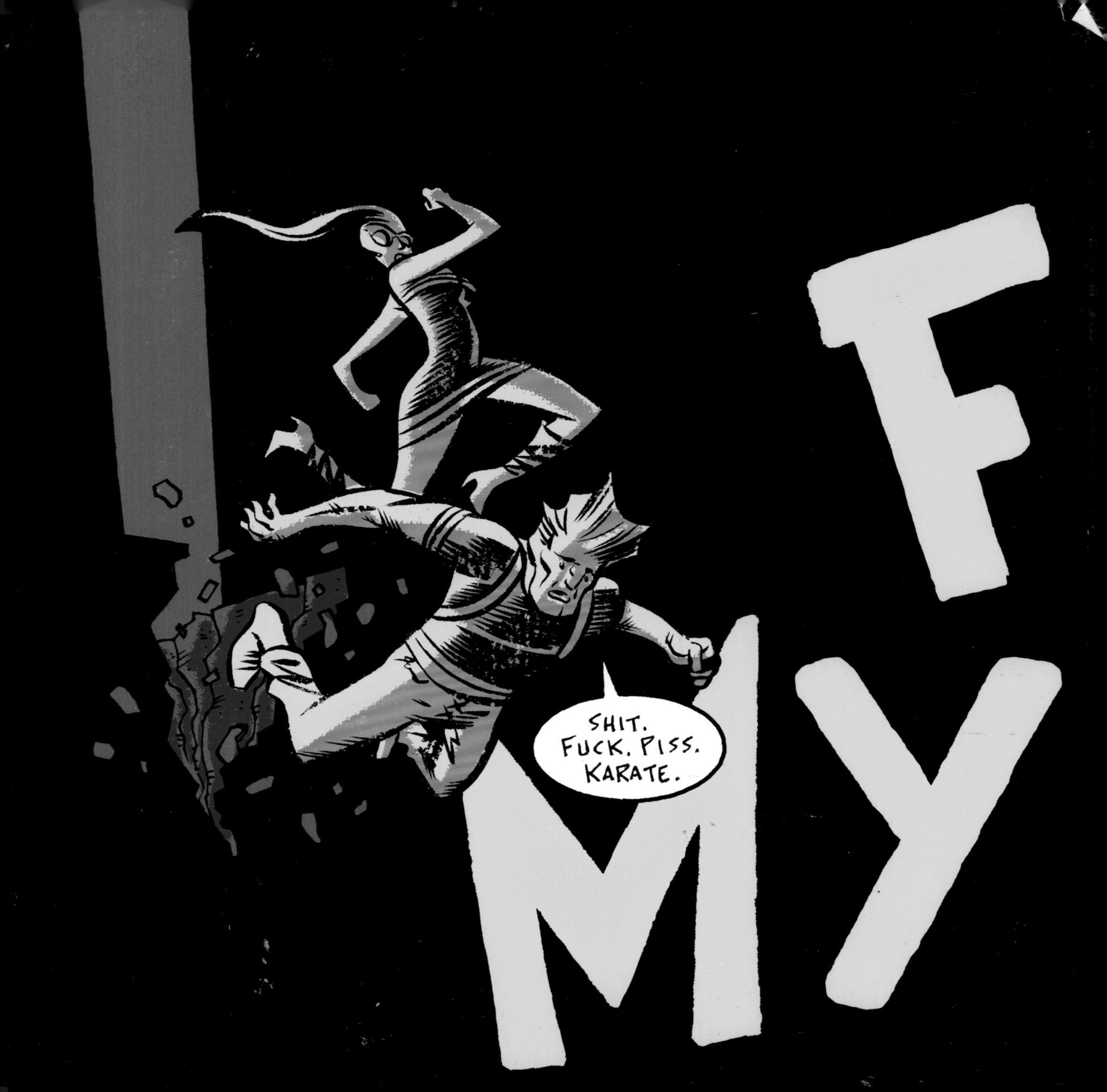
SHIT. FUCK. PISS. KARATE.
F
MY

EAR, DEAR

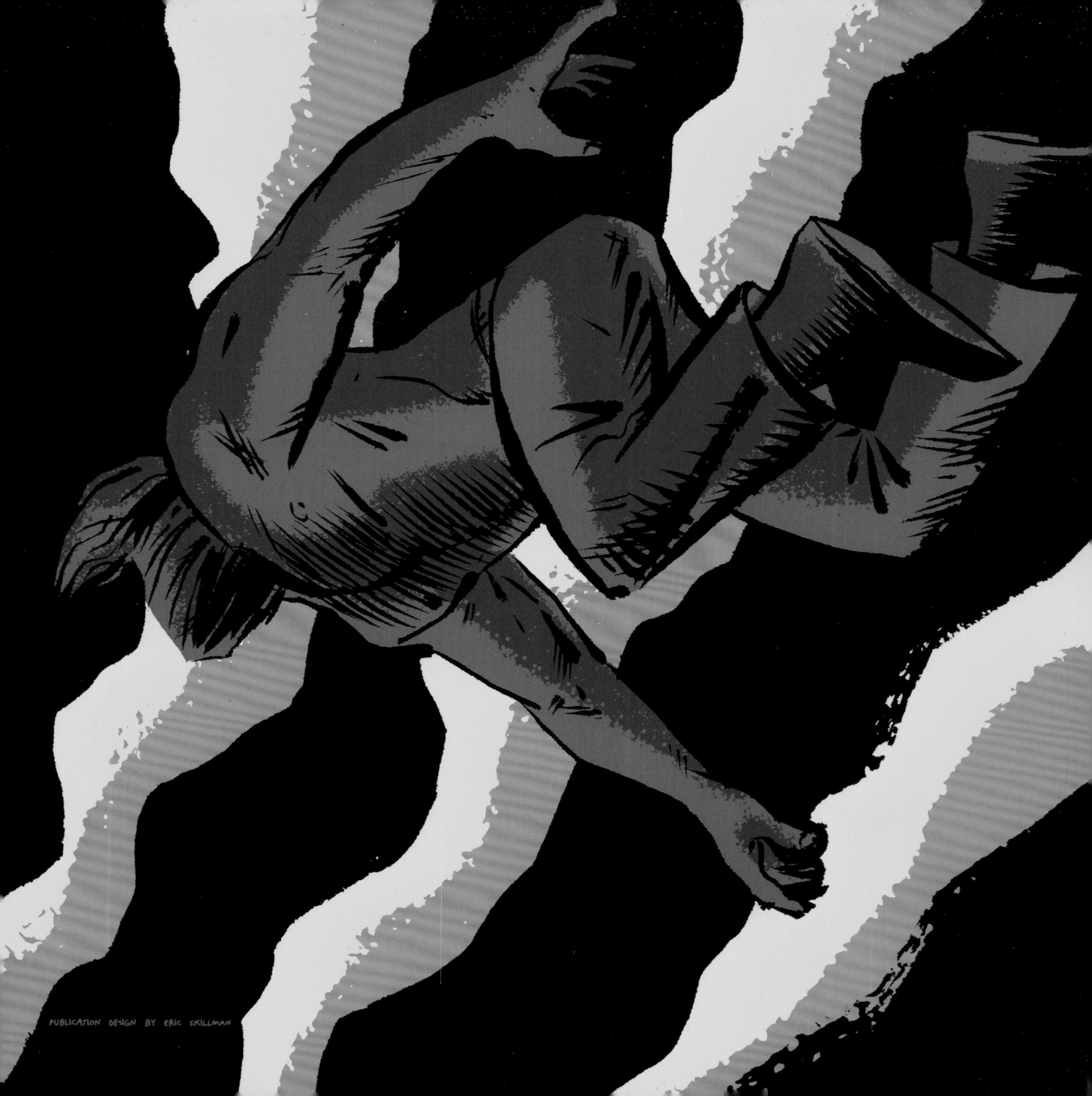

PUBLICATION DESIGN BY ERIC SKILLMAN

BY DEAN HASPIEL

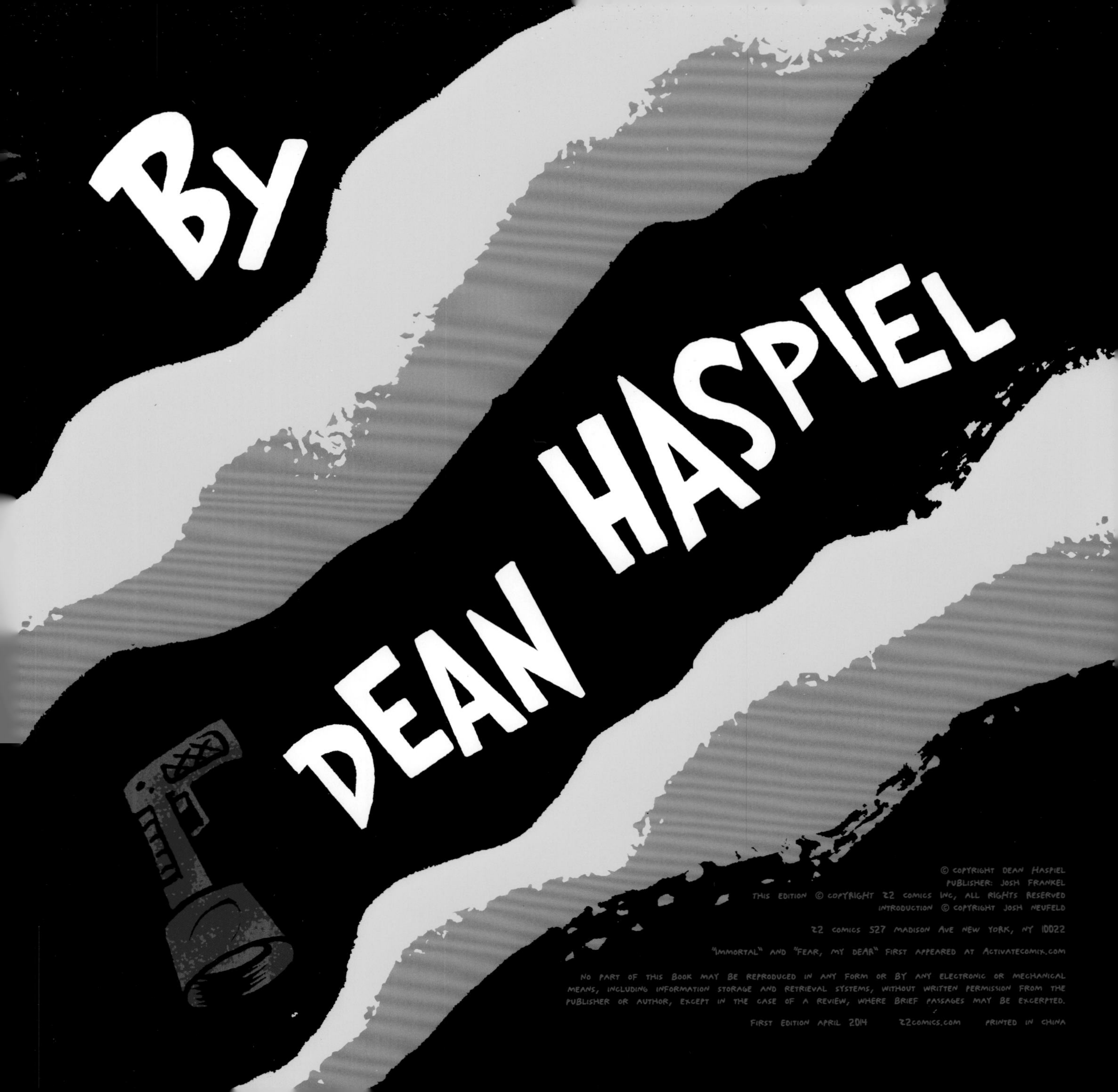

PUBLISHER: JOSH FRANKEL

22 COMICS 527 MADISON AVE NEW YORK, NY 10022

"IMMORTAL" AND "FEAR, MY DEAR" FIRST APPEARED AT ACTIVATECOMIX.COM

FIRST EDITION APRIL 2014 22COMICS.COM PRINTED IN CHINA

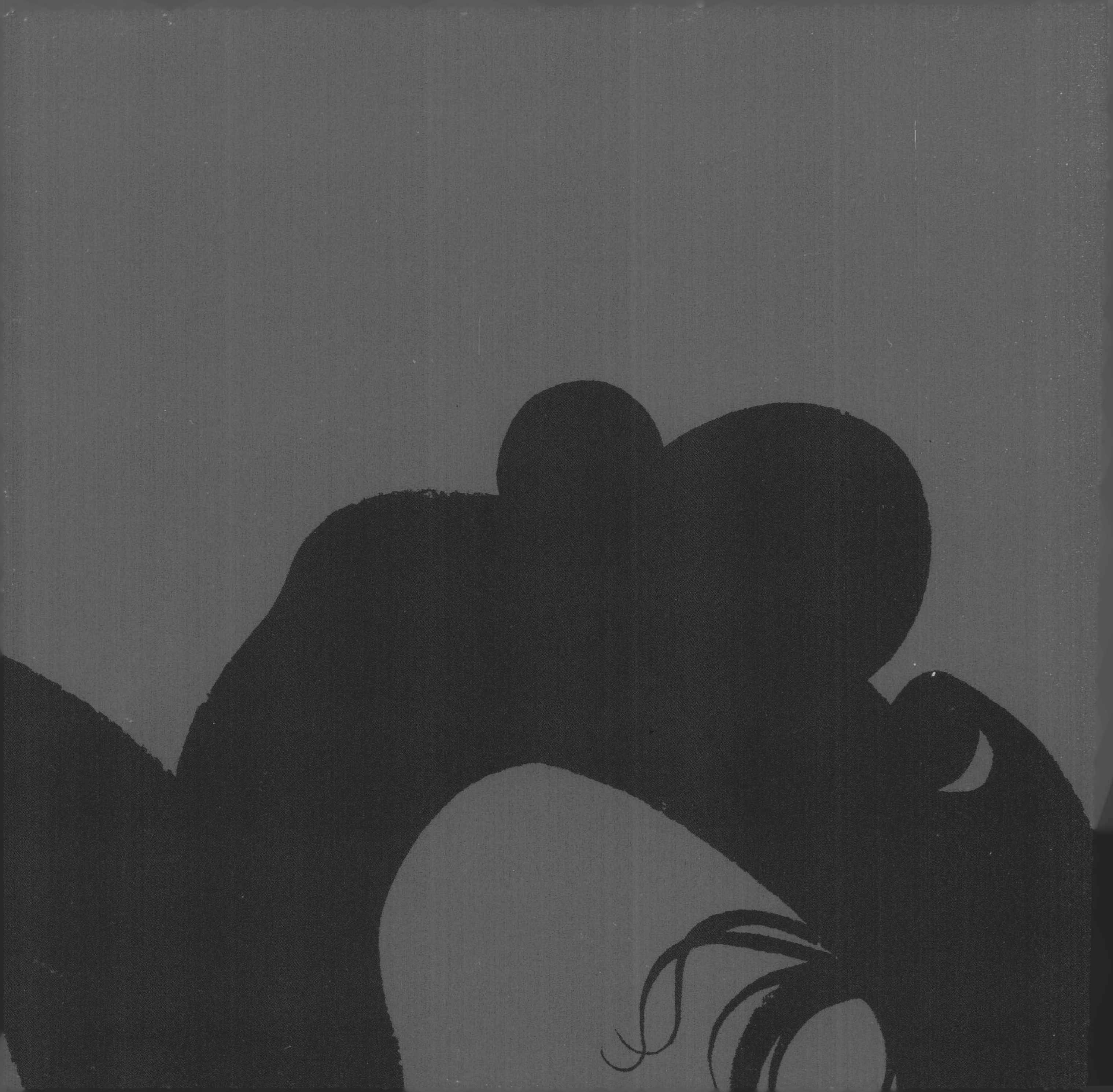

INTRODUCTION by Josh Neufeld

Friends, folks, and jackasses:

You are in for a treat: Dean Haspiel at the height of his powers. It's all here: Dino's spectacular storytelling, his gorgeous, stylish brushstrokes—and his iconic creation Billy Dogma in a way we've never seen him before: rebooted, stripped-down to his purest essence.

The original Billy was a philosopher for the 1990s, sounding off in his own unique way about the vagaries of fame, neighborliness, and the functional necessity of women's hips. There's a great moment in FEAR, MY DEAR when Billy pauses in the midst of furious action. He pauses, and he thinks! Before he acts! It's a first for the character, and it sparks a metamorphosis: the square-jawed philosopher transforms into a scruffy desert prophet. Billy Dogma 2.0 is all about the heart—and the hard lesson that "you don't get to love when you love like you love."

The primary object of Billy's love, of course, is the spectacularly bespectacled Jane Legit. And In "Immortal," the red-soaked opening story, Billy and Jane's "war of woo" is played out—disastrously—on the mean streets of Trip City. (Billy and Jane are reality stars without the mediating authority of television.) And all the inhabitants of Trip City, from the beat cops to the regulars over at Lucy's Bar, tell the tale. One of the great pleasures of all Billy Dogma stories is the language. Billy has always had the gift of gab—Jane too—and here we discover that apparently everyone in Trip City talks in the same lingo: part hard-boiled slang, part beat poetry. Thus we learn about "indulging a ruse," "a lonely monster sans purpose," and "steeping in seasons of cosmic love." Sometimes your only option is to laugh and scratch your head at Dino's unfathomable brilliance, but there's no doubt it rings a cryptic coda.

From "Immortal" we segue into the golden-accented tones of the title story, as Billy embarks on a vision quest to (literally) get his head on straight. I won't spoil the details of his heroic journey, but what emerges is Billy's "secret origin:" Who is he? Where does he come from? What's the deal with that Berserk Gun? Bite the bullet and take the bait—all shall be revealed.

Hopefully, your eyes are sensitive to feelings, because FEAR, MY DEAR is beautiful, funny, and guaranteed to make you go, "Awww"! I love Dino's Billy Dogma tales precisely because they're so completely different from my own work—fantastic, imagistic, and preoccupied by the BIG QUESTIONS. And after reading FEAR, MY DEAR, I bet you'll love them too.

FEAR, MY DEAR is Dino's most ambitious work to date. Harder than the hardest heart attack, it will spark the napalm in your apocalypse. So, sally forth, reader—it's as easy as hopscotch!

—Josh Neufeld, author of
A.D.: NEW ORLEANS AFTER THE DELUGE

PART ONE:

"IMMO

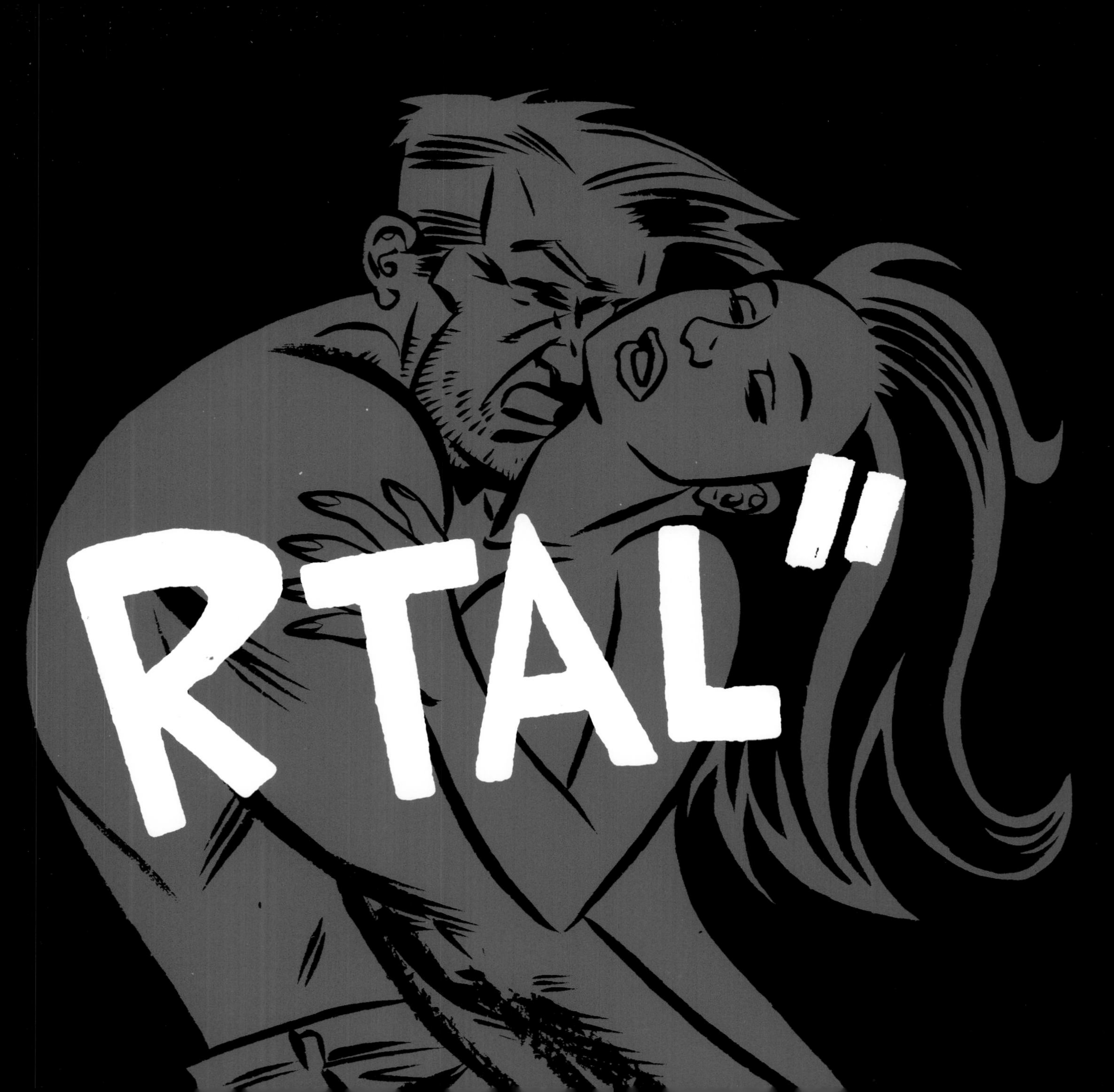
RTAL"

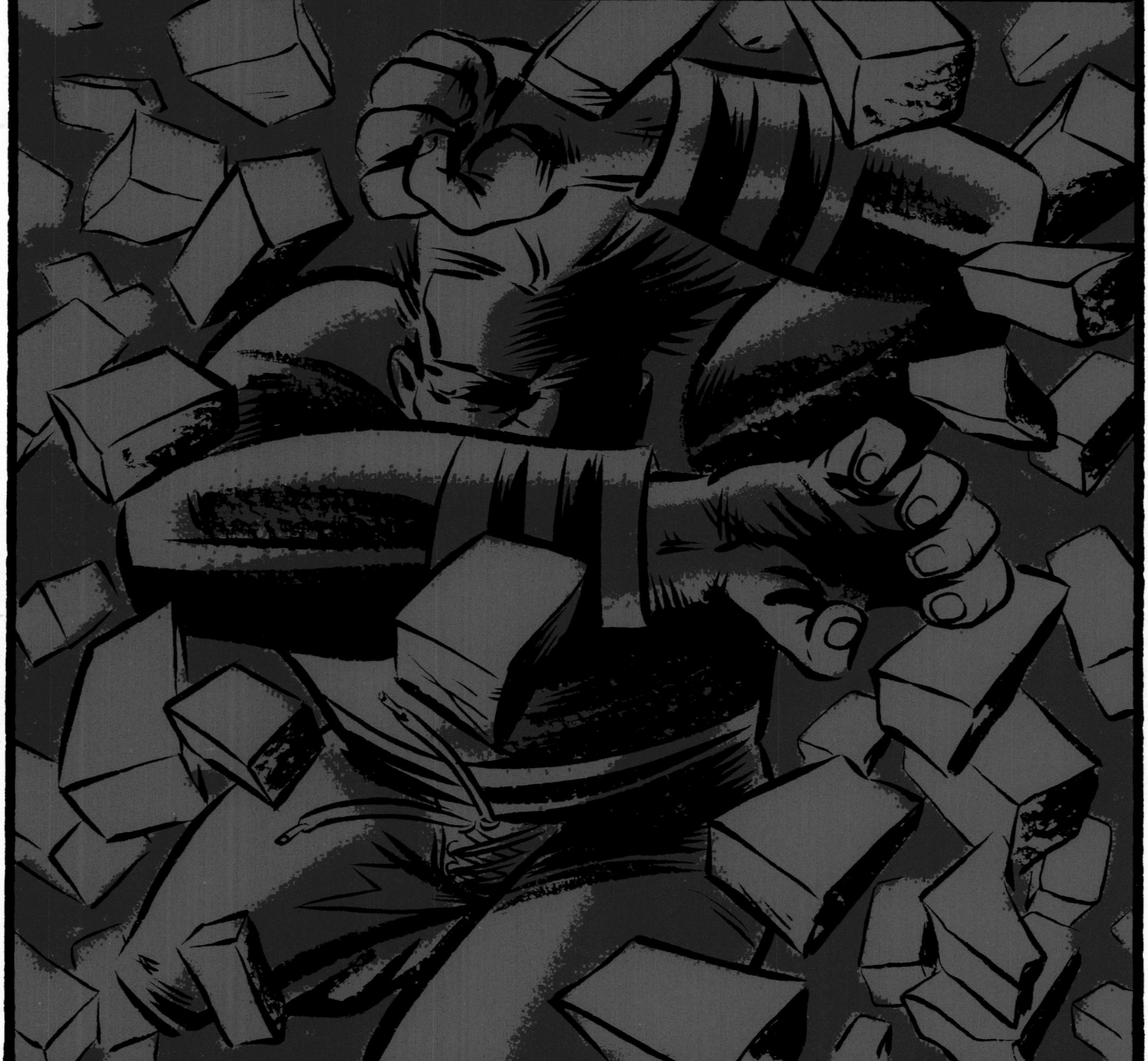

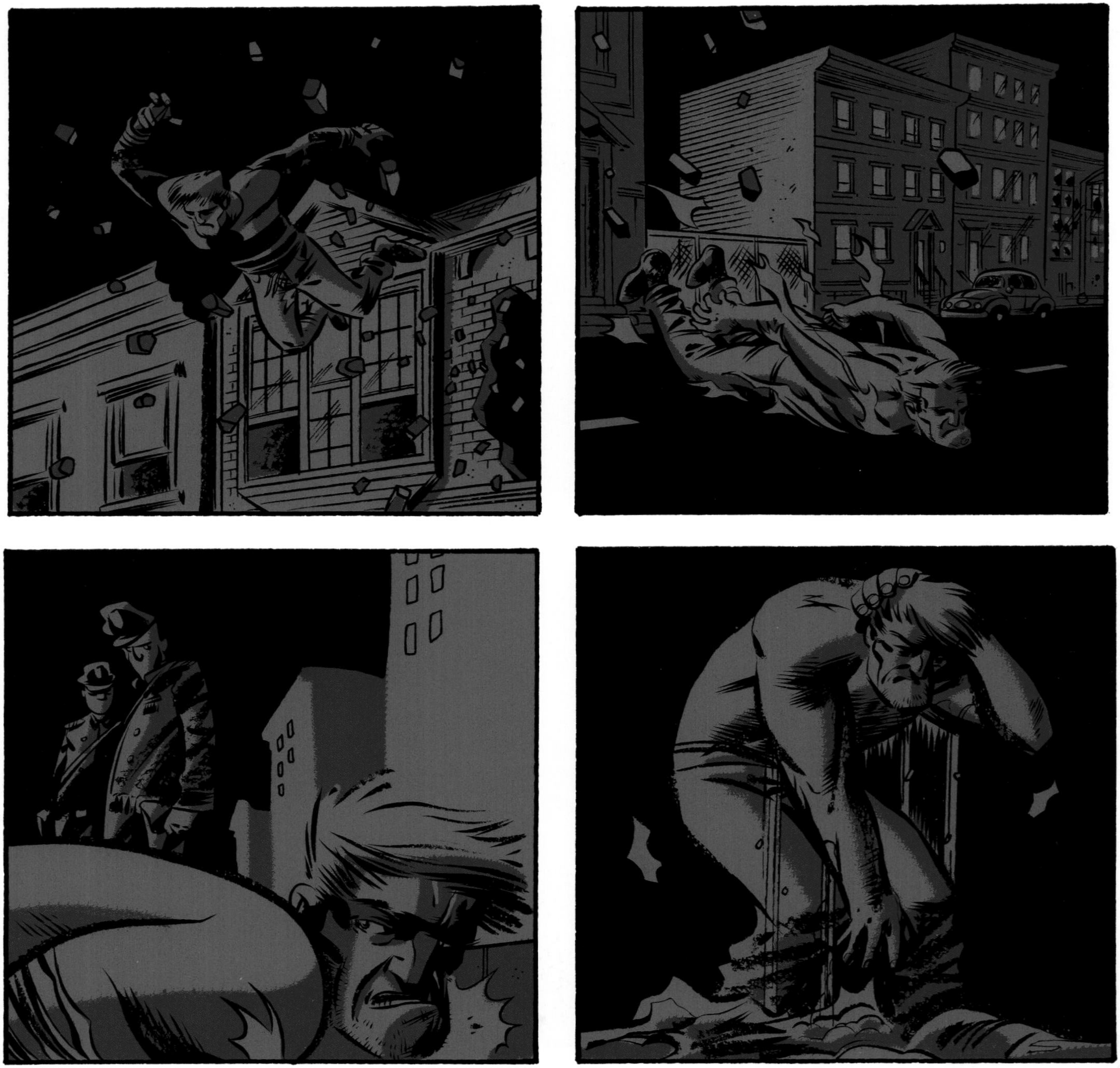

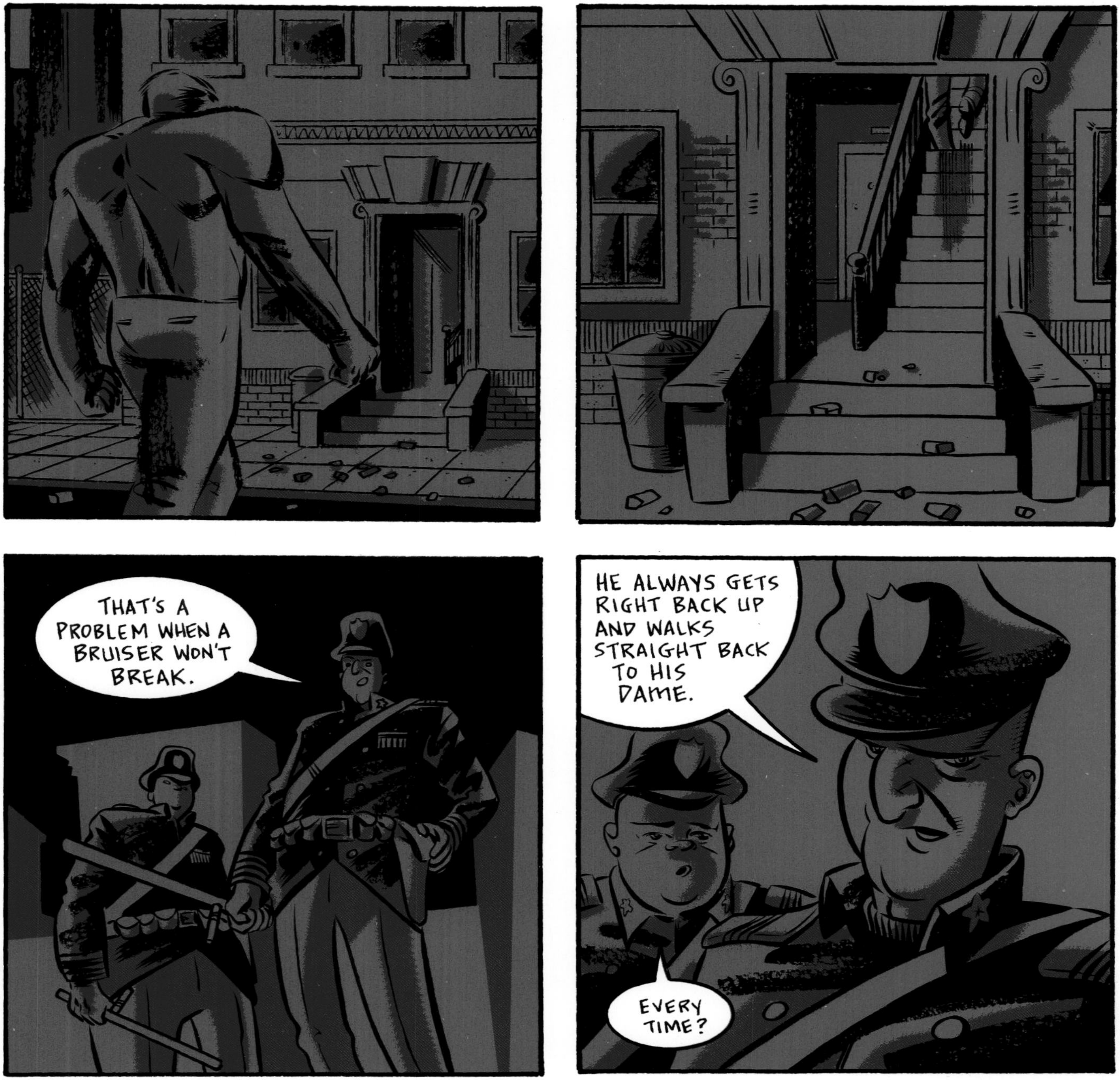
THAT'S A PROBLEM WHEN A BRUISER WON'T BREAK.
HE ALWAYS GETS RIGHT BACK UP AND WALKS STRAIGHT BACK TO HIS DAME.
EVERY TIME?

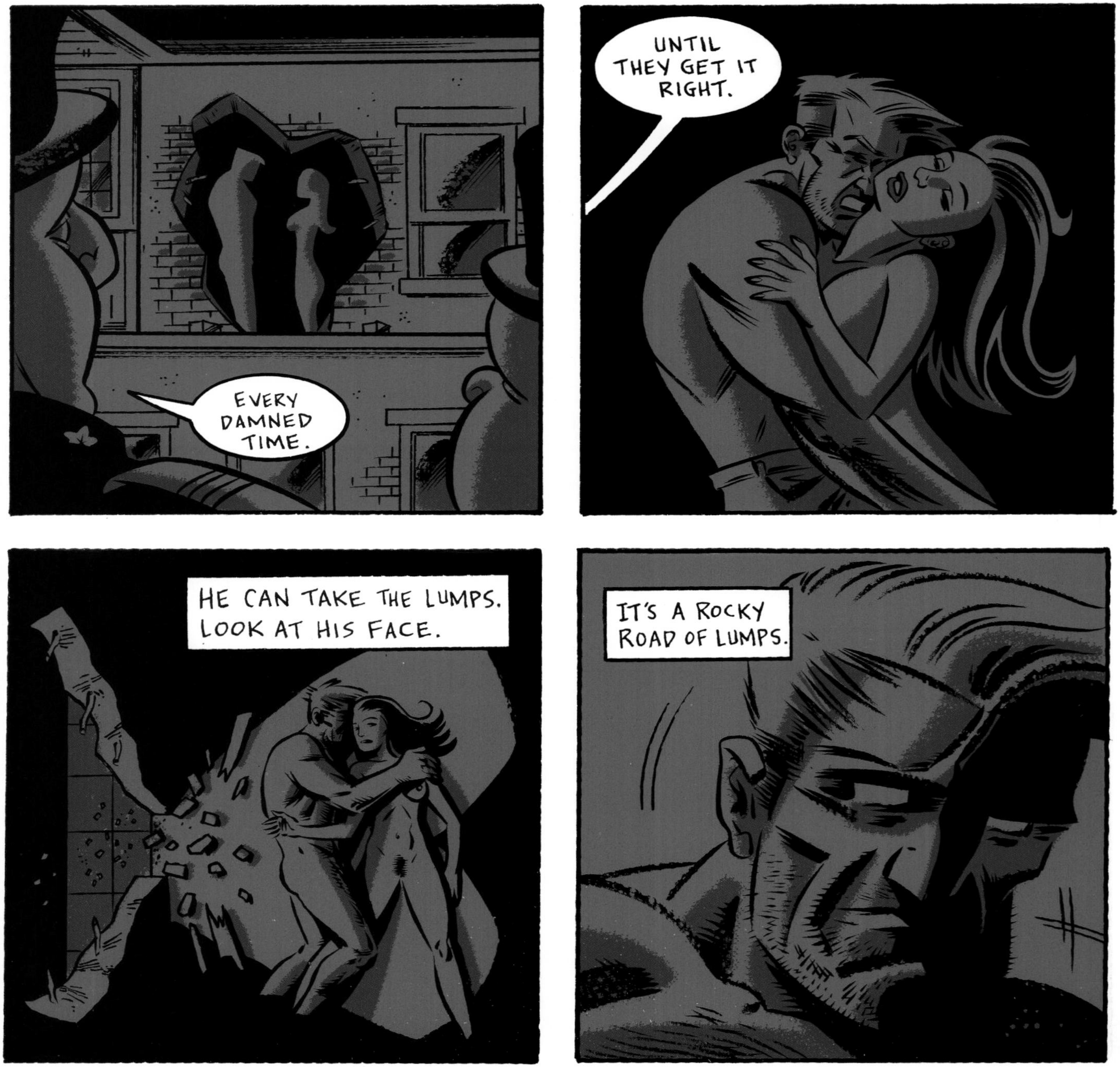
EVERY DAMNED TIME.
UNTIL THEY GET IT RIGHT.
HE CAN TAKE THE LUMPS. LOOK AT HIS FACE.
IT'S A ROCKY ROAD OF LUMPS.

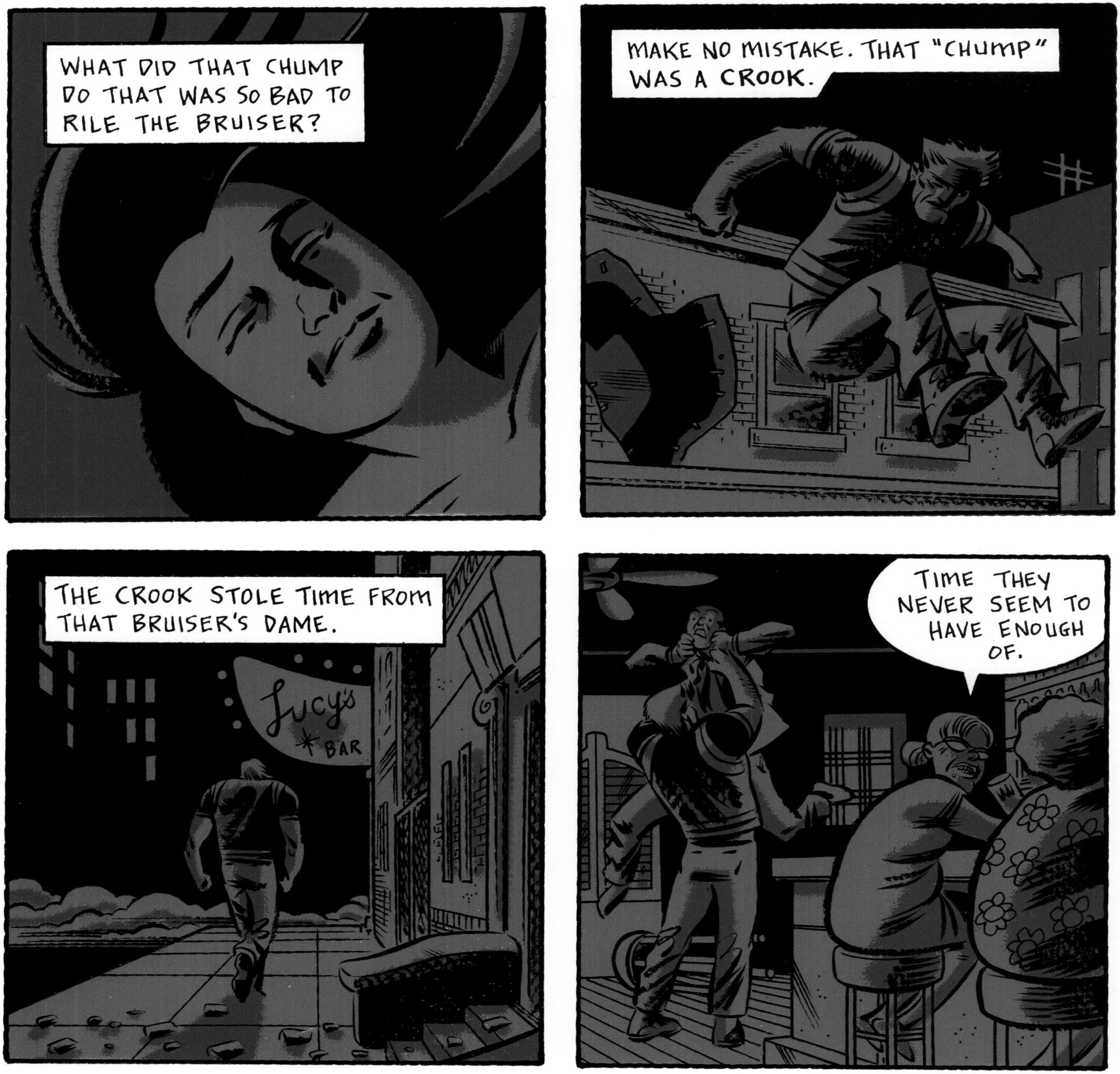
WHAT DID THAT CHUMP DO THAT WAS SO BAD TO RILE THE BRUISER?
MAKE NO MISTAKE. THAT "CHUMP" WAS A CROOK.
THE CROOK STOLE TIME FROM THAT BRUISER'S DAME.
Lucy's BAR
TIME THEY NEVER SEEM TO HAVE ENOUGH OF.

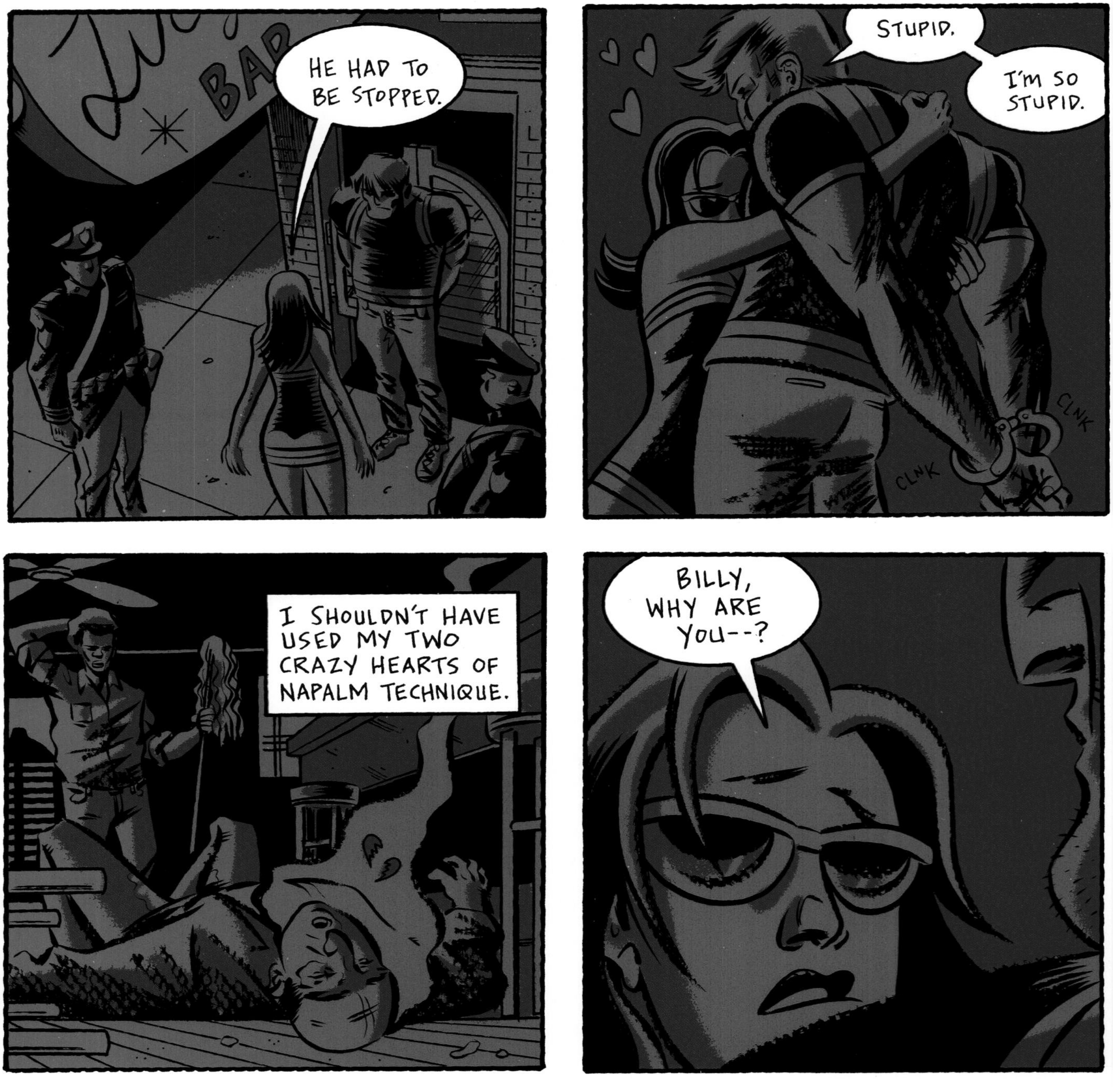
BAR
HE HAD TO BE STOPPED.
STUPID.
I'M SO STUPID.
CLNK
CLNK
I SHOULDN'T HAVE USED MY TWO CRAZY HEARTS OF NAPALM TECHNIQUE.
BILLY, WHY ARE YOU--?

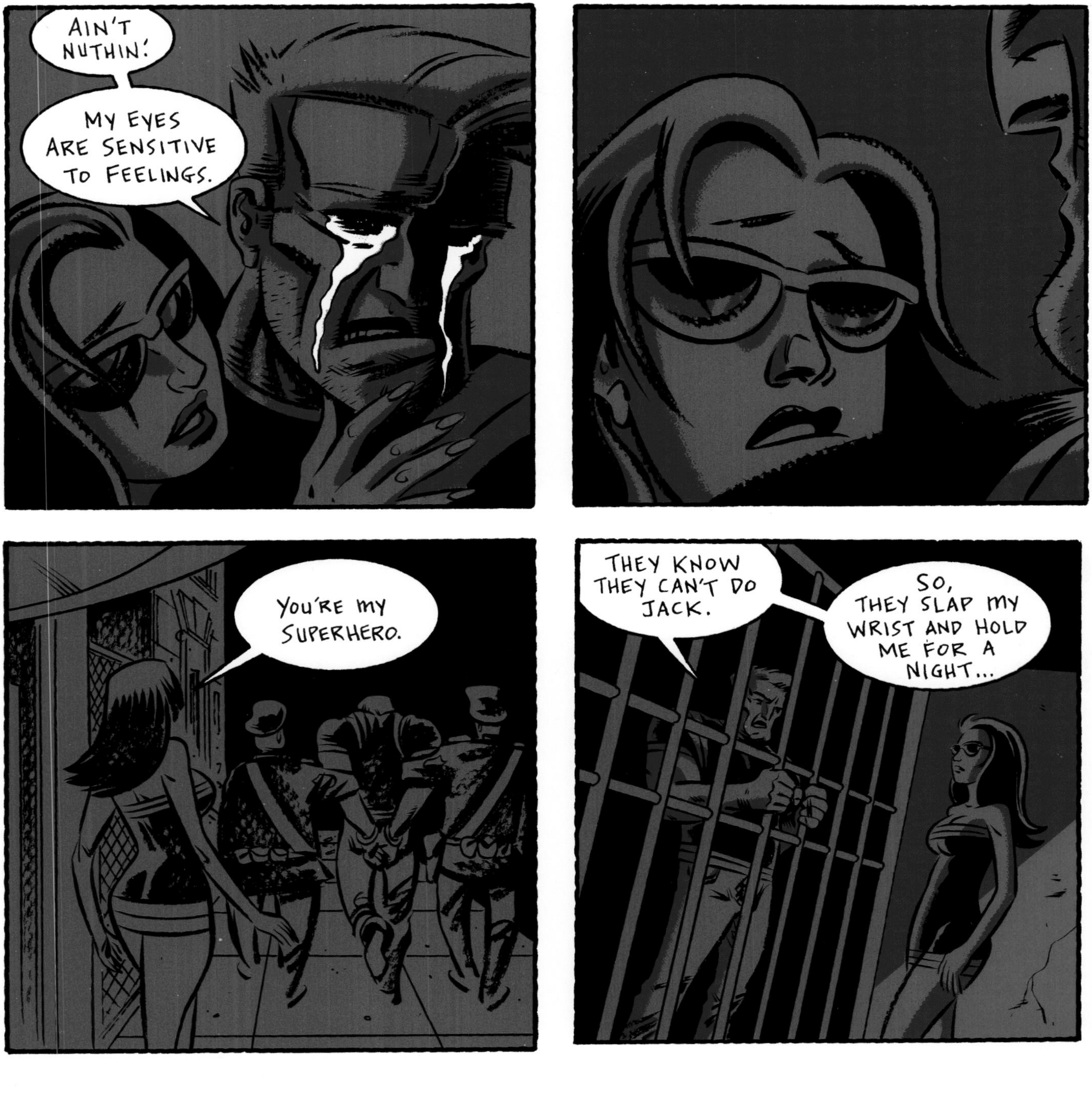
AIN'T NUTHIN'.
MY EYES ARE SENSITIVE TO FEELINGS.
YOU'RE MY SUPERHERO.
THEY KNOW THEY CAN'T DO JACK.
SO, THEY SLAP MY WRIST AND HOLD ME FOR A NIGHT...

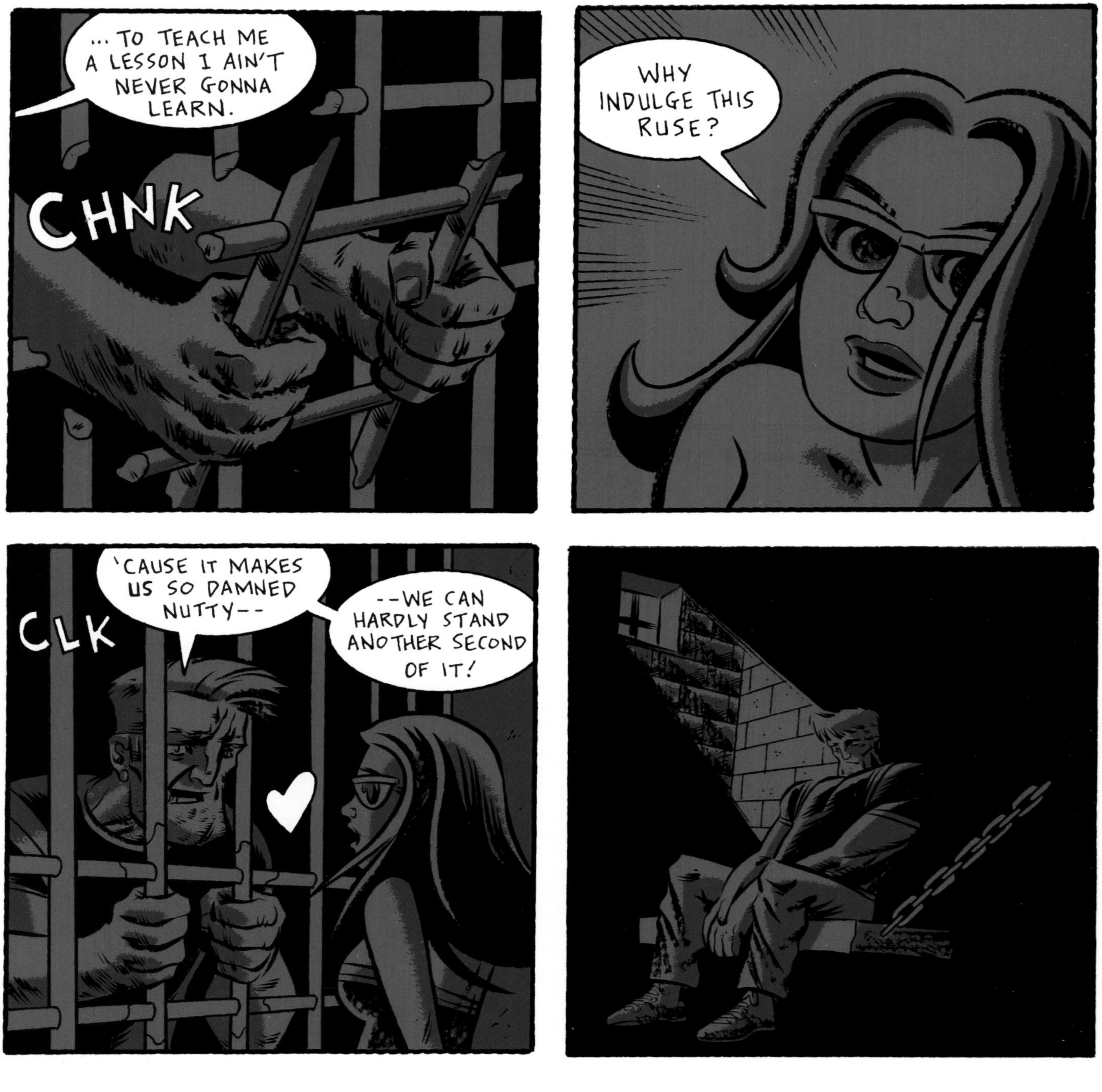
... TO TEACH ME A LESSON I AIN'T NEVER GONNA LEARN.
CHNK
WHY INDULGE THIS RUSE?
CLK
'CAUSE IT MAKES US SO DAMNED NUTTY--
--WE CAN HARDLY STAND ANOTHER SECOND OF IT!

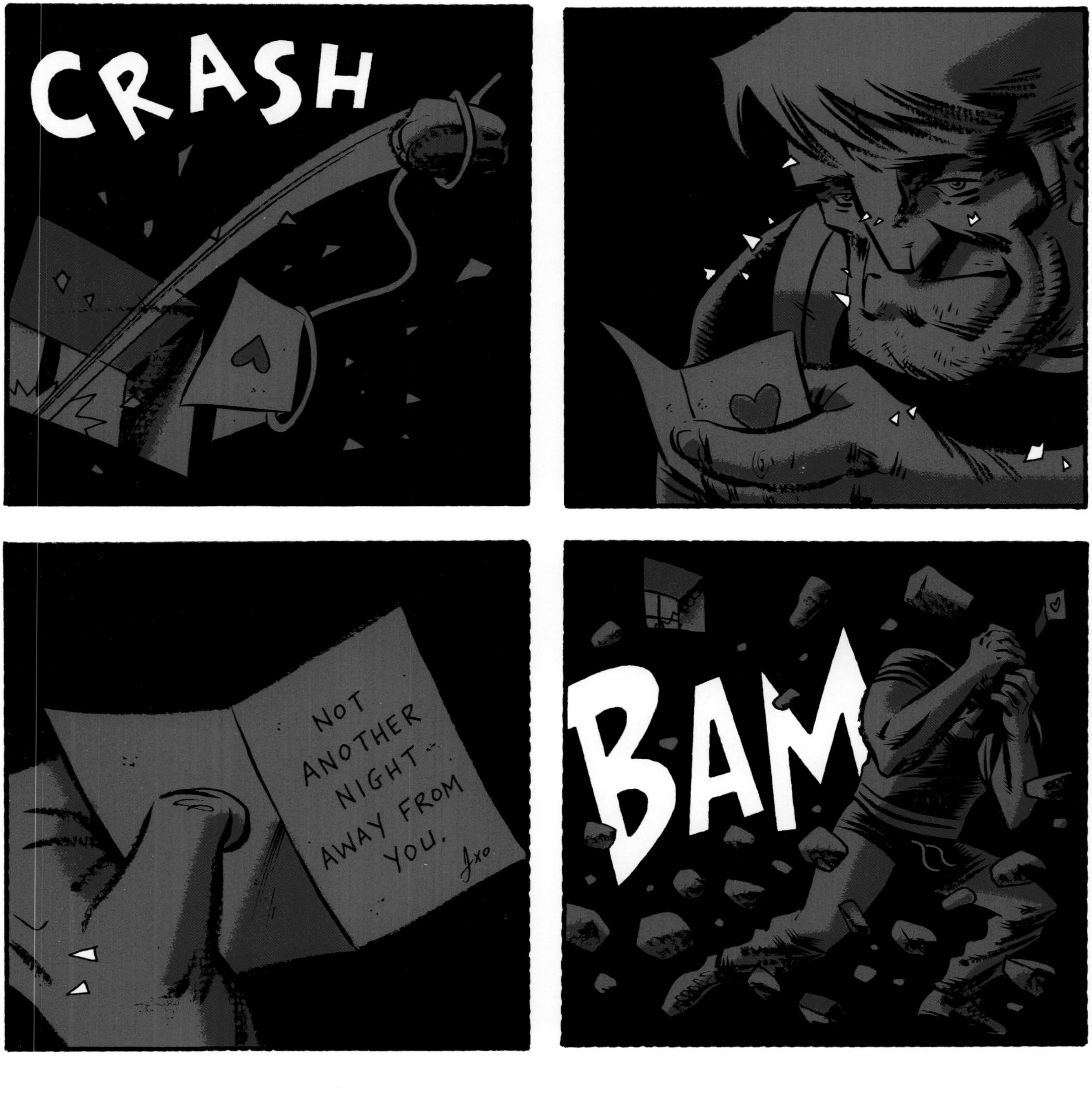
CRASH
NOT ANOTHER NIGHT AWAY FROM YOU.
Jxo
BAM

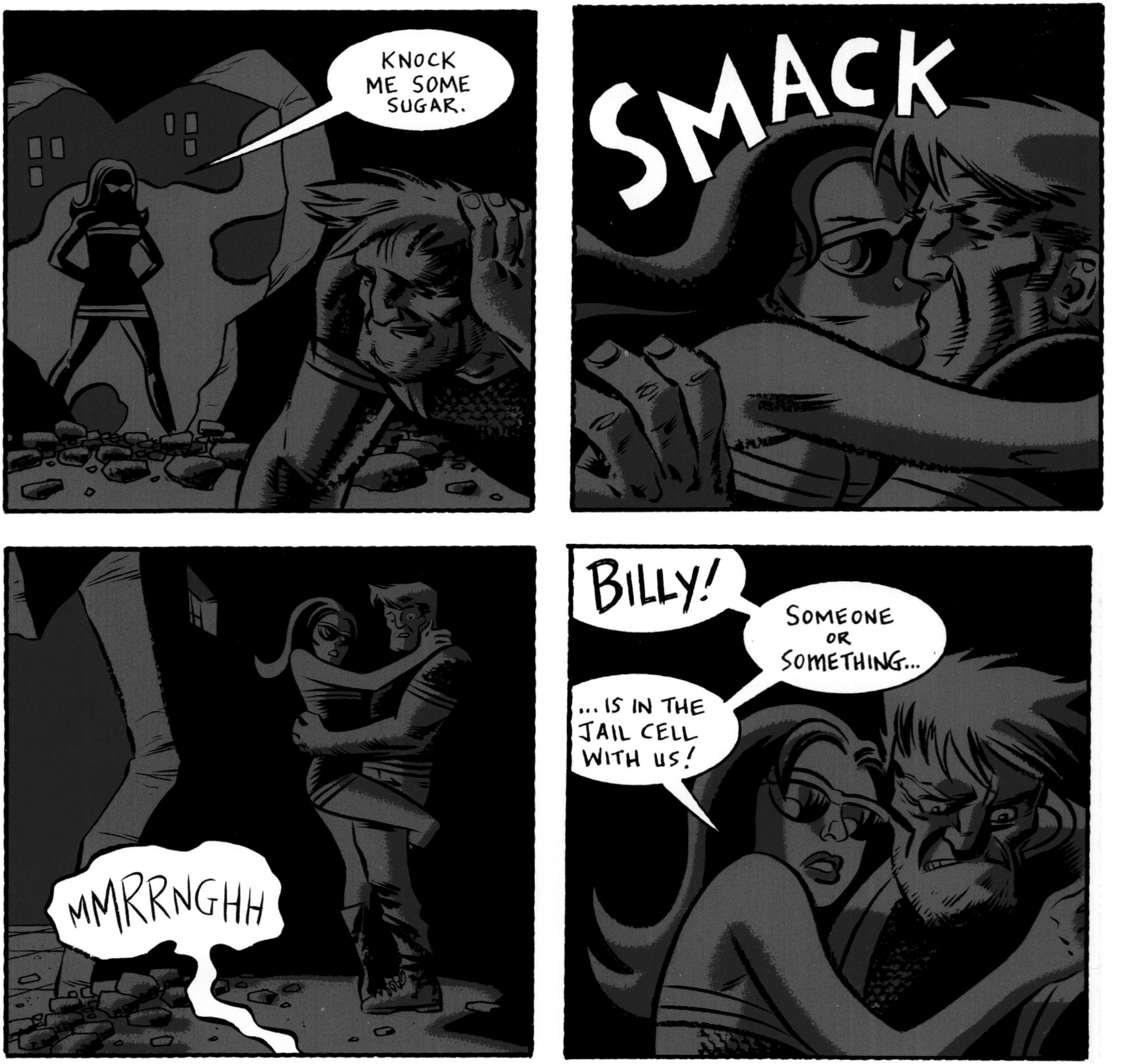
KNOCK ME SOME SUGAR.
SMACK
MMRRNGHH
BILLY!
SOMEONE OR SOMETHING...
...IS IN THE JAIL CELL WITH US!

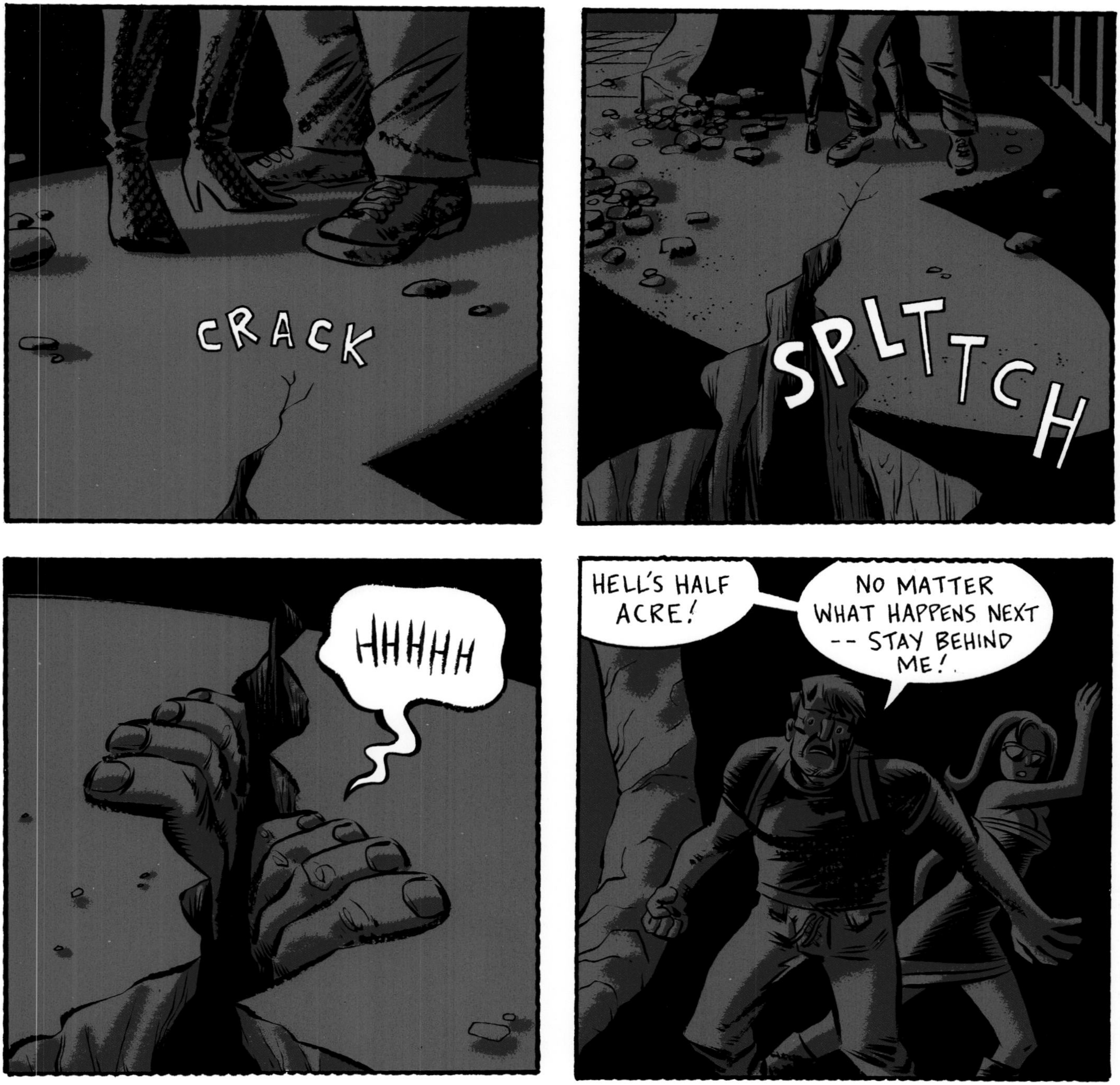
CRACK
SPLTTTCH
HHHHH
HELL'S HALF ACRE!
NO MATTER WHAT HAPPENS NEXT -- STAY BEHIND ME!

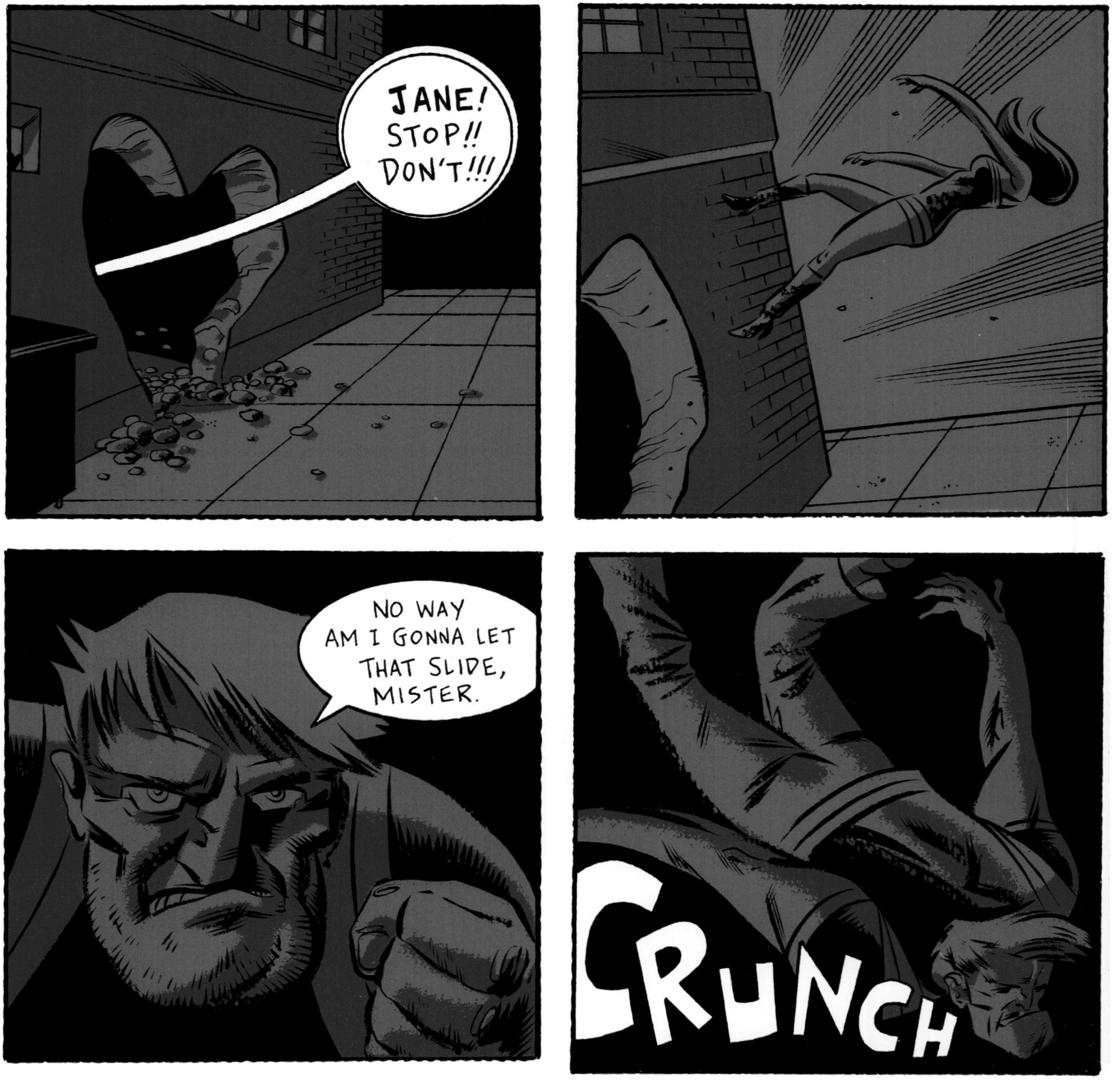
JANE! STOP!! DON'T!!!
NO WAY AM I GONNA LET THAT SLIDE, MISTER.
CRUNCH

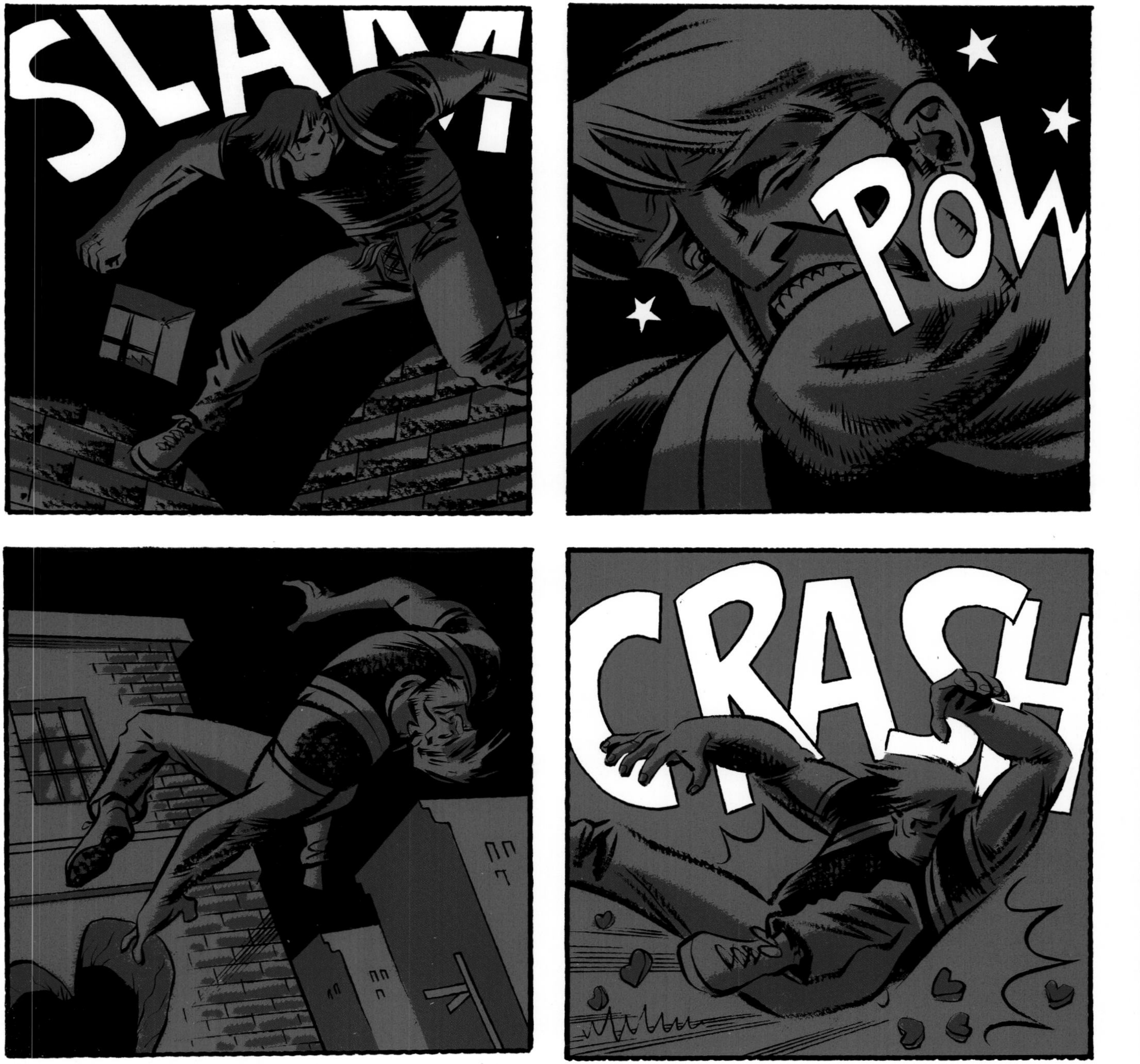
SLAM
POW
CRASH

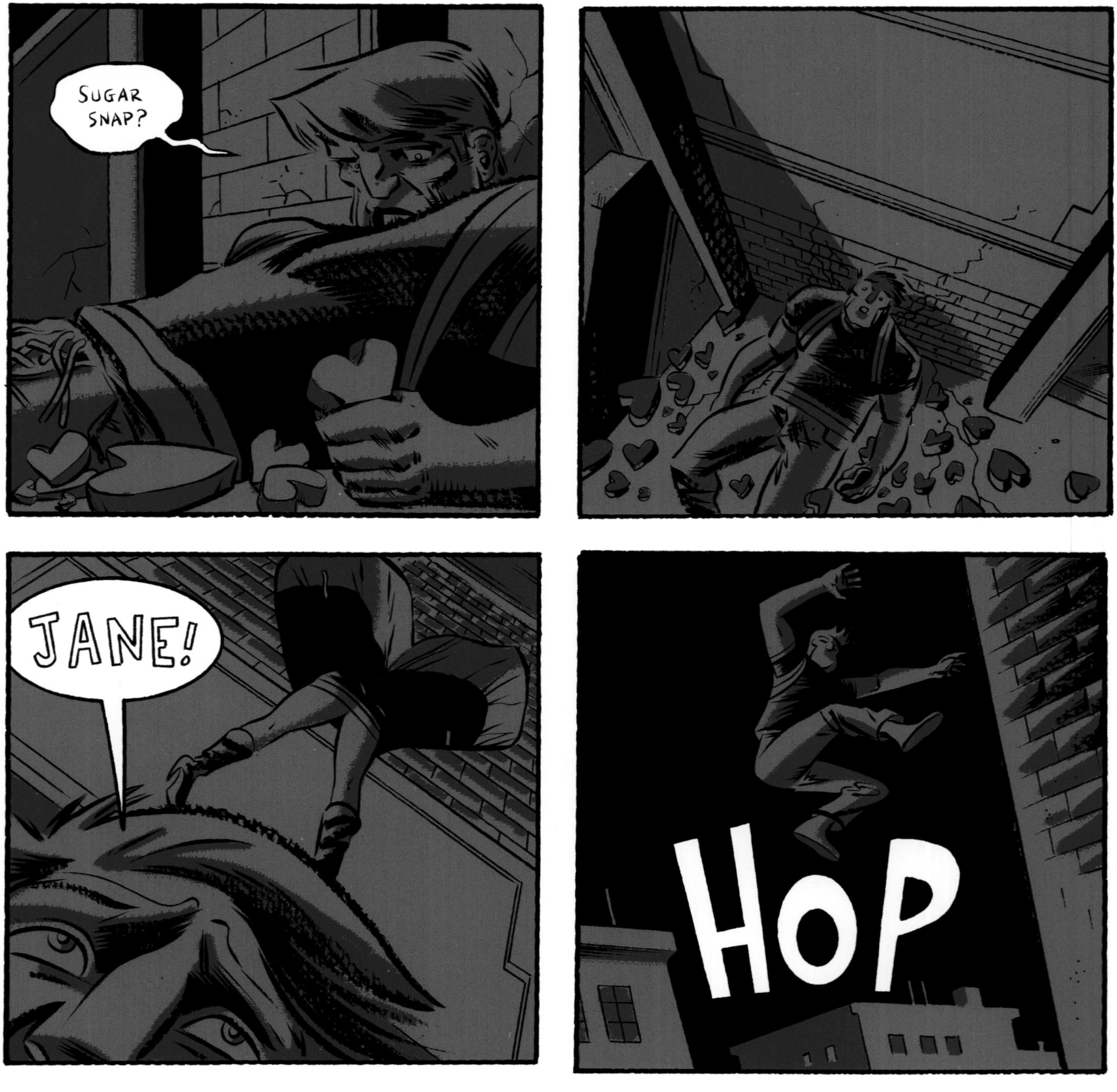
SUGAR SNAP?
JANE!
HOP

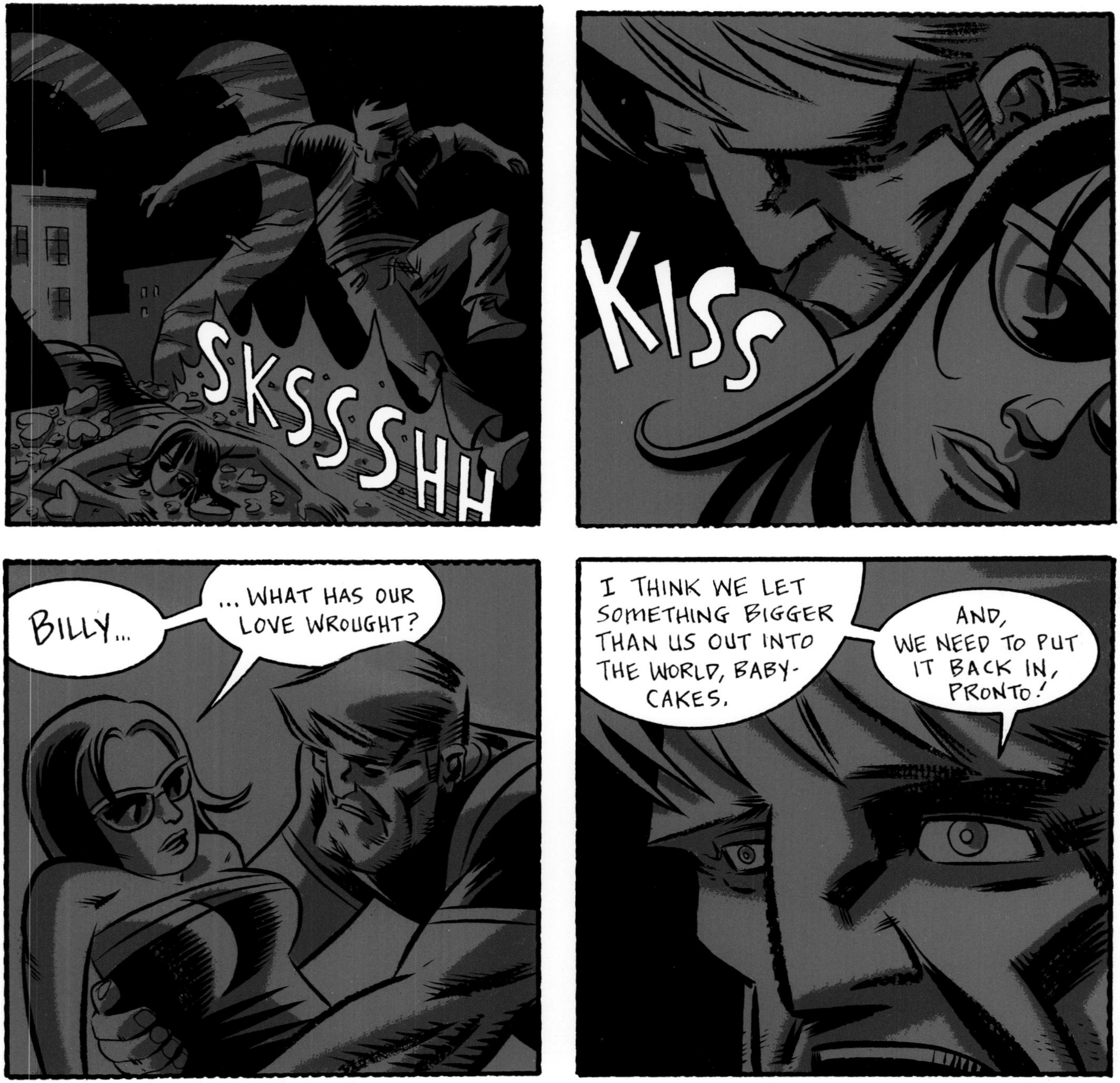
SKSSSHH
KISS
BILLY...
... WHAT HAS OUR LOVE WROUGHT?
I THINK WE LET SOMETHING BIGGER THAN US OUT INTO THE WORLD, BABY-CAKES.
AND, WE NEED TO PUT IT BACK IN, PRONTO!

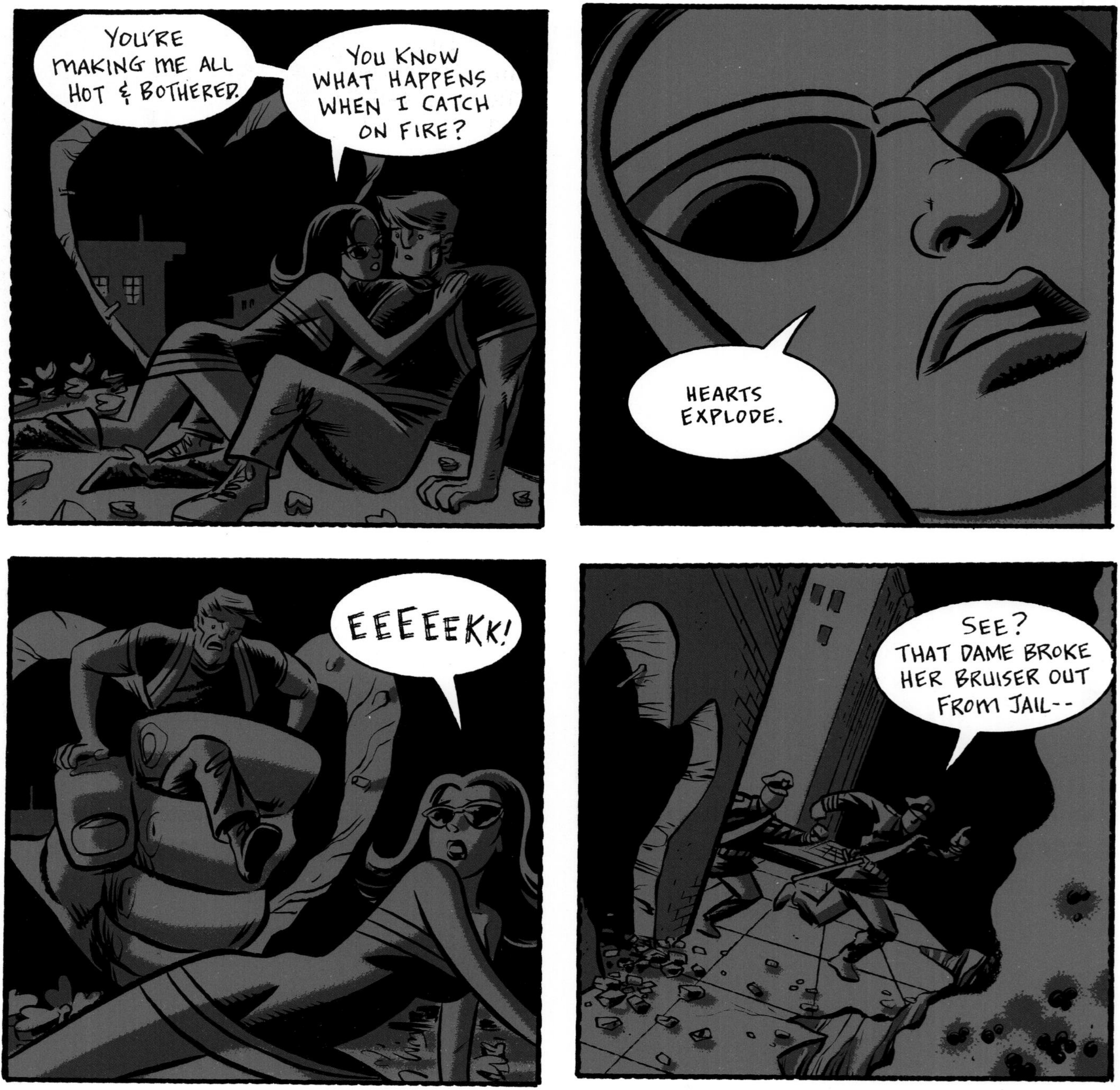
YOU'RE MAKING ME ALL HOT & BOTHERED.
YOU KNOW WHAT HAPPENS WHEN I CATCH ON FIRE?
HEARTS EXPLODE.
EEEEEKK!
SEE? THAT DAME BROKE HER BRUISER OUT FROM JAIL--

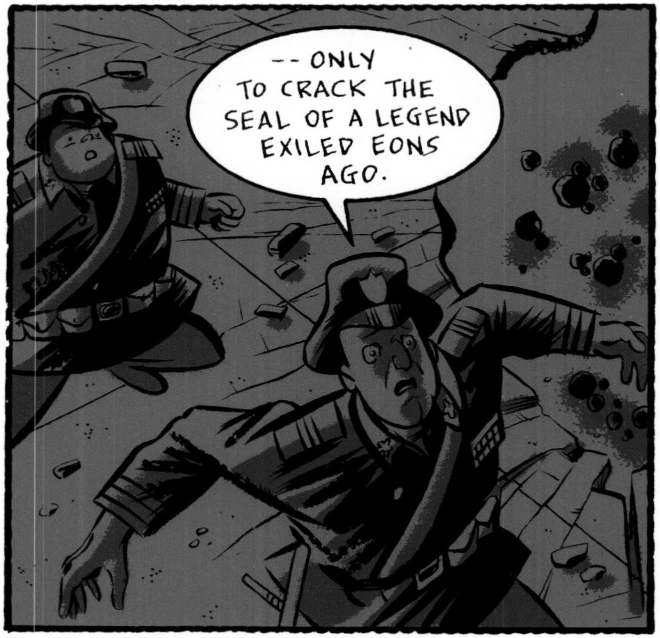
-- ONLY TO CRACK THE SEAL OF A LEGEND EXILED EONS AGO.

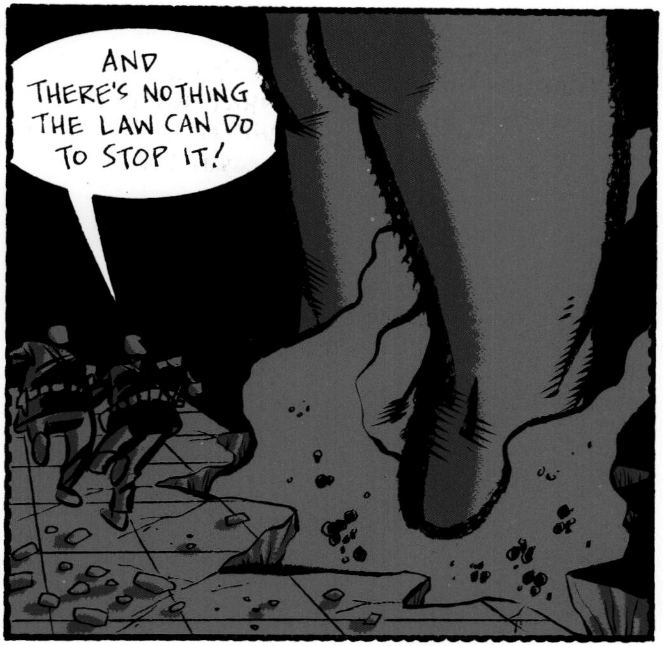
AND THERE'S NOTHING THE LAW CAN DO TO STOP IT!

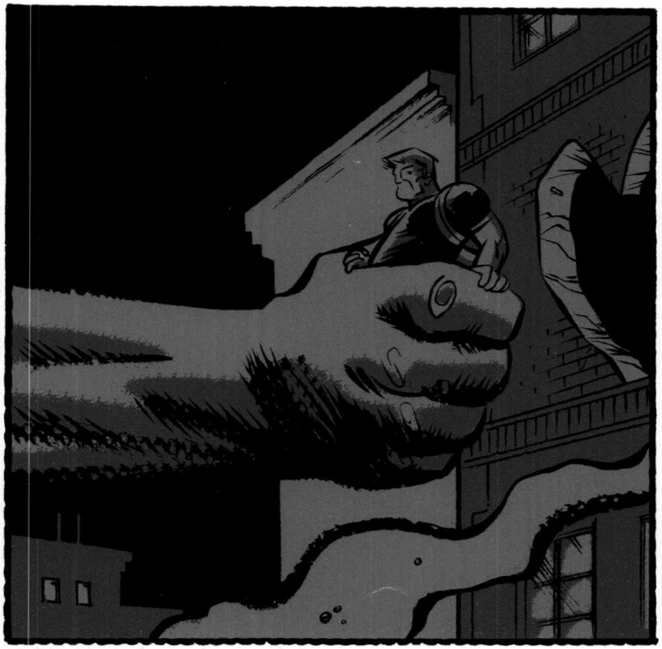

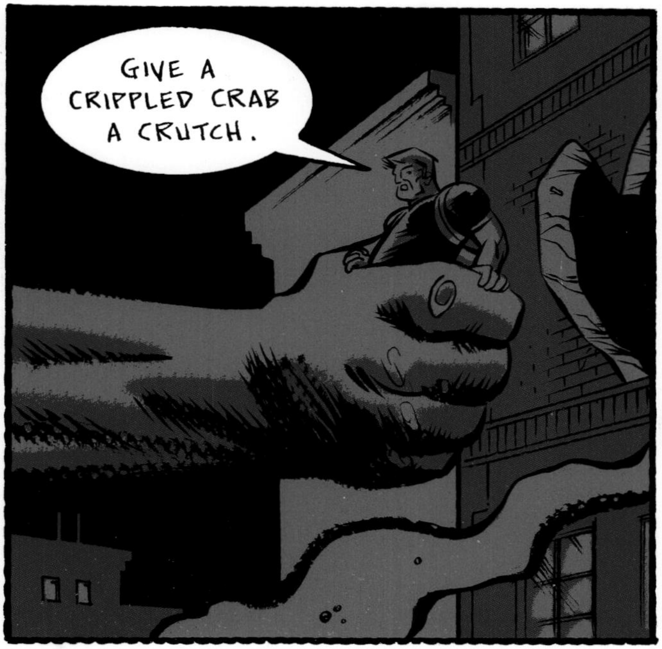
GIVE A CRIPPLED CRAB A CRUTCH.

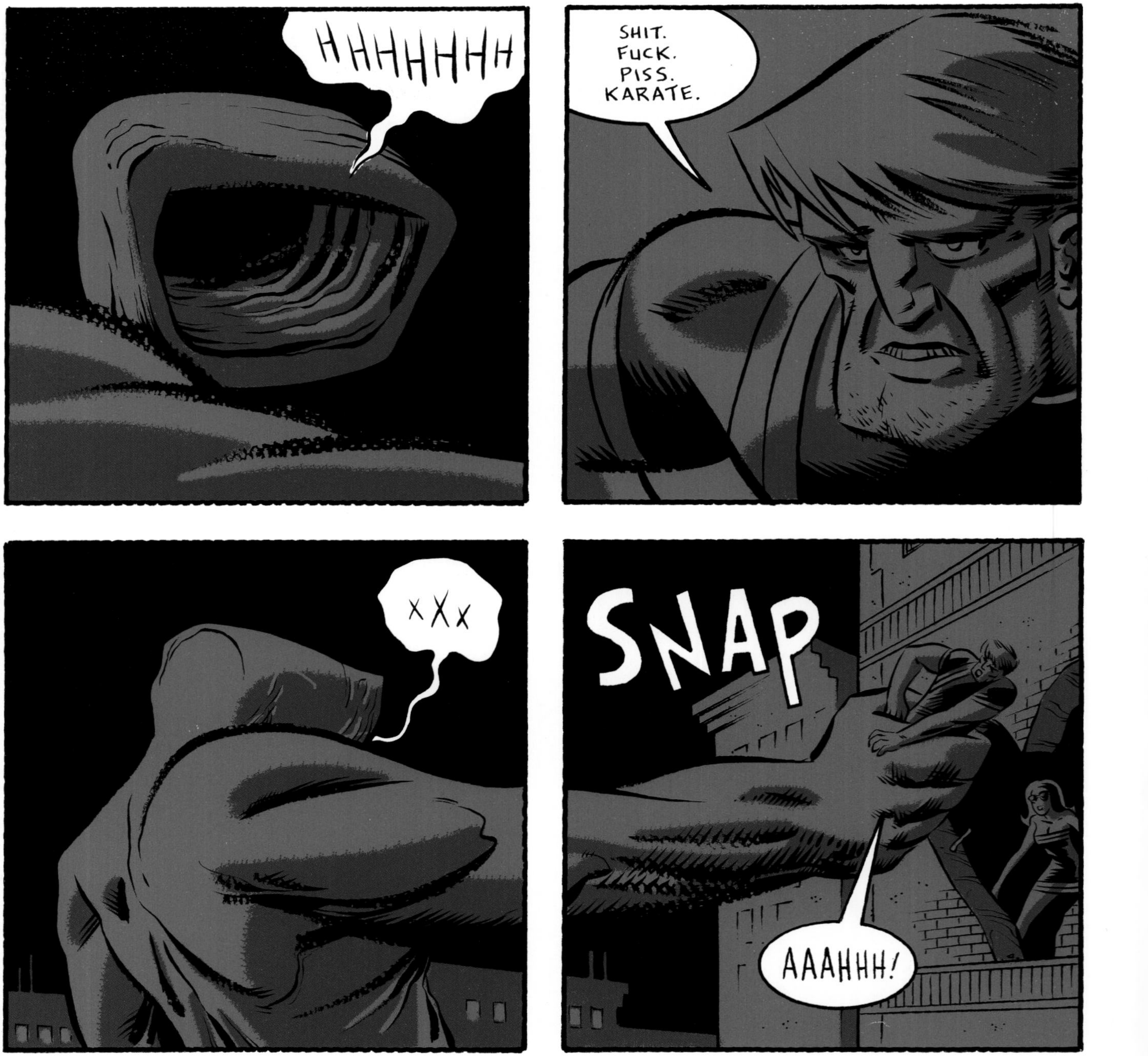
HHHHHHHH
SHIT. FUCK. PISS. KARATE.
XXX
SNAP
AAAHHH!

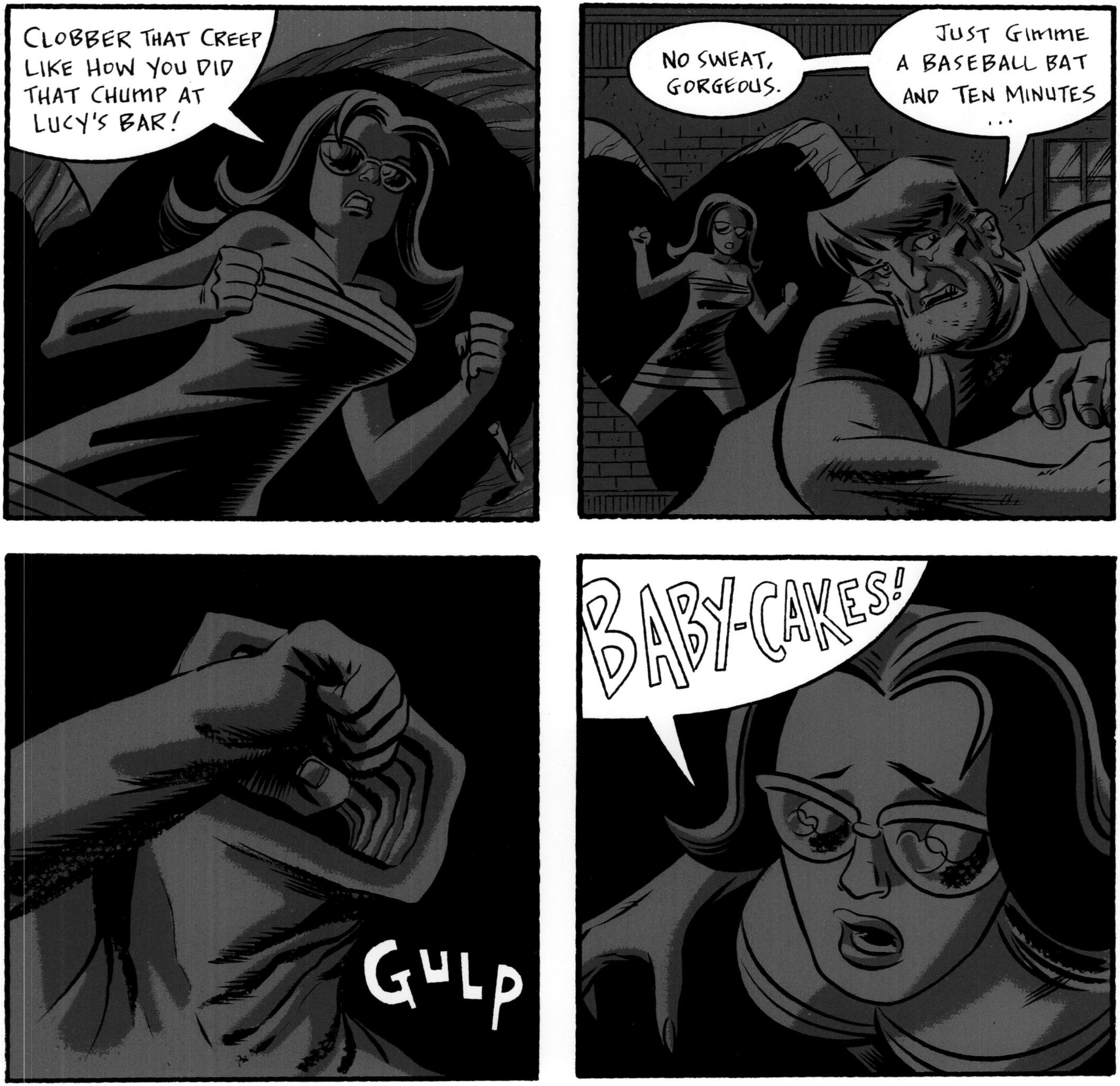
CLOBBER THAT CREEP LIKE HOW YOU DID THAT CHUMP AT LUCY'S BAR!
NO SWEAT, GORGEOUS.
JUST GIMME A BASEBALL BAT AND TEN MINUTES ...
GULP
BABY-CAKES!

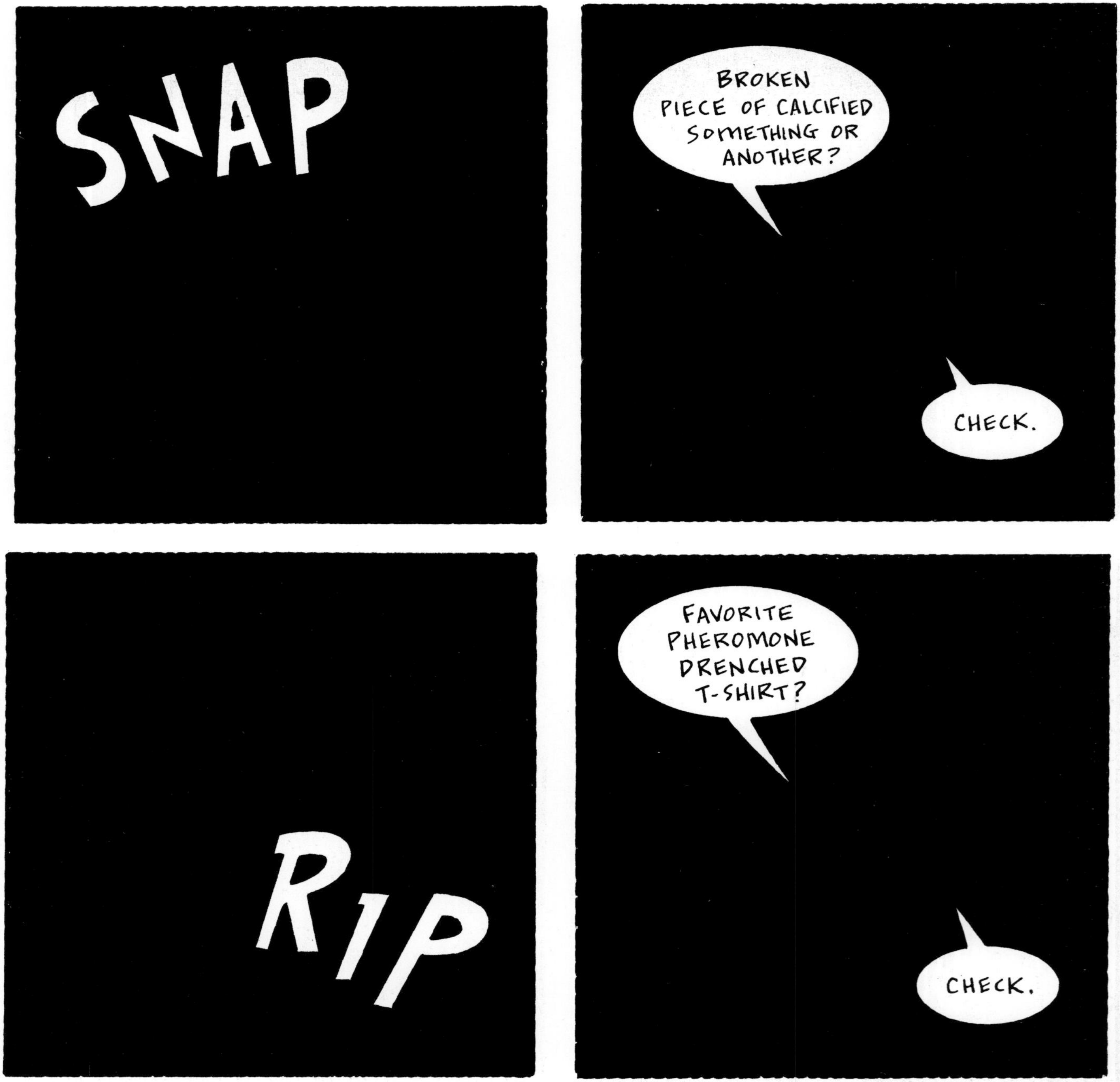
SNAP
BROKEN PIECE OF CALCIFIED SOMETHING OR ANOTHER?
CHECK.
RIP
FAVORITE PHEROMONE DRENCHED T-SHIRT?
CHECK.

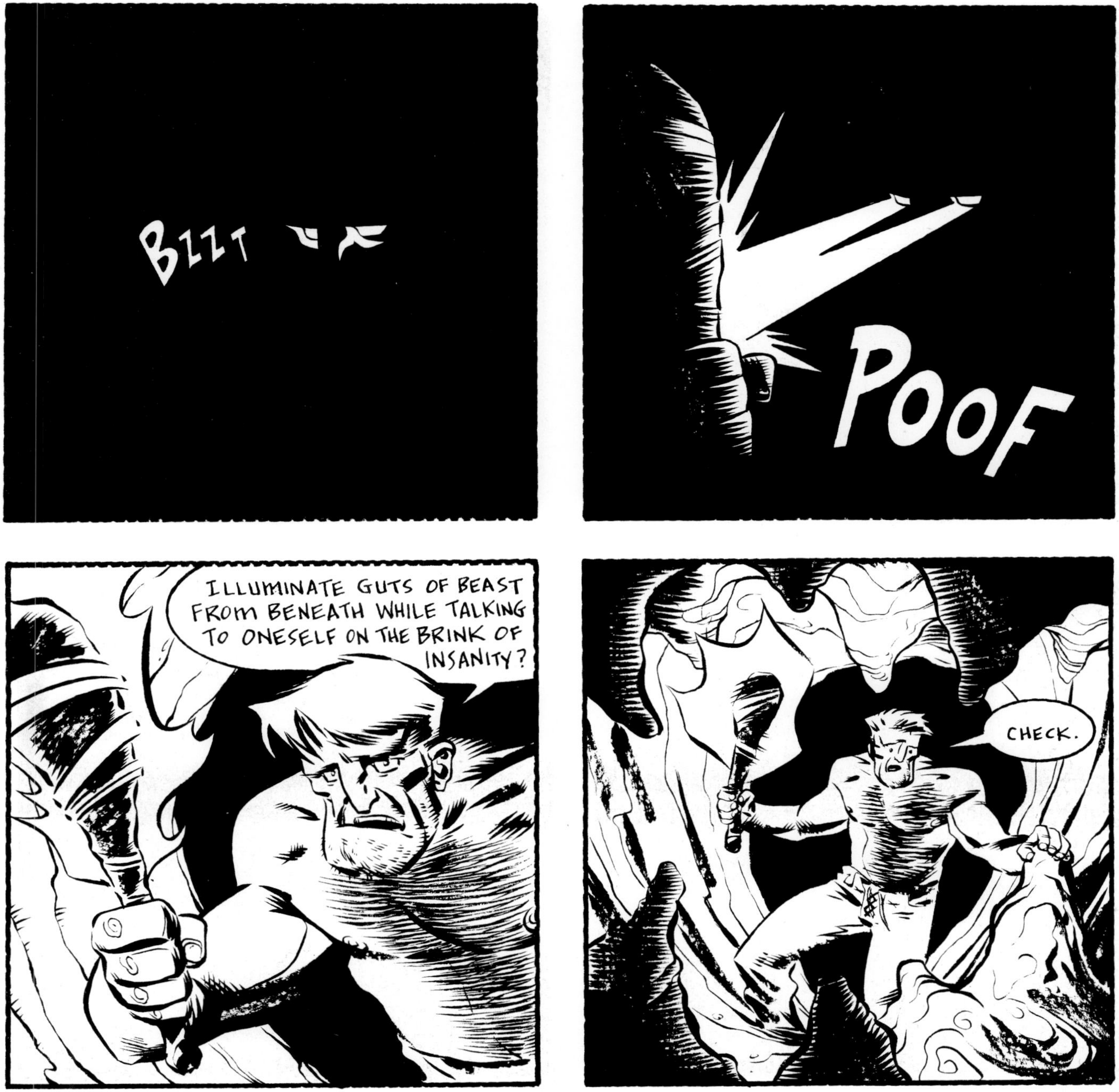
BZZT
POOF
ILLUMINATE GUTS OF BEAST FROM BENEATH WHILE TALKING TO ONESELF ON THE BRINK OF INSANITY?
CHECK.

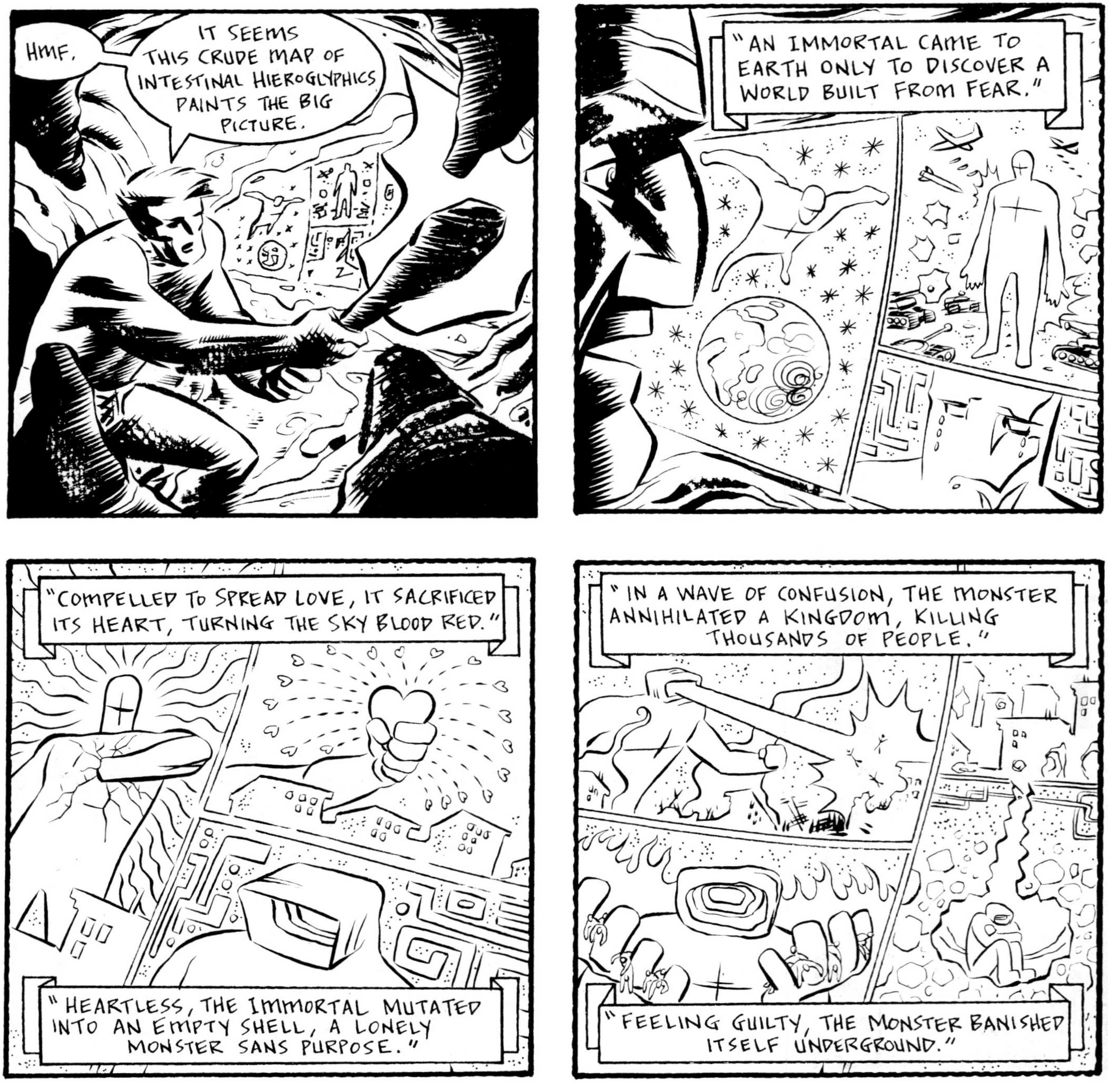
HMF.
IT SEEMS THIS CRUDE MAP OF INTESTINAL HIEROGLYPHICS PAINTS THE BIG PICTURE.
"AN IMMORTAL CAME TO EARTH ONLY TO DISCOVER A WORLD BUILT FROM FEAR."
"COMPELLED TO SPREAD LOVE, IT SACRIFICED ITS HEART, TURNING THE SKY BLOOD RED."
"HEARTLESS, THE IMMORTAL MUTATED INTO AN EMPTY SHELL, A LONELY MONSTER SANS PURPOSE."
"IN A WAVE OF CONFUSION, THE MONSTER ANNIHILATED A KINGDOM, KILLING THOUSANDS OF PEOPLE."
"FEELING GUILTY, THE MONSTER BANISHED ITSELF UNDERGROUND."

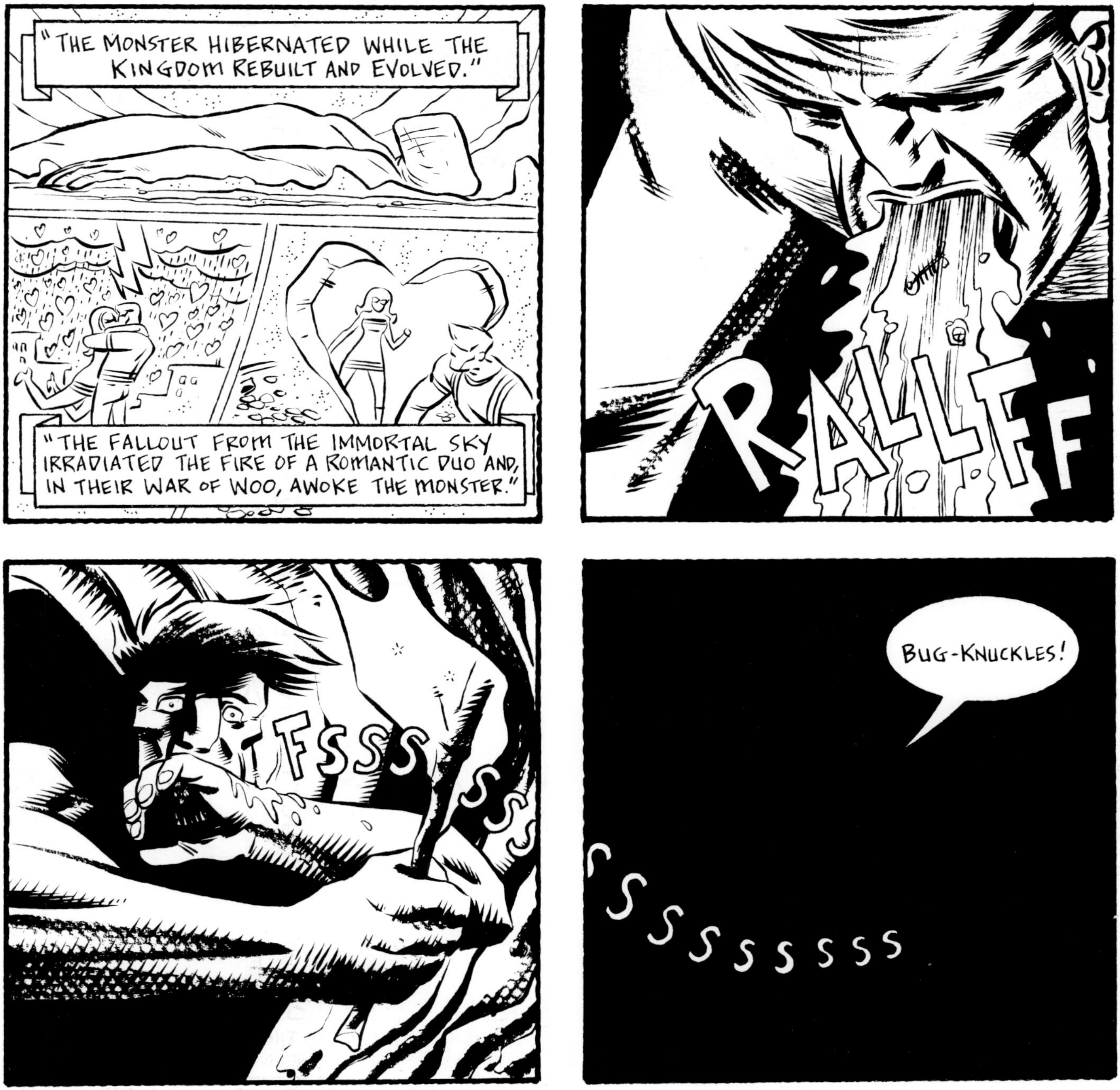
"THE MONSTER HIBERNATED WHILE THE KINGDOM REBUILT AND EVOLVED."
"THE FALLOUT FROM THE IMMORTAL SKY IRRADIATED THE FIRE OF A ROMANTIC DUO AND, IN THEIR WAR OF WOO, AWOKE THE MONSTER."
RALLFF
FSSSSSS
BUG-KNUCKLES!
SSSSSSSSS

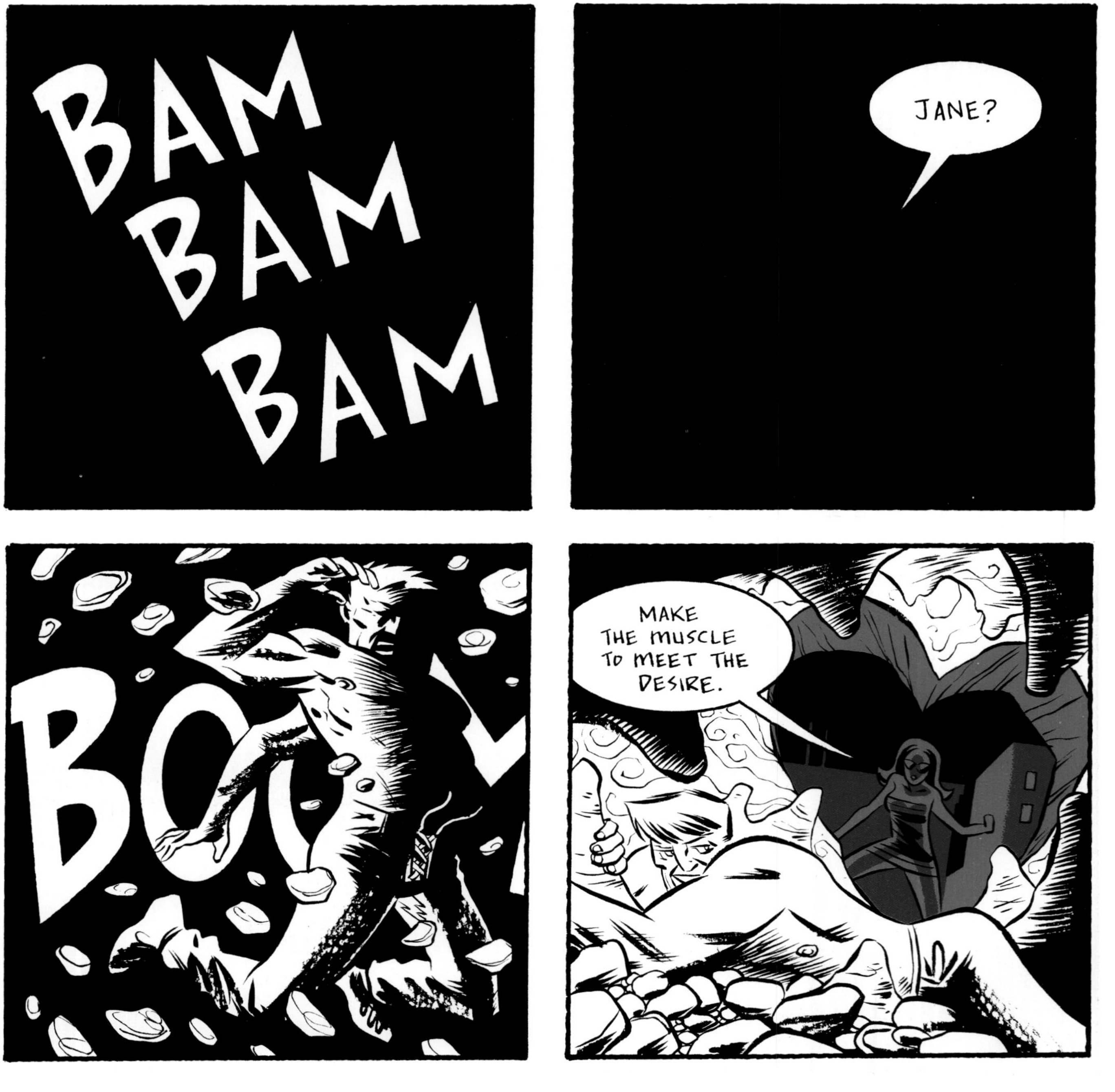
BAM
BAM
BAM
JANE?
BO
MAKE THE MUSCLE TO MEET THE DESIRE.

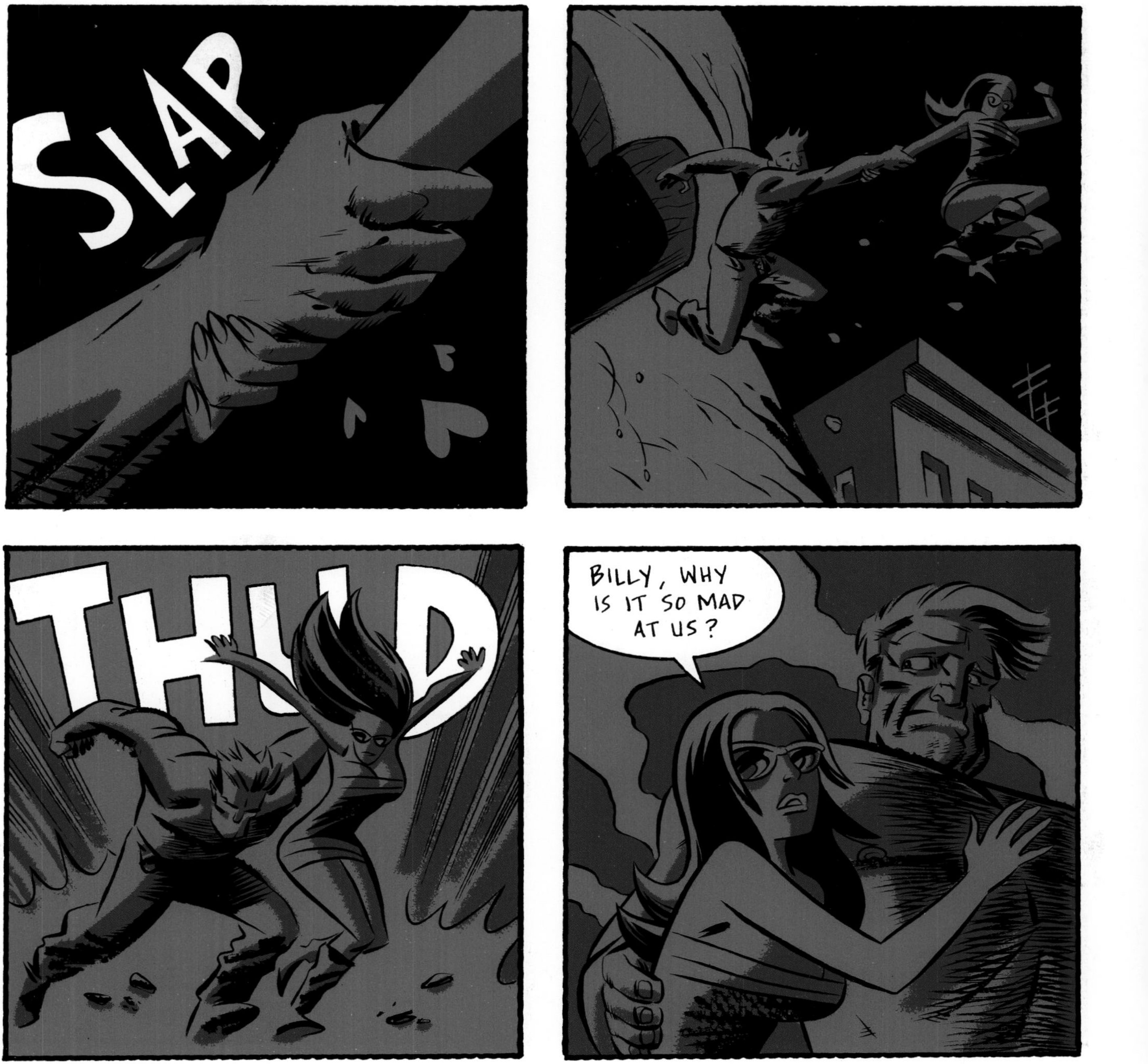
SLAP
THUD
BILLY, WHY IS IT SO MAD AT US?

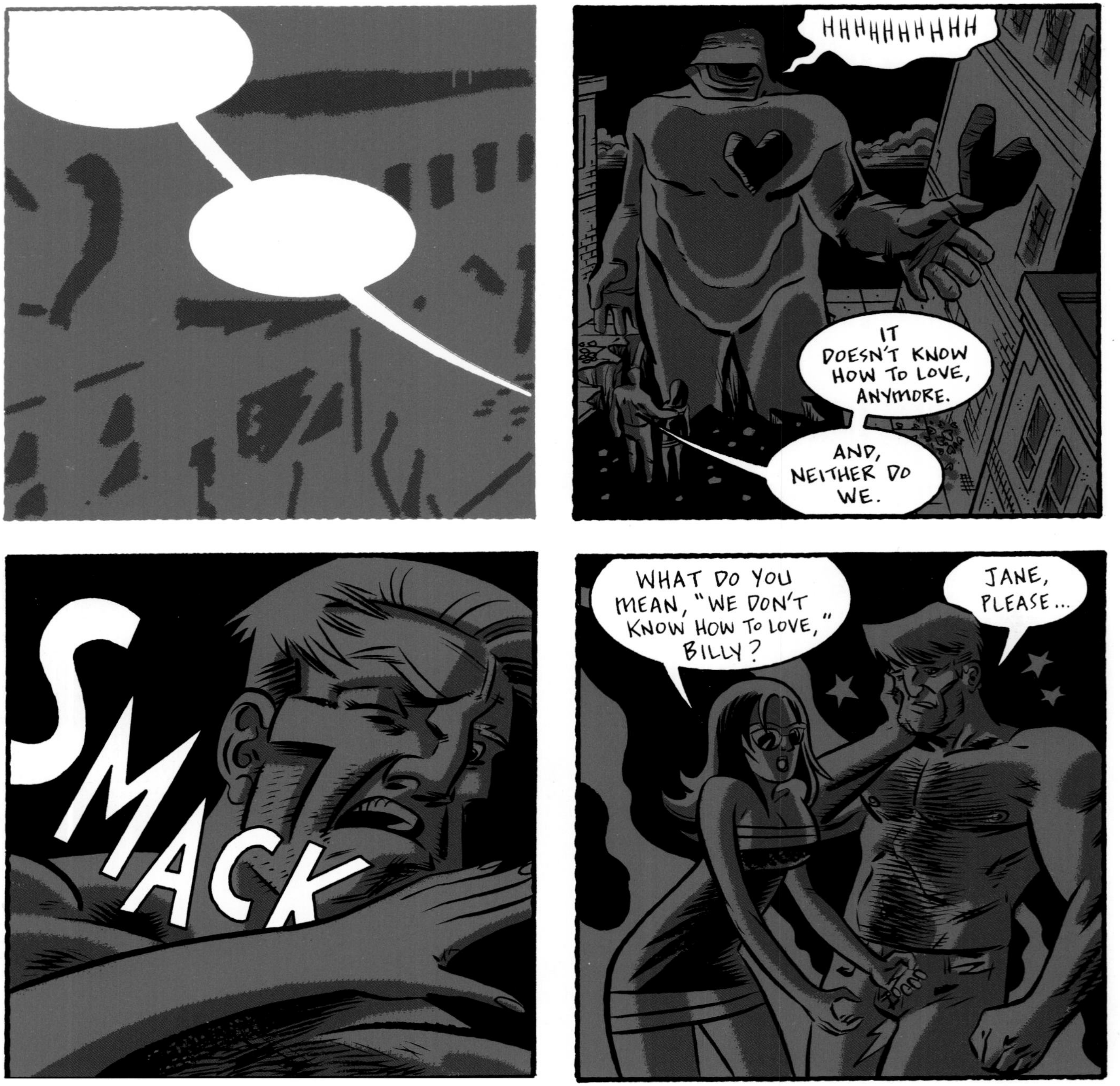
HHHHHHHHHH
IT DOESN'T KNOW HOW TO LOVE, ANYMORE.
AND, NEITHER DO WE.
SMACK
WHAT DO YOU MEAN, "WE DON'T KNOW HOW TO LOVE," BILLY?
JANE, PLEASE...

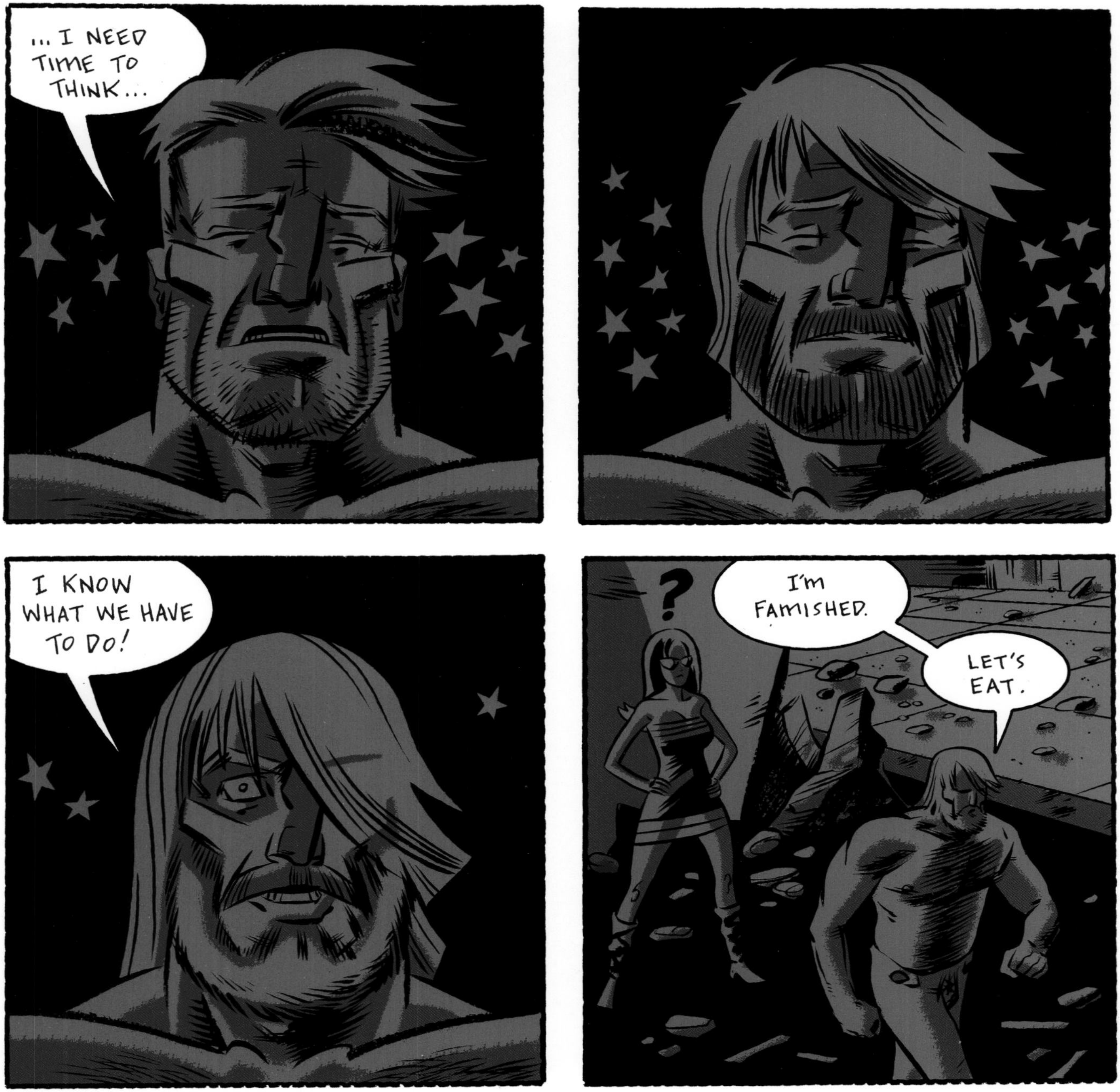
... I NEED TIME TO THINK...
I KNOW WHAT WE HAVE TO DO!
?
I'M FAMISHED.
LET'S EAT.

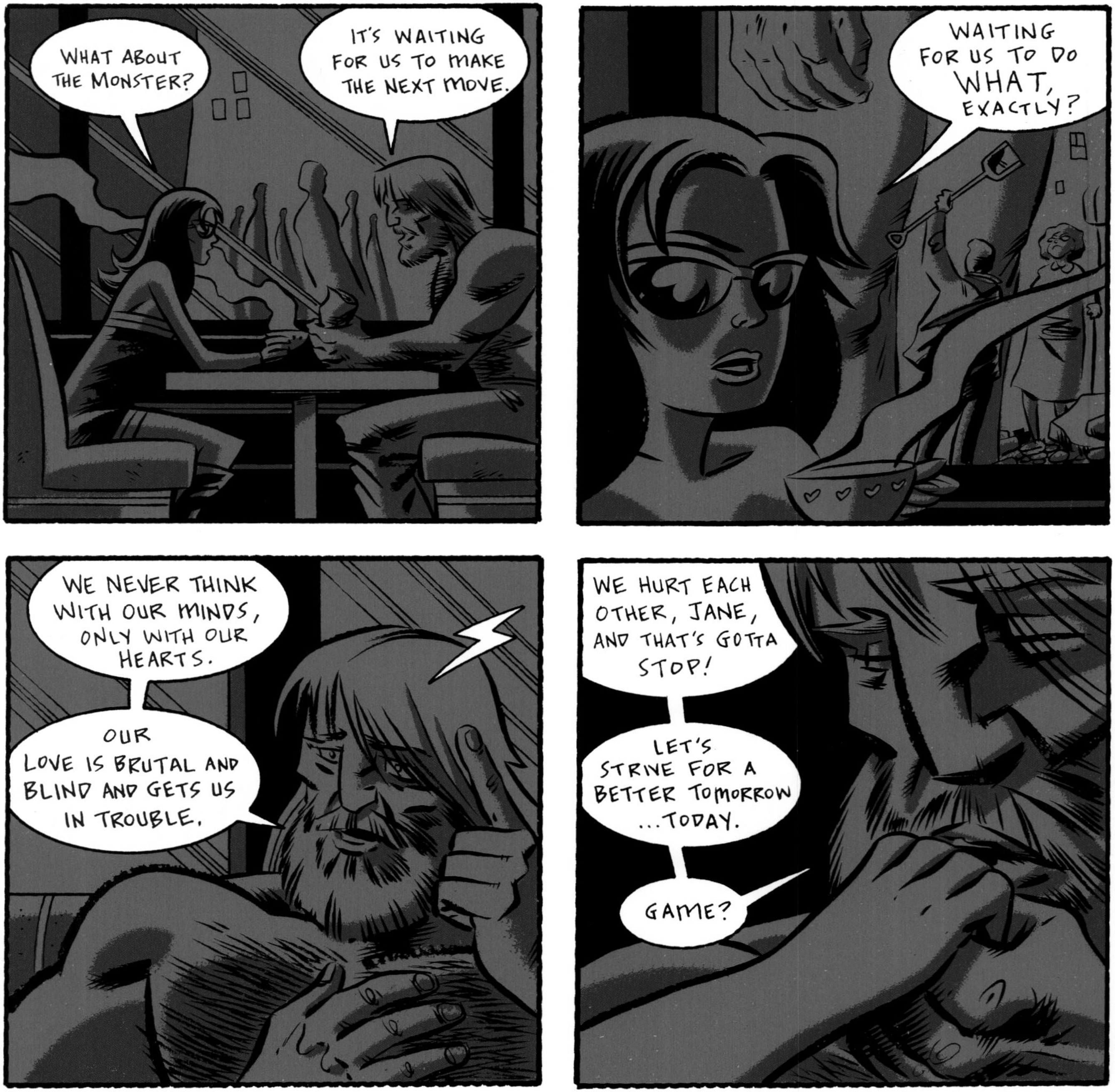
WHAT ABOUT THE MONSTER?
IT'S WAITING FOR US TO MAKE THE NEXT MOVE.
WAITING FOR US TO DO WHAT, EXACTLY?
WE NEVER THINK WITH OUR MINDS, ONLY WITH OUR HEARTS.
OUR LOVE IS BRUTAL AND BLIND AND GETS US IN TROUBLE.
WE HURT EACH OTHER, JANE, AND THAT'S GOTTA STOP!
LET'S STRIVE FOR A BETTER TOMORROW ...TODAY.
GAME?

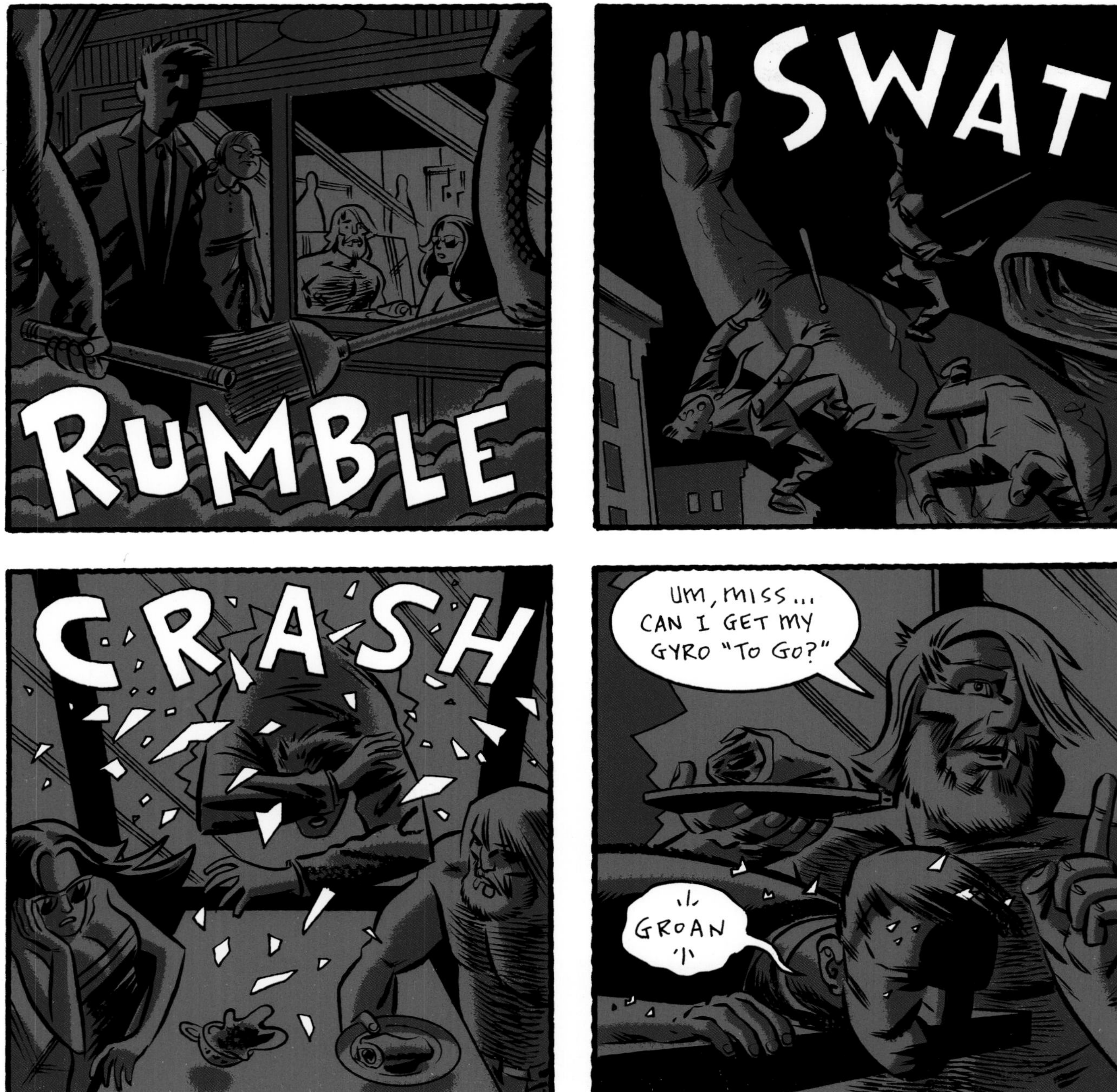
RUMBLE
SWAT
CRASH
UM, MISS... CAN I GET MY GYRO "TO GO?"
GROAN

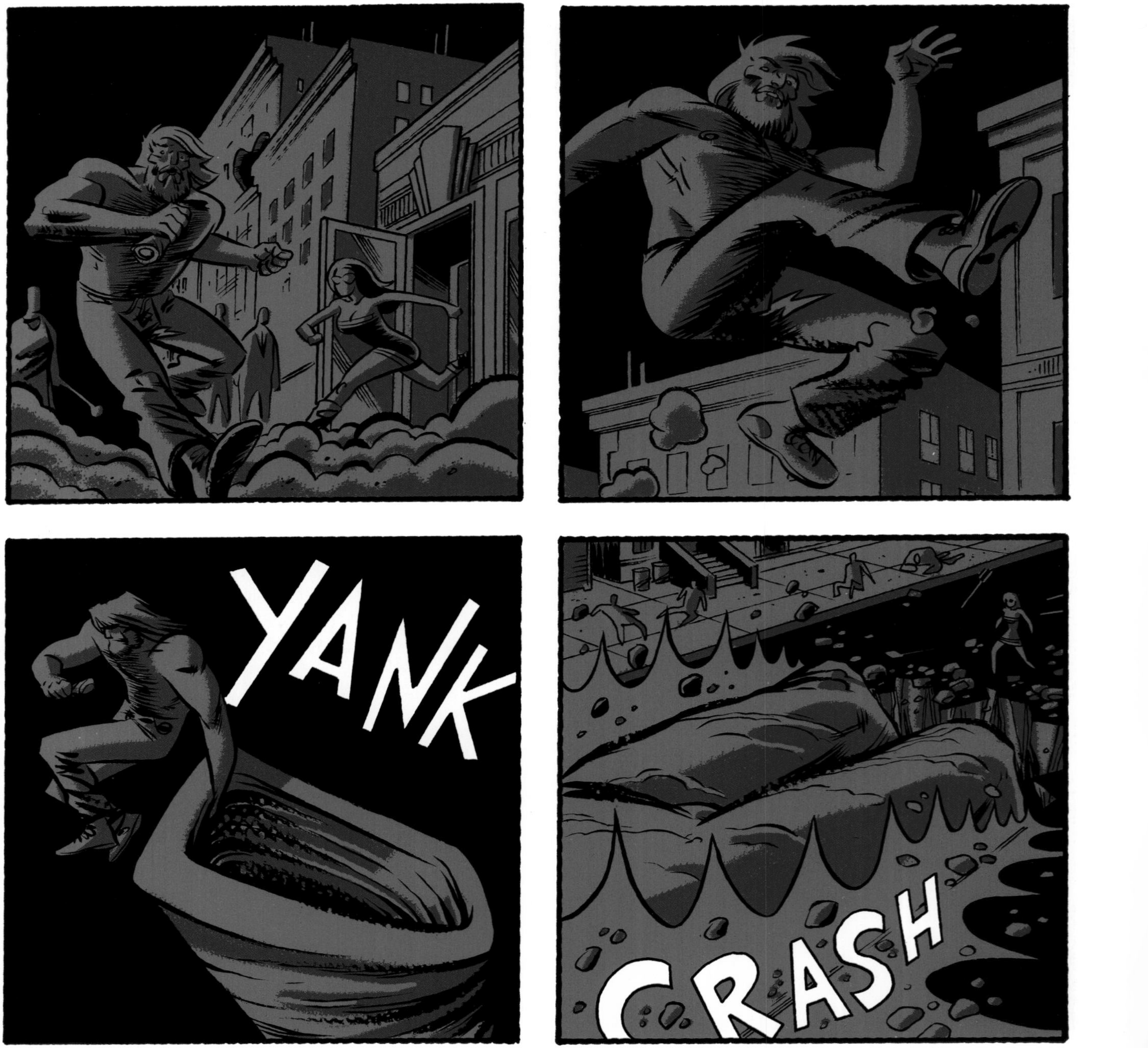
YANK
CRASH

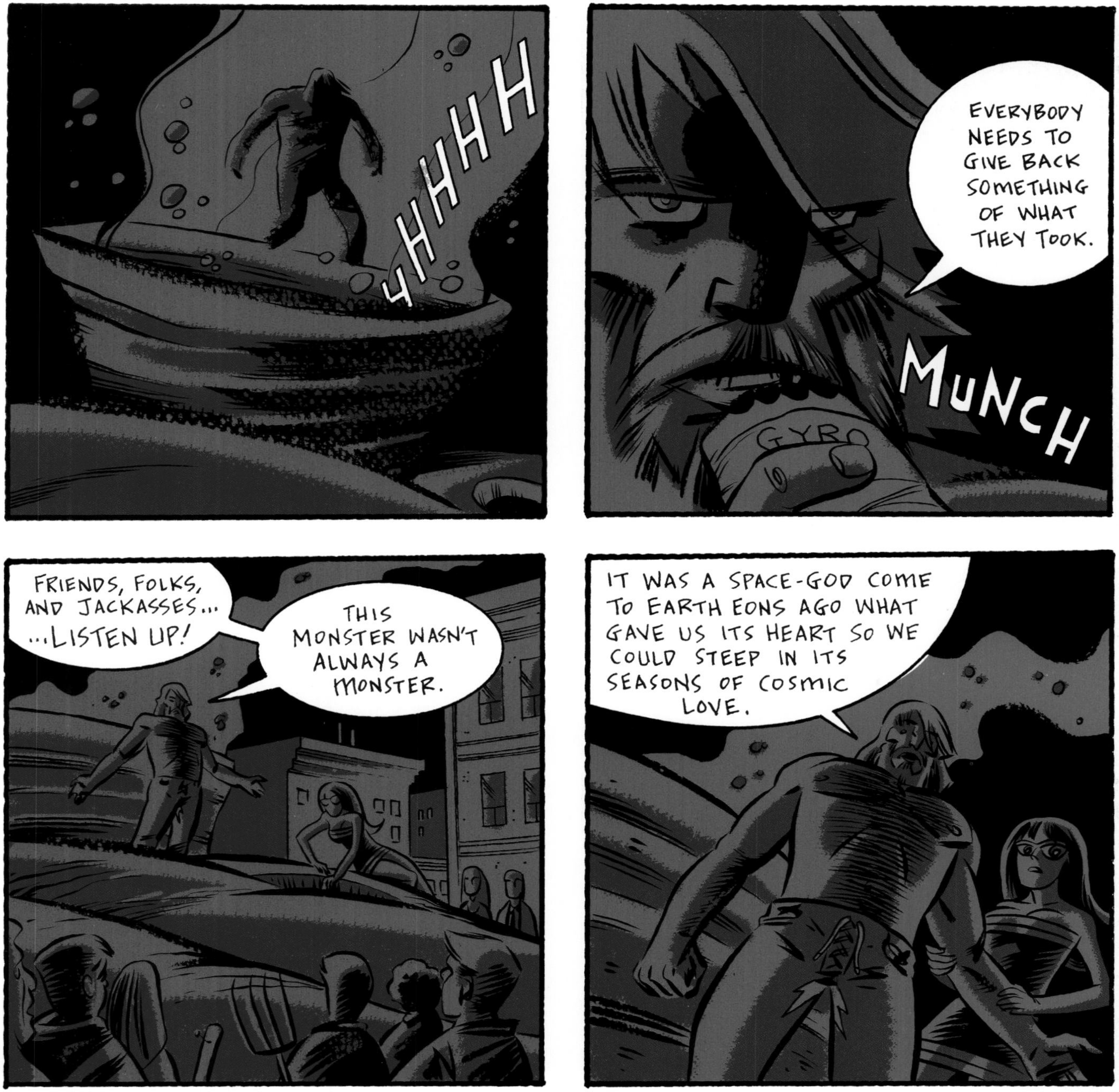
HHHHH
EVERYBODY NEEDS TO GIVE BACK SOMETHING OF WHAT THEY TOOK.
MUNCH
GYRO
FRIENDS, FOLKS, AND JACKASSES... ...LISTEN UP!
THIS MONSTER WASN'T ALWAYS A MONSTER.
IT WAS A SPACE-GOD COME TO EARTH EONS AGO WHAT GAVE US ITS HEART SO WE COULD STEEP IN ITS SEASONS OF COSMIC LOVE.

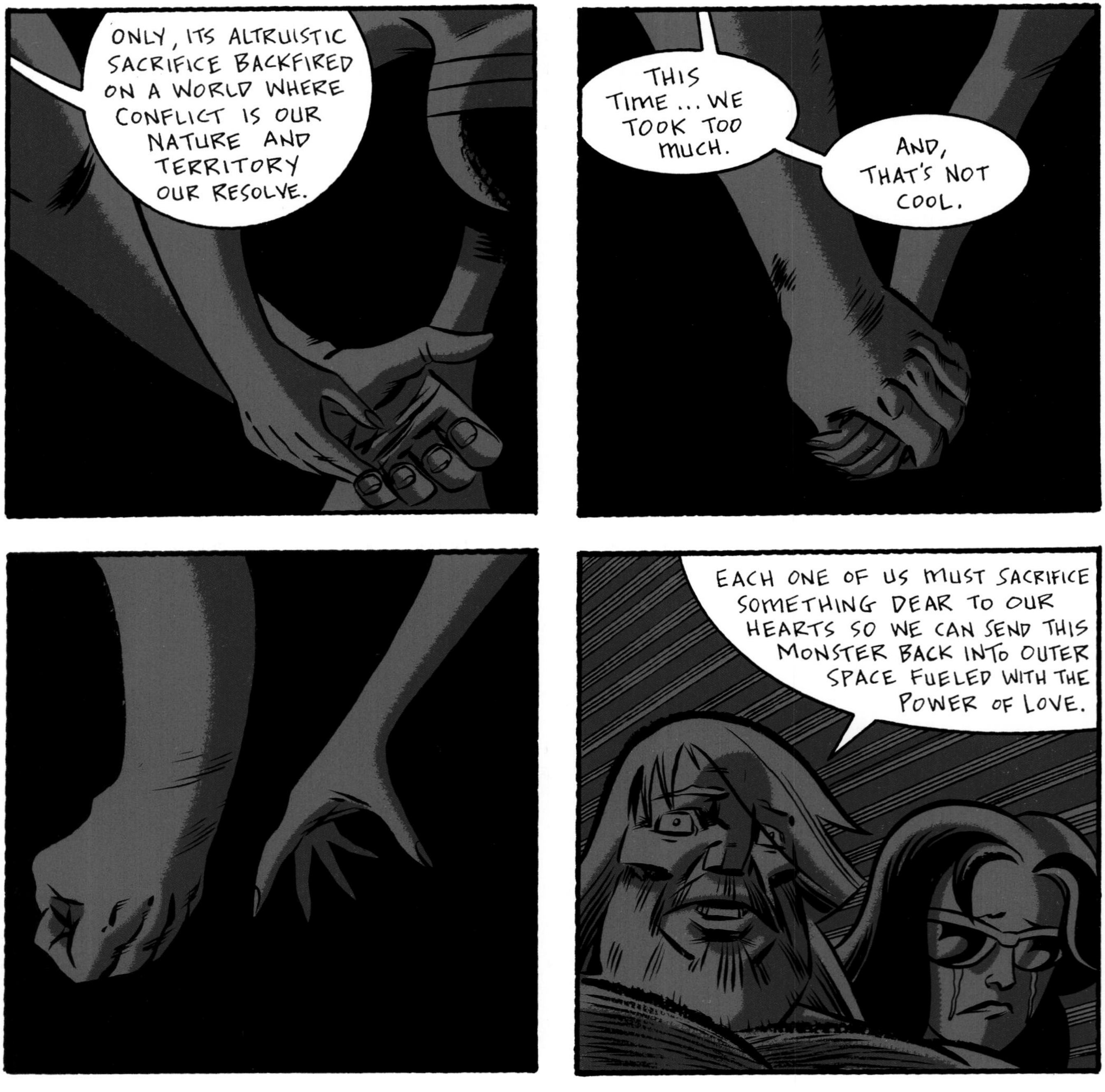
ONLY, ITS ALTRUISTIC SACRIFICE BACKFIRED ON A WORLD WHERE CONFLICT IS OUR NATURE AND TERRITORY OUR RESOLVE.
THIS TIME... WE TOOK TOO MUCH.
AND, THAT'S NOT COOL.
EACH ONE OF US MUST SACRIFICE SOMETHING DEAR TO OUR HEARTS SO WE CAN SEND THIS MONSTER BACK INTO OUTER SPACE FUELED WITH THE POWER OF LOVE.

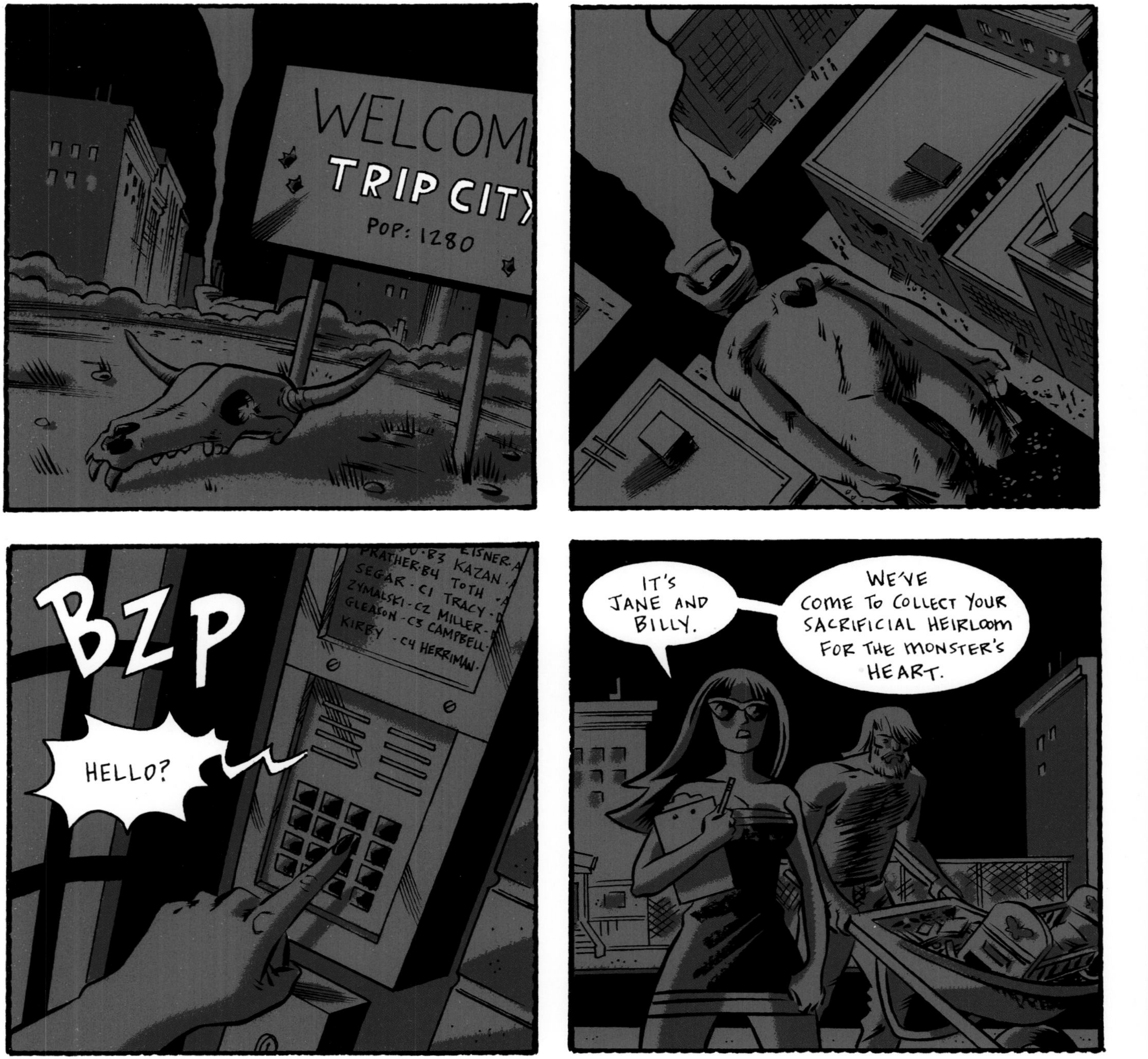
WELCOM
TRIP CIT
POP: 1280
PRATHER·B4 KAZAN
SEGAR - C1 TOTH
ZYMALSKI - C2 TRACY
GLEASON - C3 MILLER
KIRBY - C4 CAMPBELL
HERRIMAN
BZP
HELLO?
IT'S JANE AND BILLY.
WE'VE COME TO COLLECT YOUR SACRIFICIAL HEIRLOOM FOR THE MONSTER'S HEART.

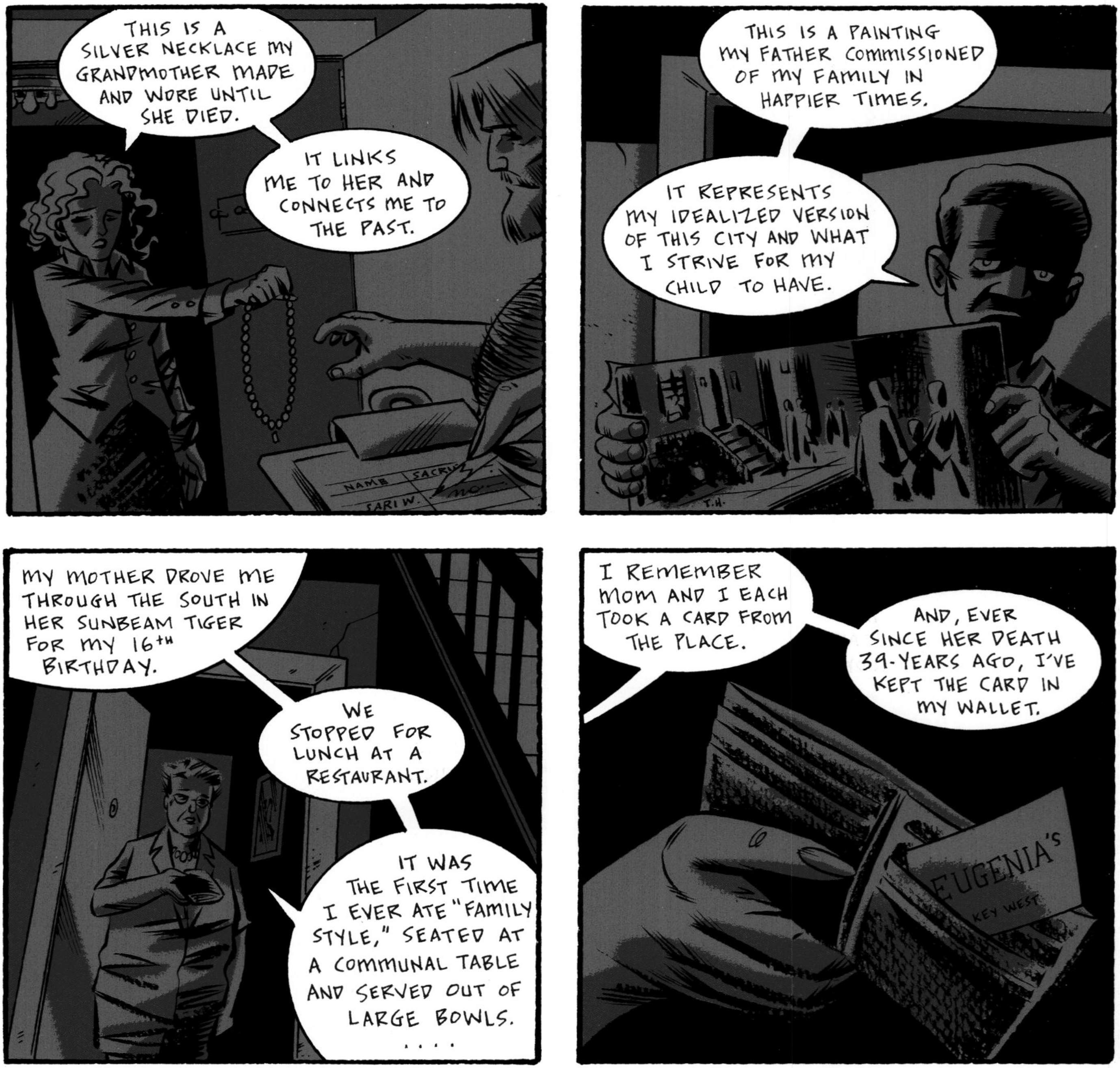
THIS IS A SILVER NECKLACE MY GRANDMOTHER MADE AND WORE UNTIL SHE DIED.
IT LINKS ME TO HER AND CONNECTS ME TO THE PAST.
THIS IS A PAINTING MY FATHER COMMISSIONED OF MY FAMILY IN HAPPIER TIMES.
IT REPRESENTS MY IDEALIZED VERSION OF THIS CITY AND WHAT I STRIVE FOR MY CHILD TO HAVE.
MY MOTHER DROVE ME THROUGH THE SOUTH IN HER SUNBEAM TIGER FOR MY 16TH BIRTHDAY.
WE STOPPED FOR LUNCH AT A RESTAURANT.
IT WAS THE FIRST TIME I EVER ATE "FAMILY STYLE," SEATED AT A COMMUNAL TABLE AND SERVED OUT OF LARGE BOWLS. . . . .
I REMEMBER MOM AND I EACH TOOK A CARD FROM THE PLACE.
AND, EVER SINCE HER DEATH 39-YEARS AGO, I'VE KEPT THE CARD IN MY WALLET.
EUGENIA'S
KEY WEST

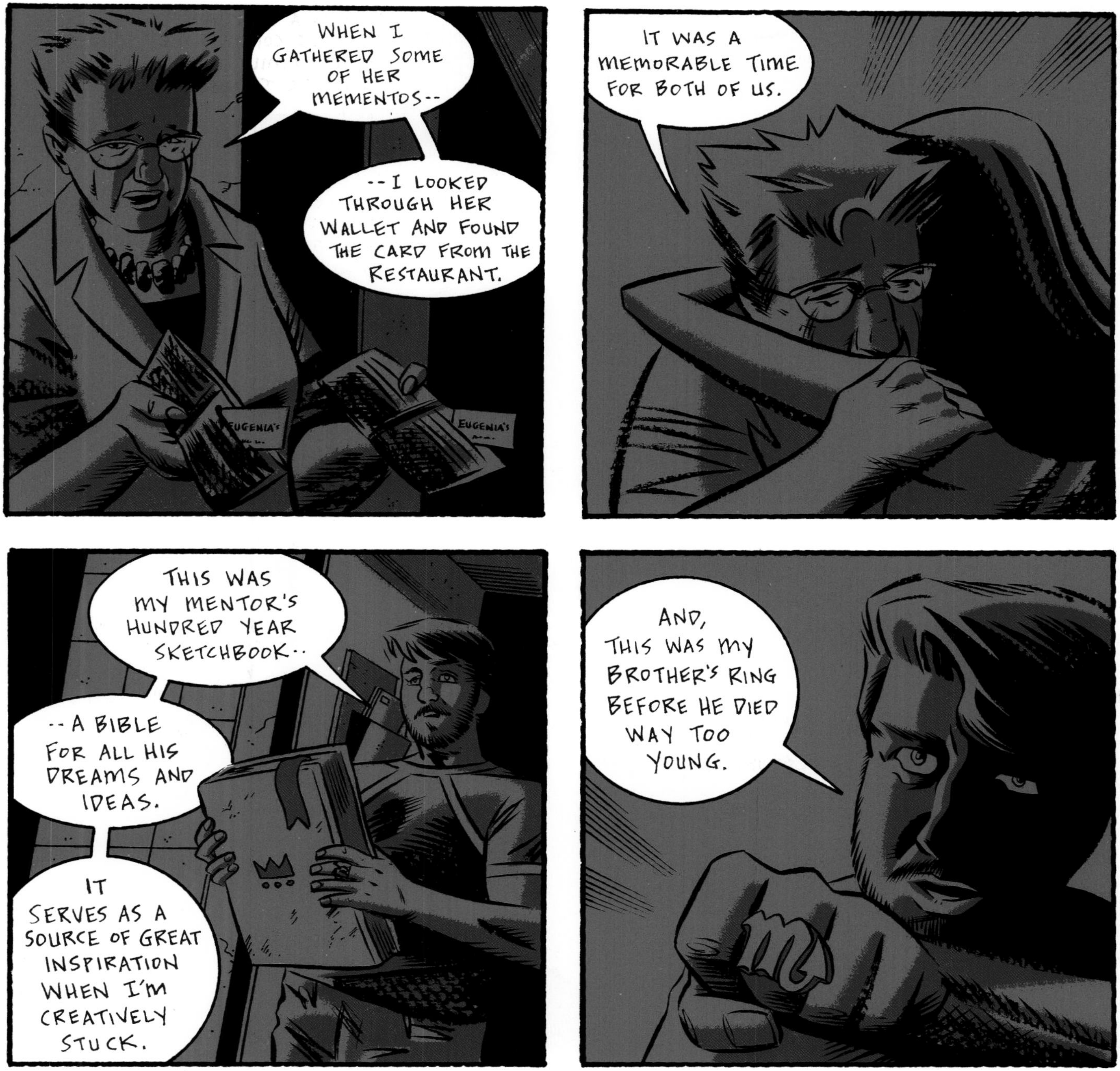
WHEN I GATHERED SOME OF HER MEMENTOS--
--I LOOKED THROUGH HER WALLET AND FOUND THE CARD FROM THE RESTAURANT.
EUGENIA'S
EUGENIA'S
IT WAS A MEMORABLE TIME FOR BOTH OF US.
THIS WAS MY MENTOR'S HUNDRED YEAR SKETCHBOOK..
--A BIBLE FOR ALL HIS DREAMS AND IDEAS.
IT SERVES AS A SOURCE OF GREAT INSPIRATION WHEN I'M CREATIVELY STUCK.
AND, THIS WAS MY BROTHER'S RING BEFORE HE DIED WAY TOO YOUNG.

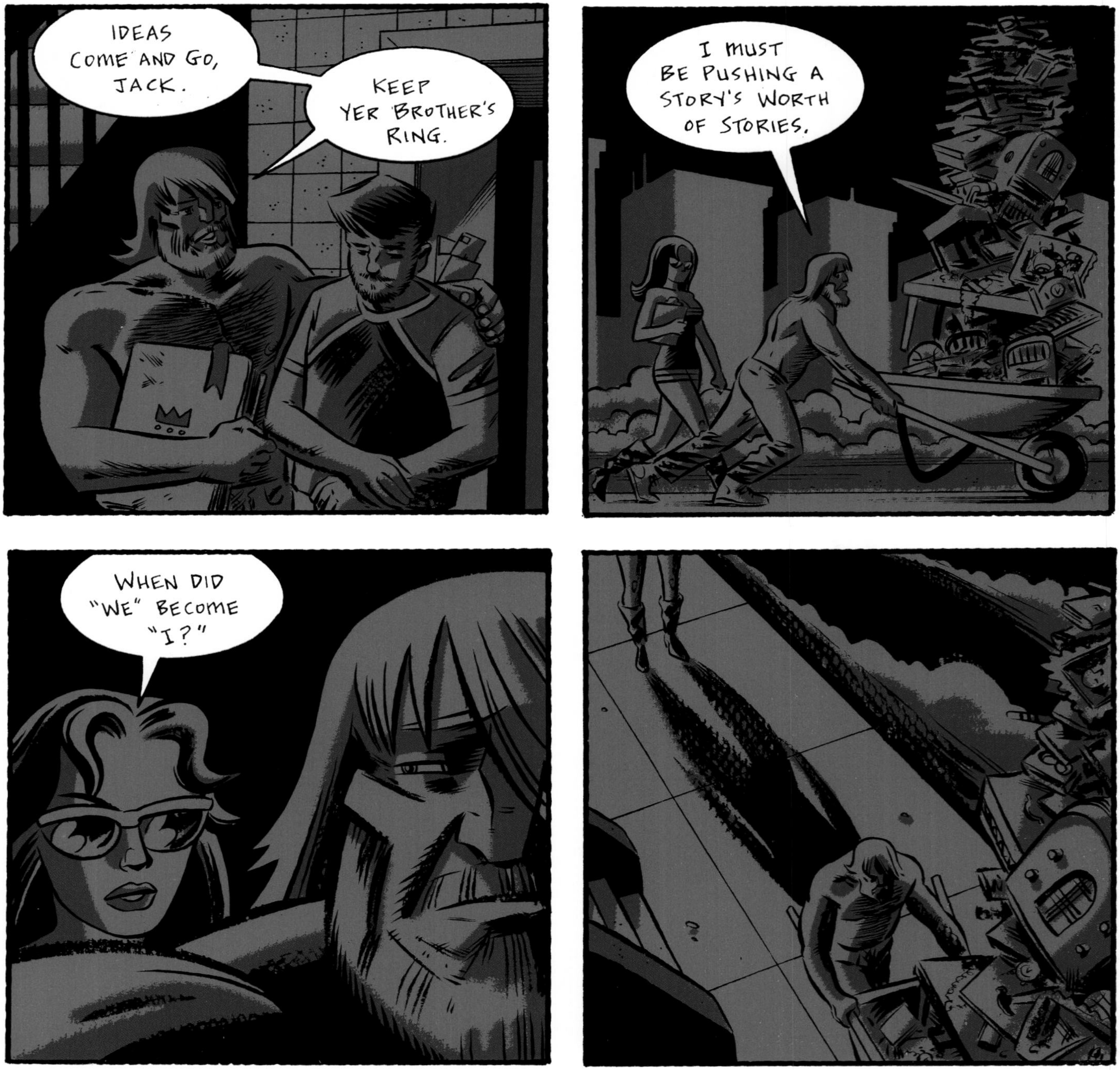
IDEAS COME AND GO, JACK.
KEEP YER BROTHER'S RING.
I MUST BE PUSHING A STORY'S WORTH OF STORIES.
WHEN DID "WE" BECOME "I?"

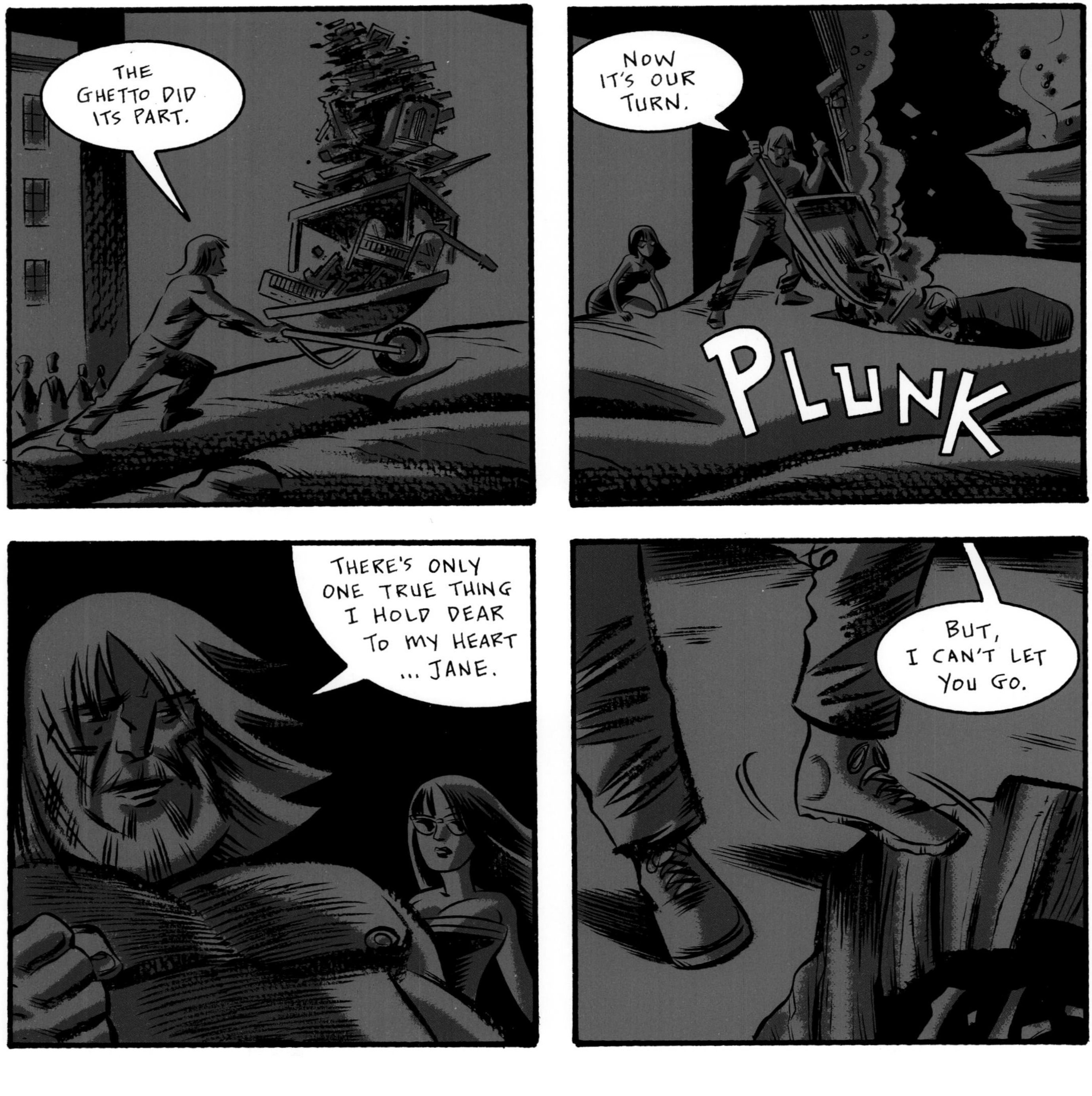
THE GHETTO DID ITS PART.
NOW IT'S OUR TURN.
PLUNK
THERE'S ONLY ONE TRUE THING I HOLD DEAR TO MY HEART ...JANE.
BUT, I CAN'T LET YOU GO.

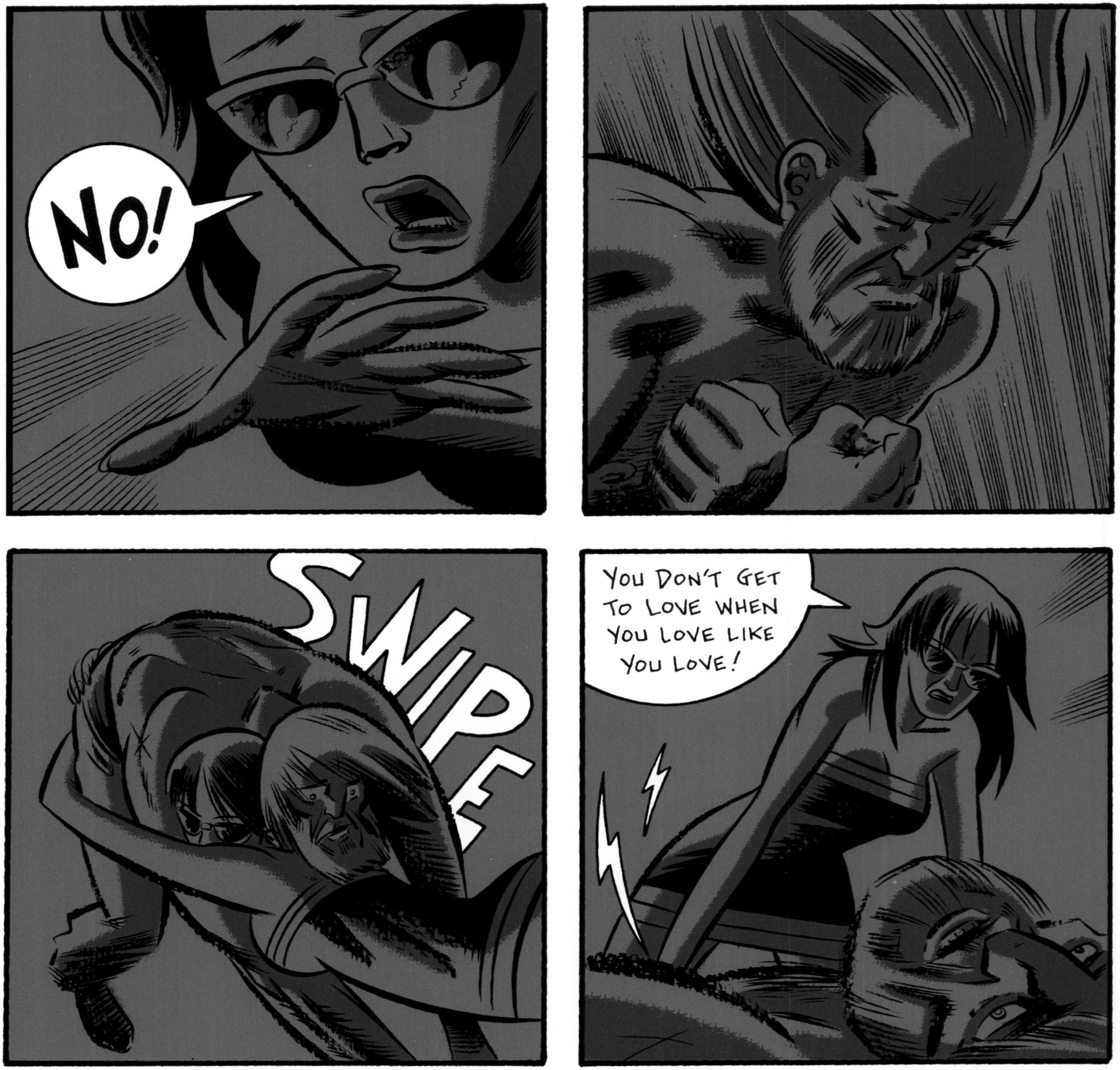
NO!
SWIPE
YOU DON'T GET TO LOVE WHEN YOU LOVE LIKE YOU LOVE!

FIRST THINGS FIRST, BILLY.
WE MUST MAKE AMMENDS.
YOU HAVE TO REVERSE THE APPLICATION OF YOUR "TWO CRAZY HEARTS OF NAPALM" TECHNIQUE.
HE SHOULDN'T SUFFER FOR WHAT COMES NATURAL.
BESIDES, FLIRTING IS ONLY MADE POTENT BY INSECURITY.
AND IT ONLY GETS YOU A NIGHT IN JAIL.
180
90
WELL, JANE, A MAN SHOULDN'T MESS WITH ANOTHER MAN'S LADY LIKE THAT!
...GRUMBLE...
MAKE WHAT'S RIGHT AND APOLOGIZE TO THIS POOR MAN.

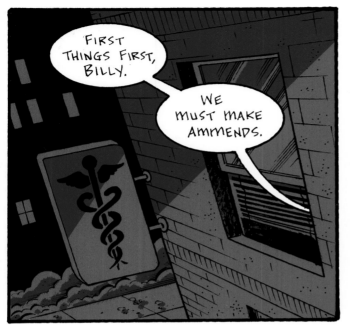

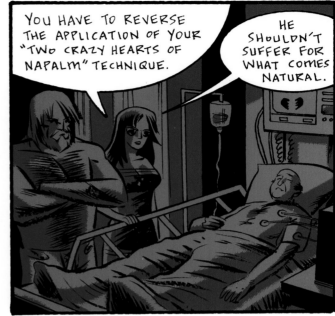

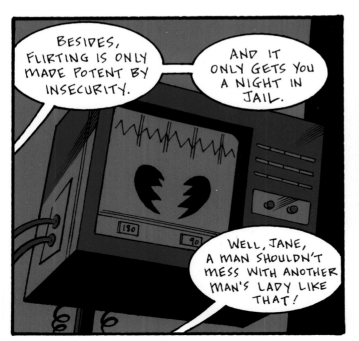

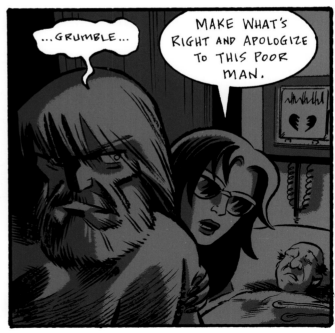

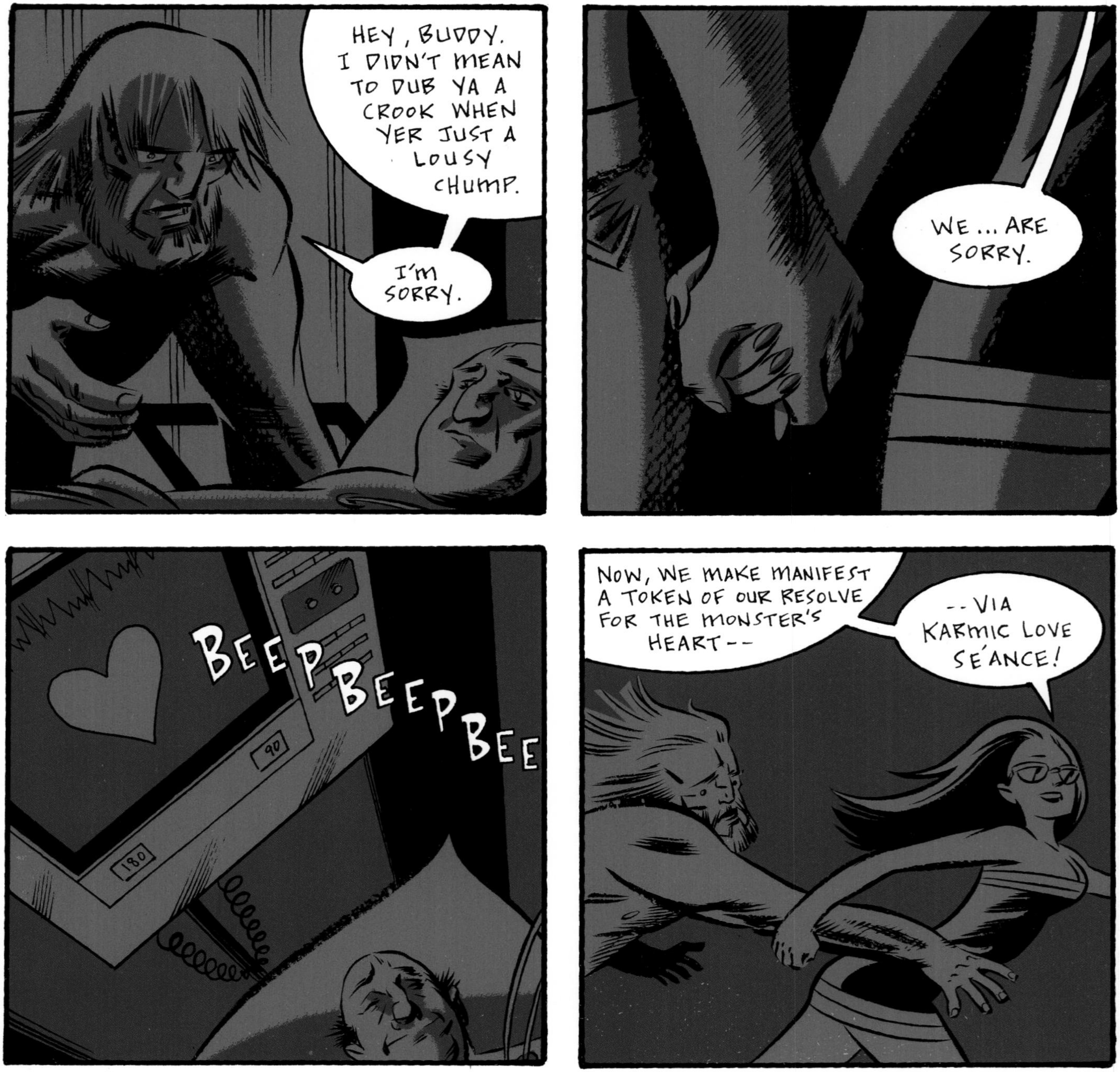
HEY, BUDDY. I DIDN'T MEAN TO DUB YA A CROOK WHEN YER JUST A LOUSY CHUMP.
I'M SORRY.
WE... ARE SORRY.
BEEP BEEP BEE
90
180
NOW, WE MAKE MANIFEST A TOKEN OF OUR RESOLVE FOR THE MONSTER'S HEART--
--VIA KARMIC LOVE SÉANCE!

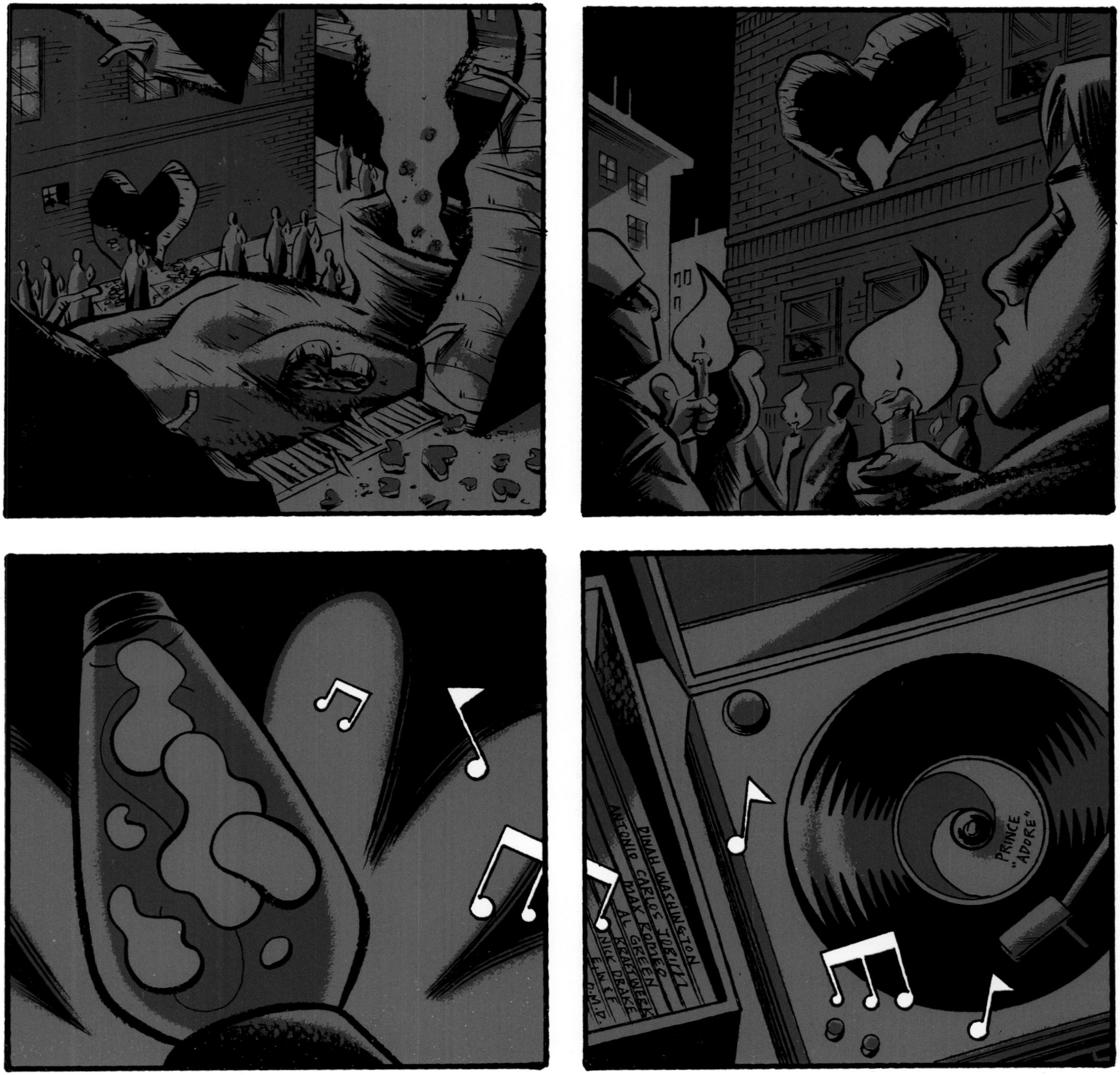
DINAH WASHINGTON
ANTONIO CARLOS JOBIM
MAX ROMEO
AL GREEN
KRAFTWERK
NICK DRAKE
E.W.&F.
D.M.D.
PRINCE
"ADORE"

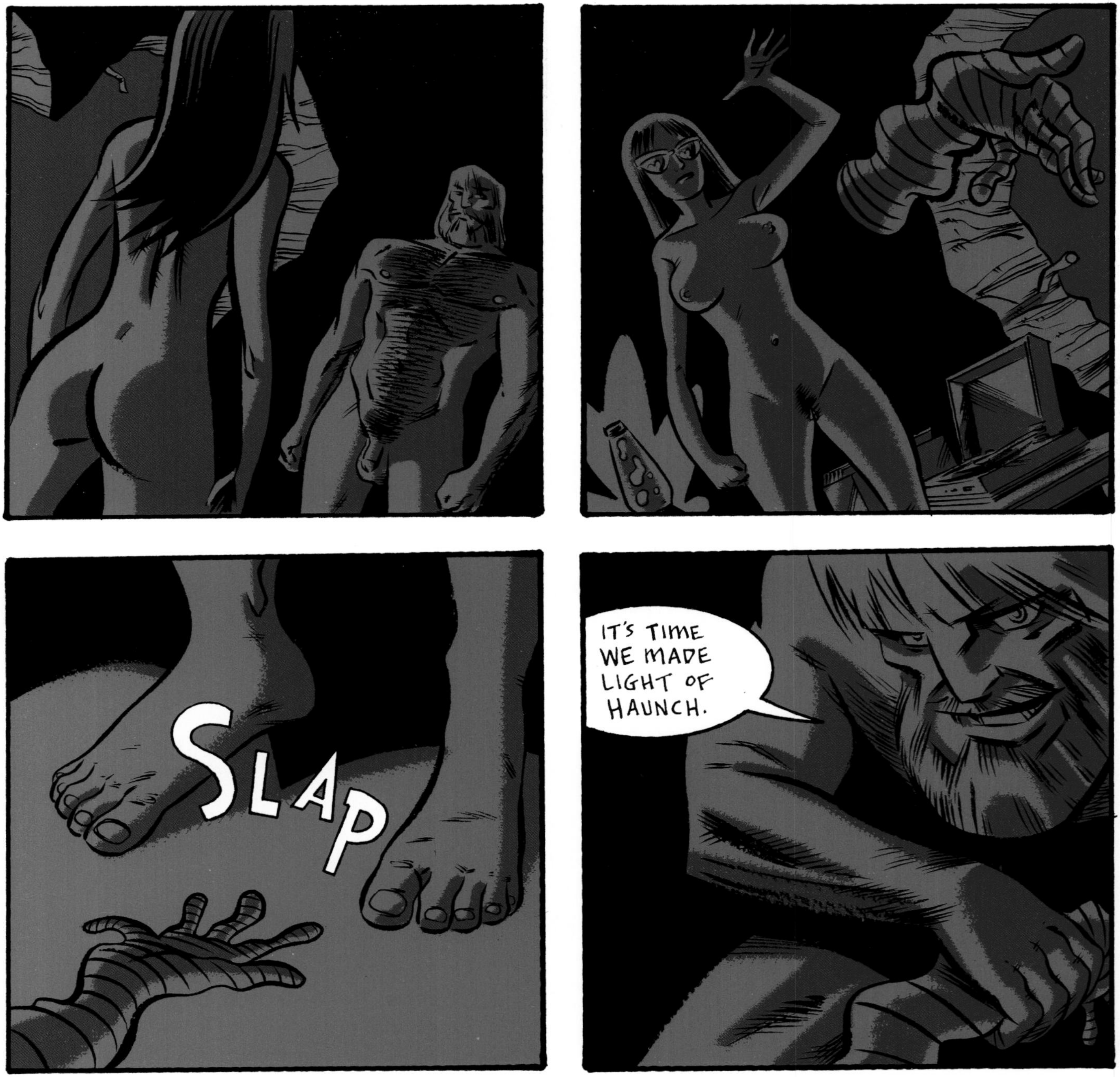
SLAP
IT'S TIME WE MADE LIGHT OF HAUNCH.

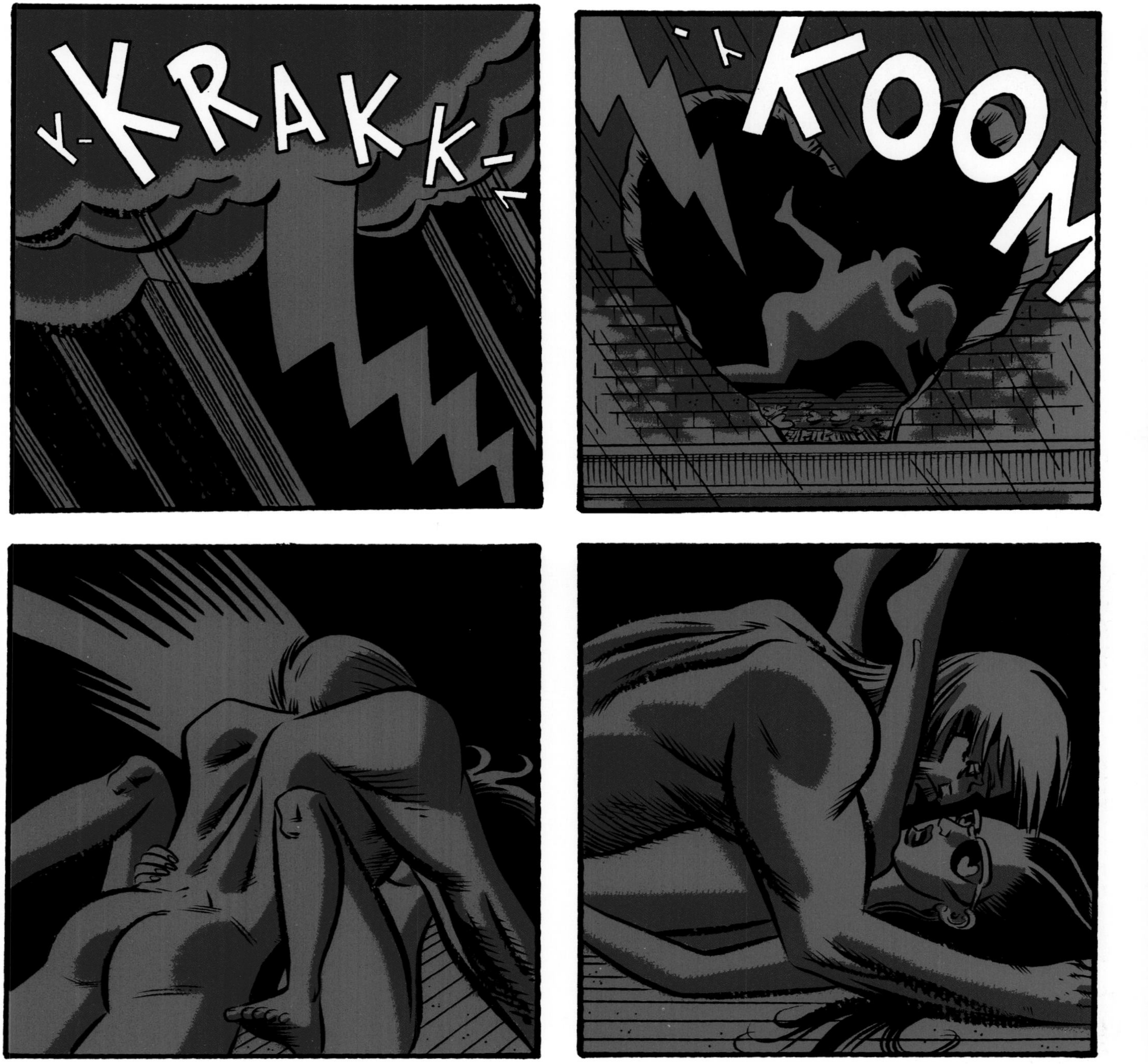
Y-KRAKK-
KOOM

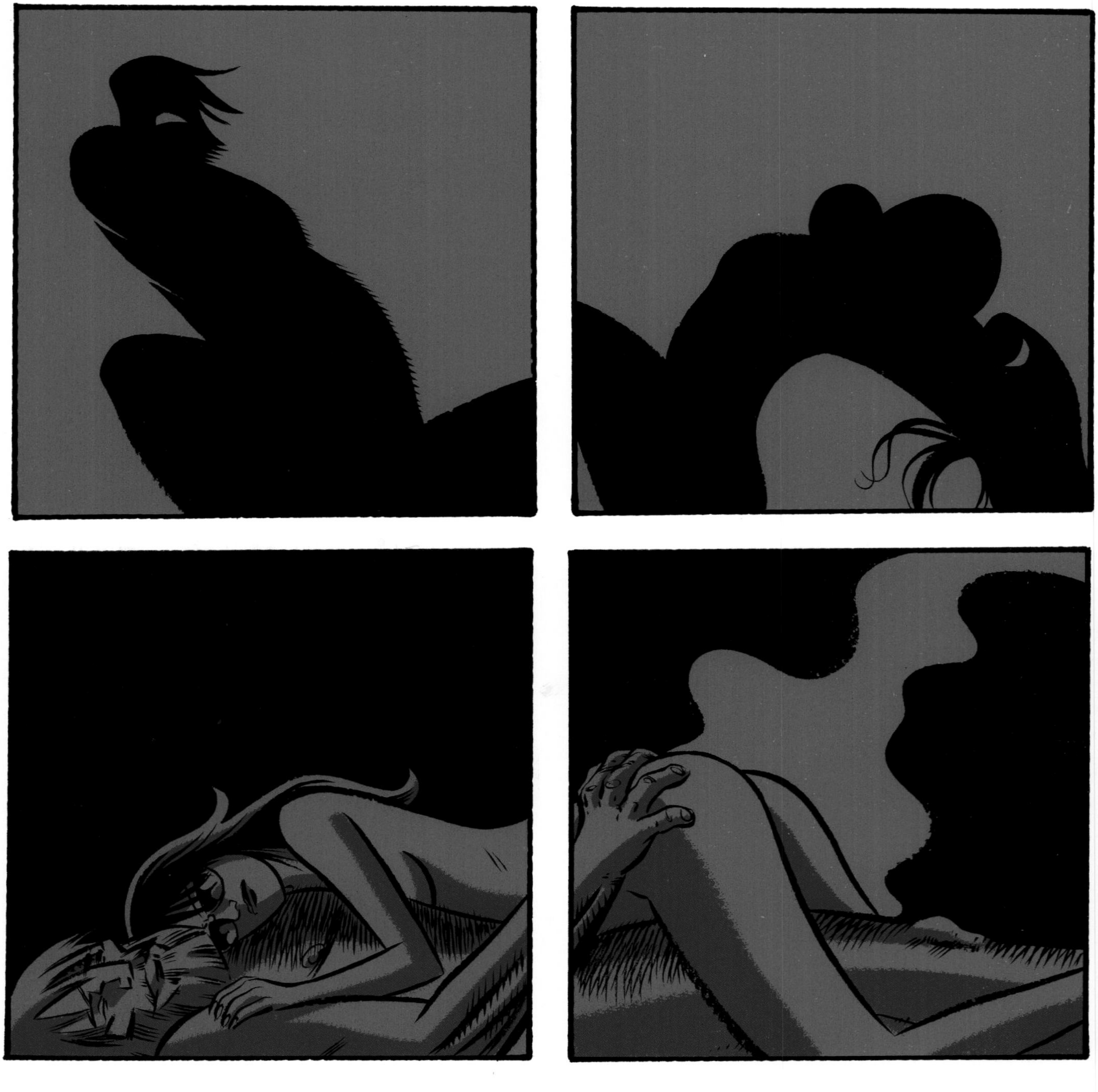

SPLT
!

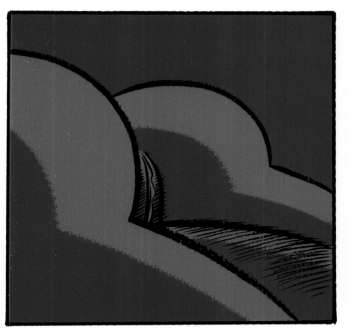

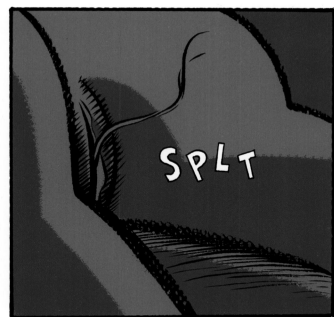

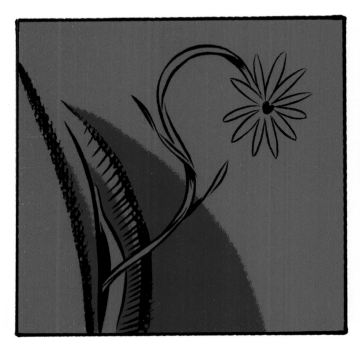

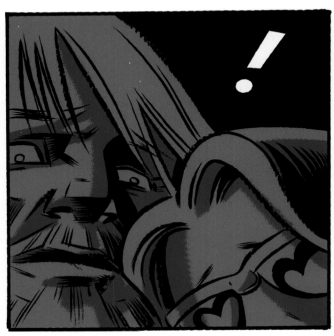

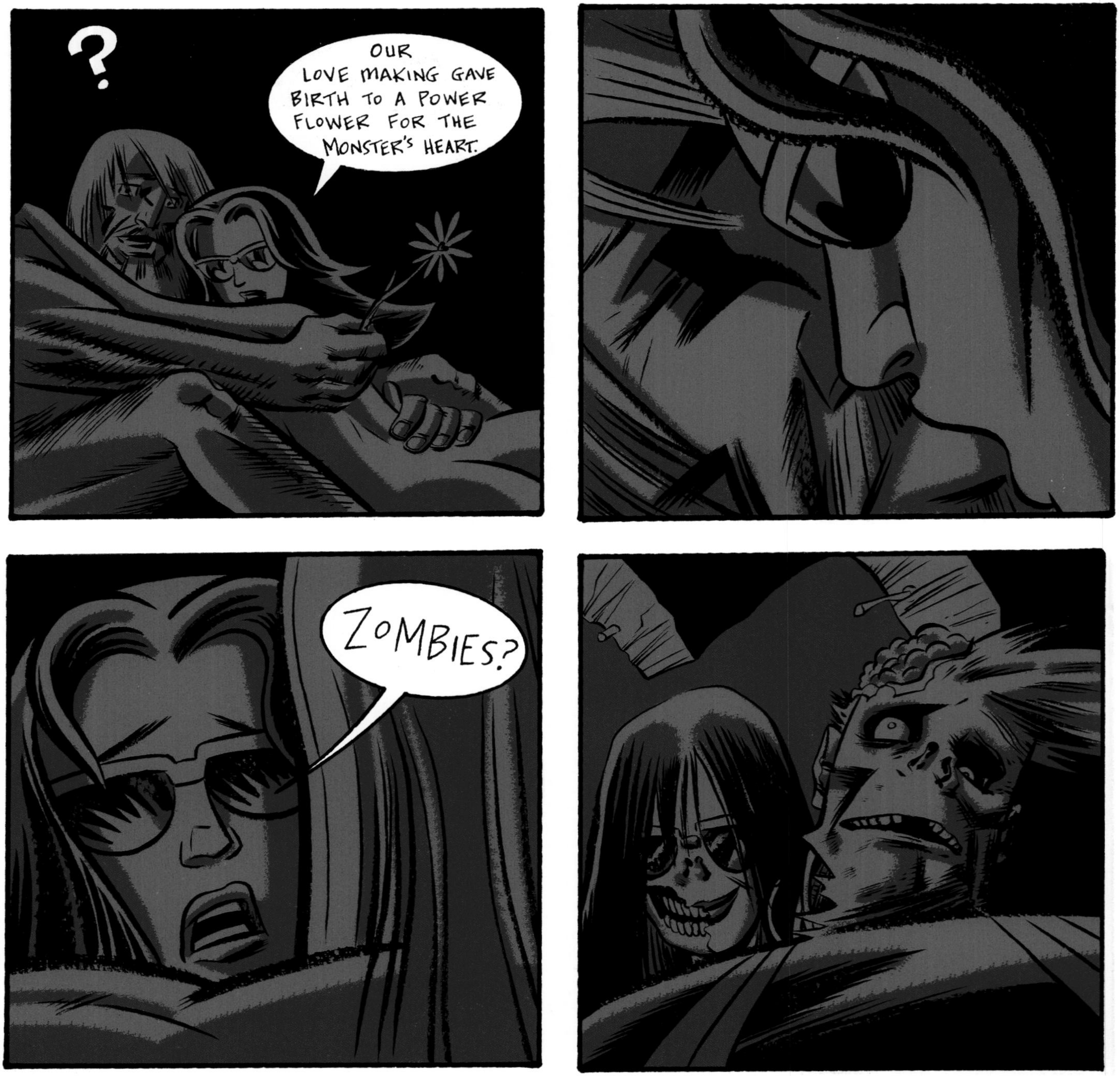
?
OUR LOVE MAKING GAVE BIRTH TO A POWER FLOWER FOR THE MONSTER'S HEART.
ZOMBIES?

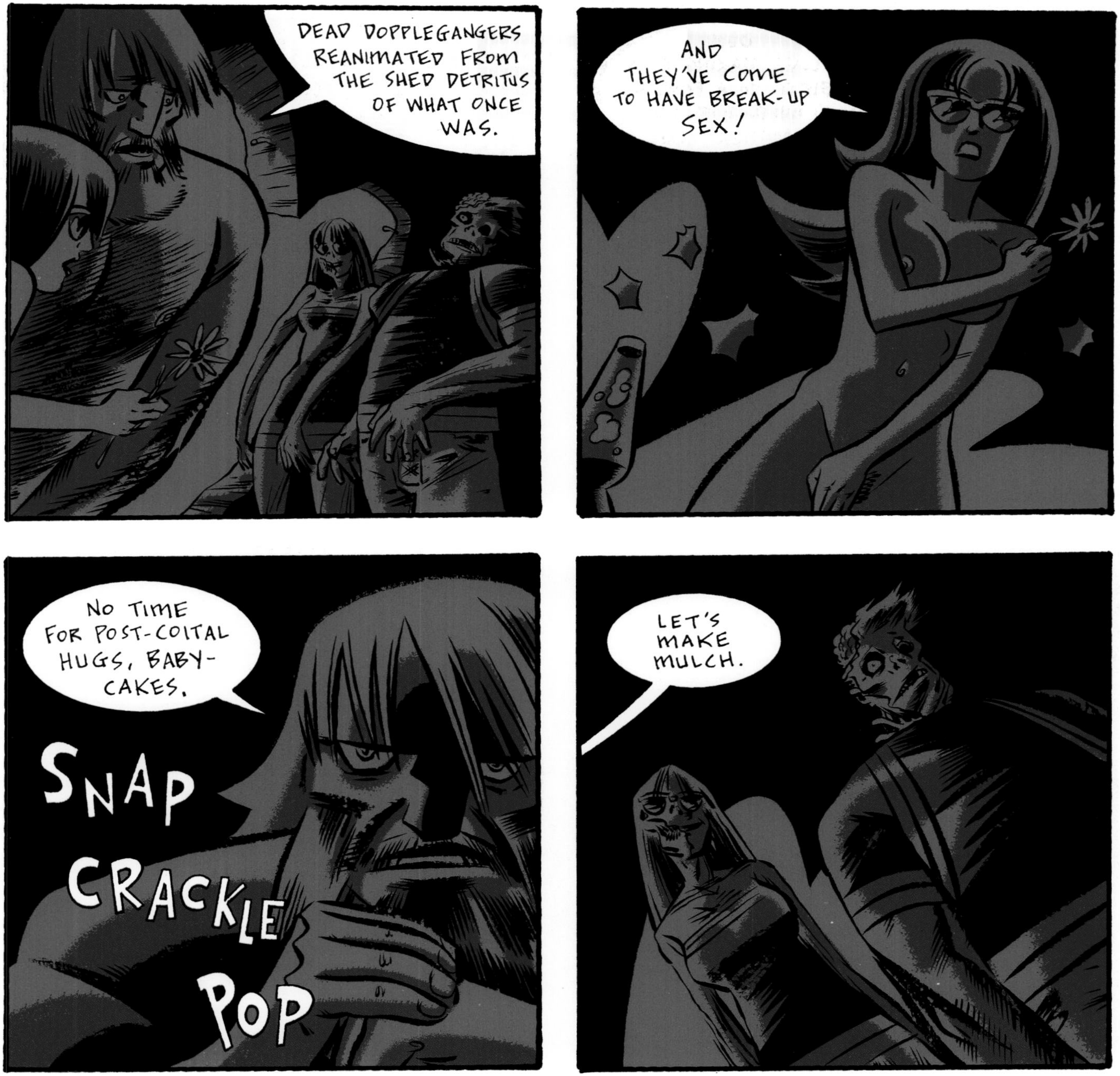
DEAD DOPPLEGANGERS REANIMATED FROM THE SHED DETRITUS OF WHAT ONCE WAS.
AND THEY'VE COME TO HAVE BREAK-UP SEX!
NO TIME FOR POST-COITAL HUGS, BABY-CAKES.
SNAP
CRACKLE
POP
LET'S MAKE MULCH.

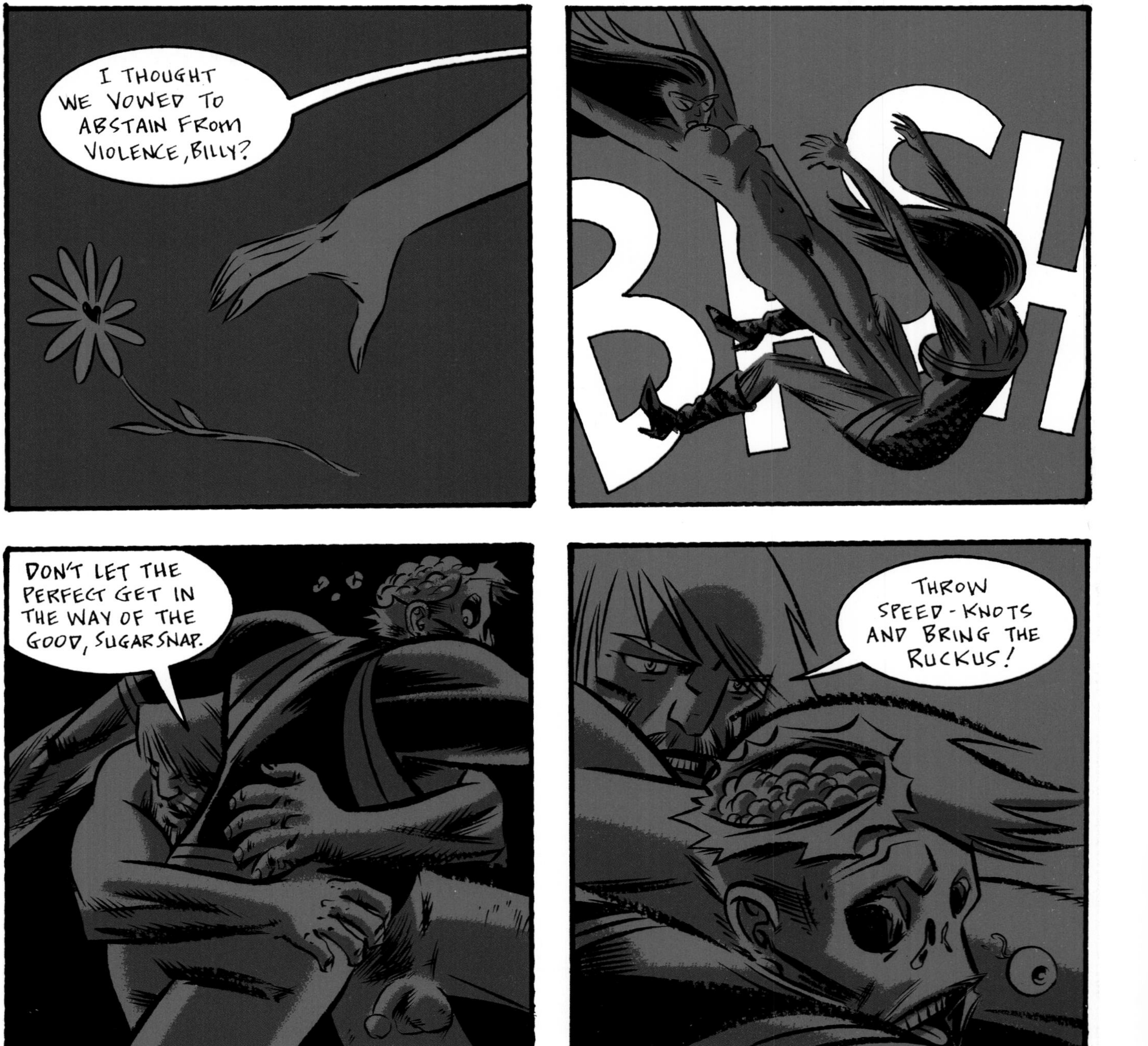
I THOUGHT WE VOWED TO ABSTAIN FROM VIOLENCE, BILLY?
BASH
DON'T LET THE PERFECT GET IN THE WAY OF THE GOOD, SUGARSNAP.
THROW SPEED-KNOTS AND BRING THE RUCKUS!

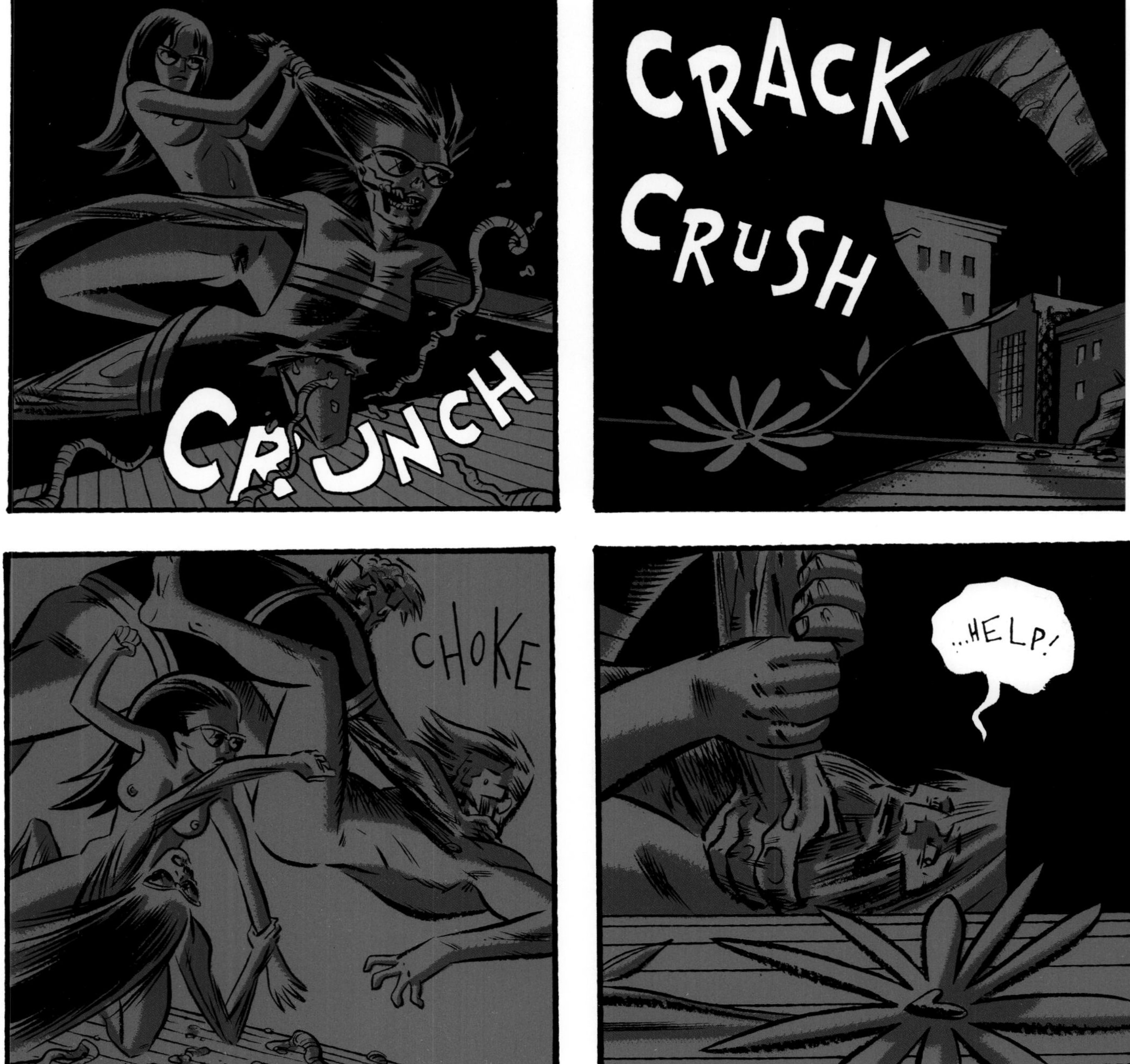
CRUNCH
CRACK
CRUSH
CHOKE
...HELP!

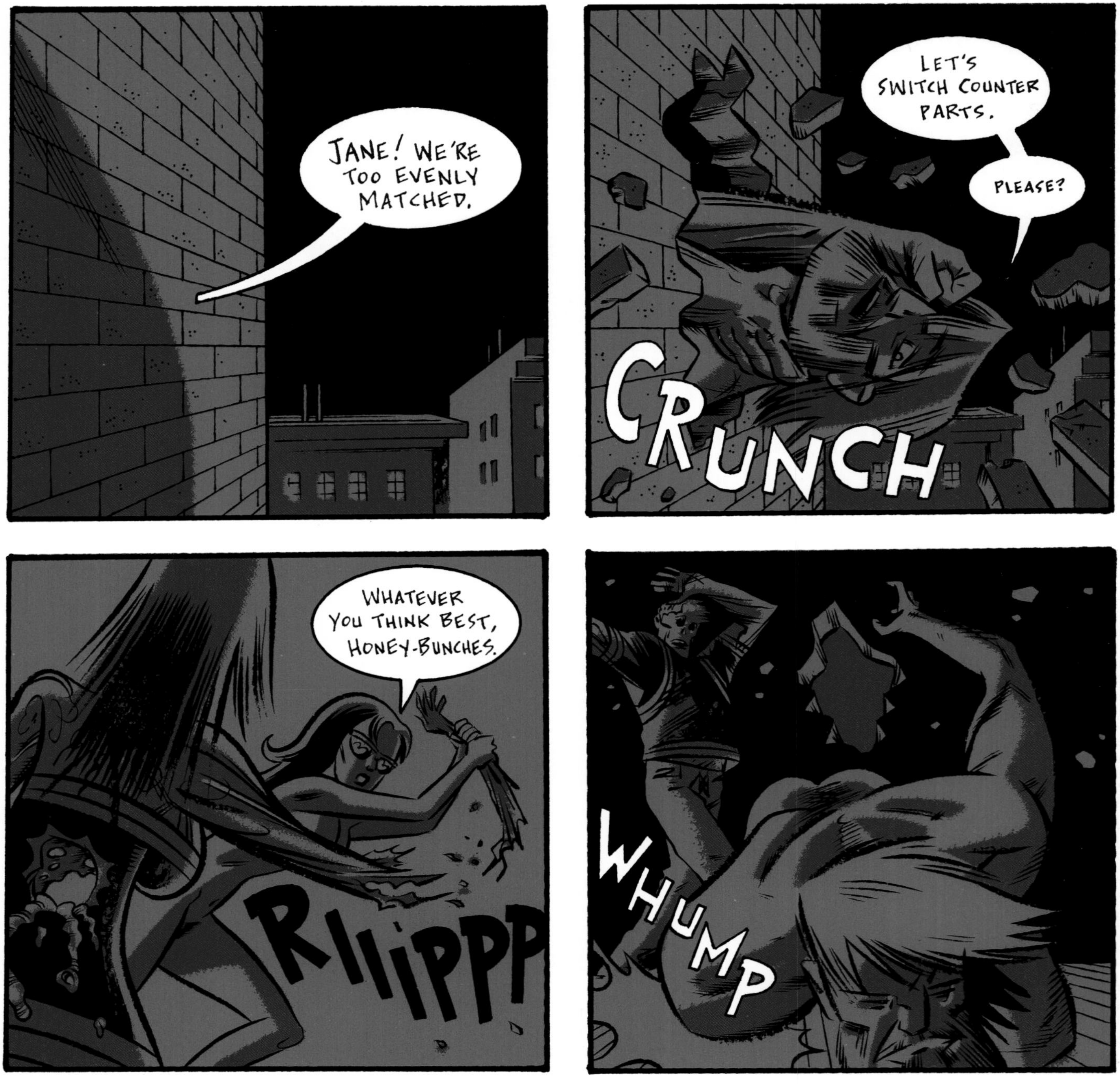
JANE! WE'RE TOO EVENLY MATCHED.
LET'S SWITCH COUNTER PARTS.
PLEASE?
CRUNCH
WHATEVER YOU THINK BEST, HONEY-BUNCHES.
RIIIPPP
WHUMP

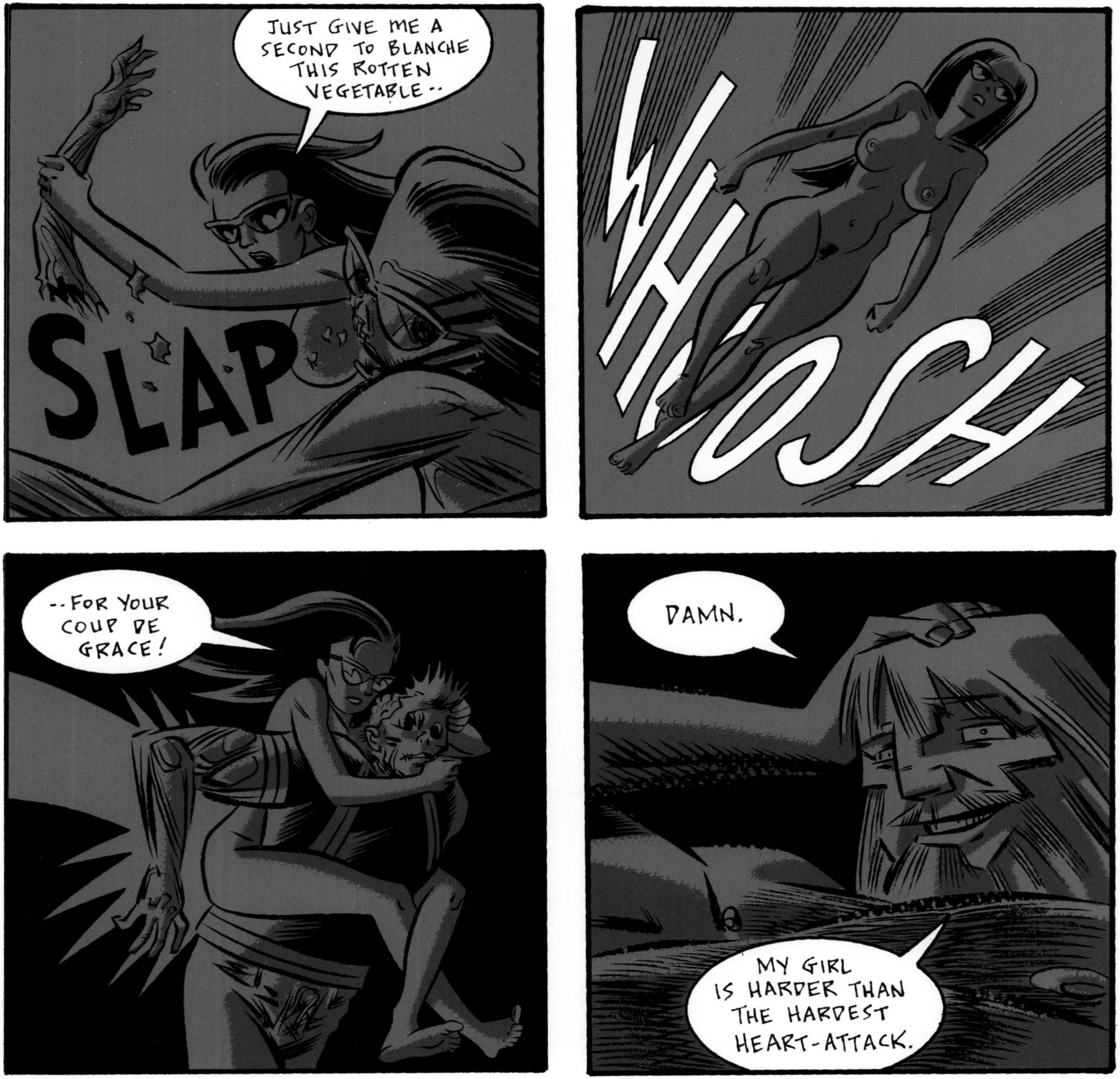
JUST GIVE ME A SECOND TO BLANCHE THIS ROTTEN VEGETABLE--
SLAP
WHOOSH
--FOR YOUR COUP DE GRACE!
DAMN.
MY GIRL IS HARDER THAN THE HARDEST HEART-ATTACK.

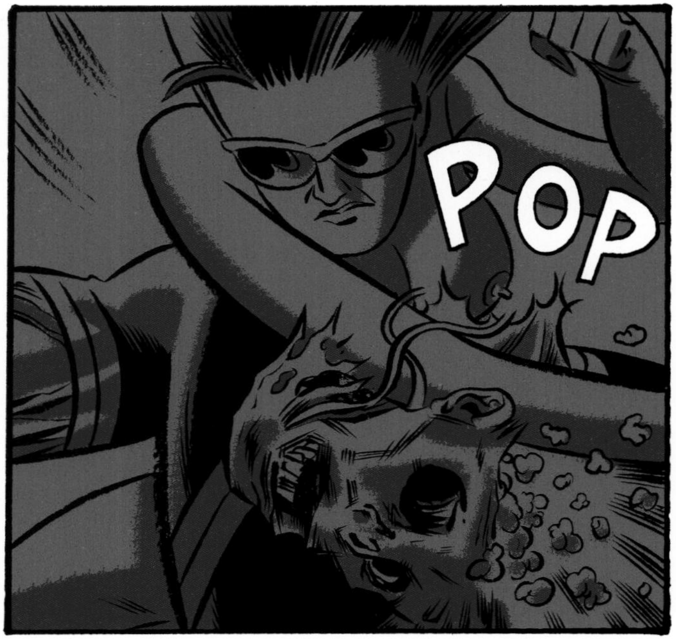
POP

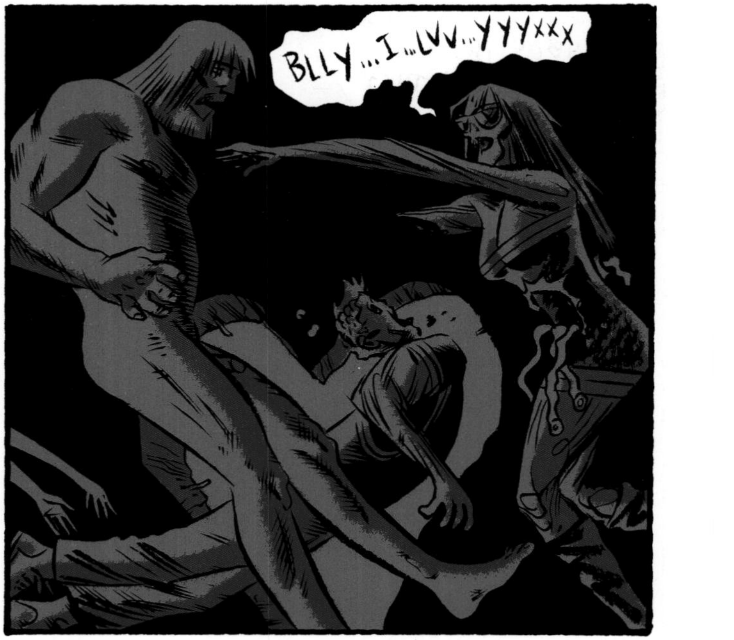
BLLY...I...LVV...YYYXXX

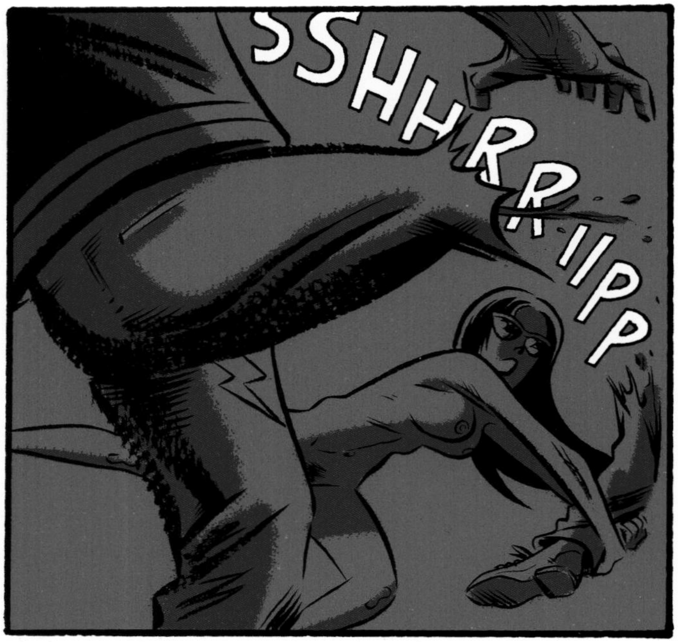
SSHHRRRIIPP

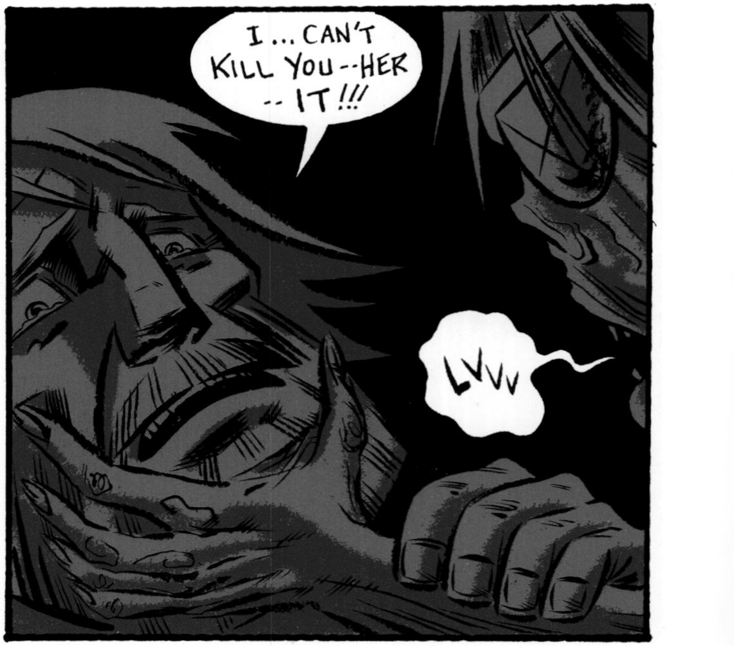
I ... CAN'T KILL YOU--HER --IT!!!
LVVV

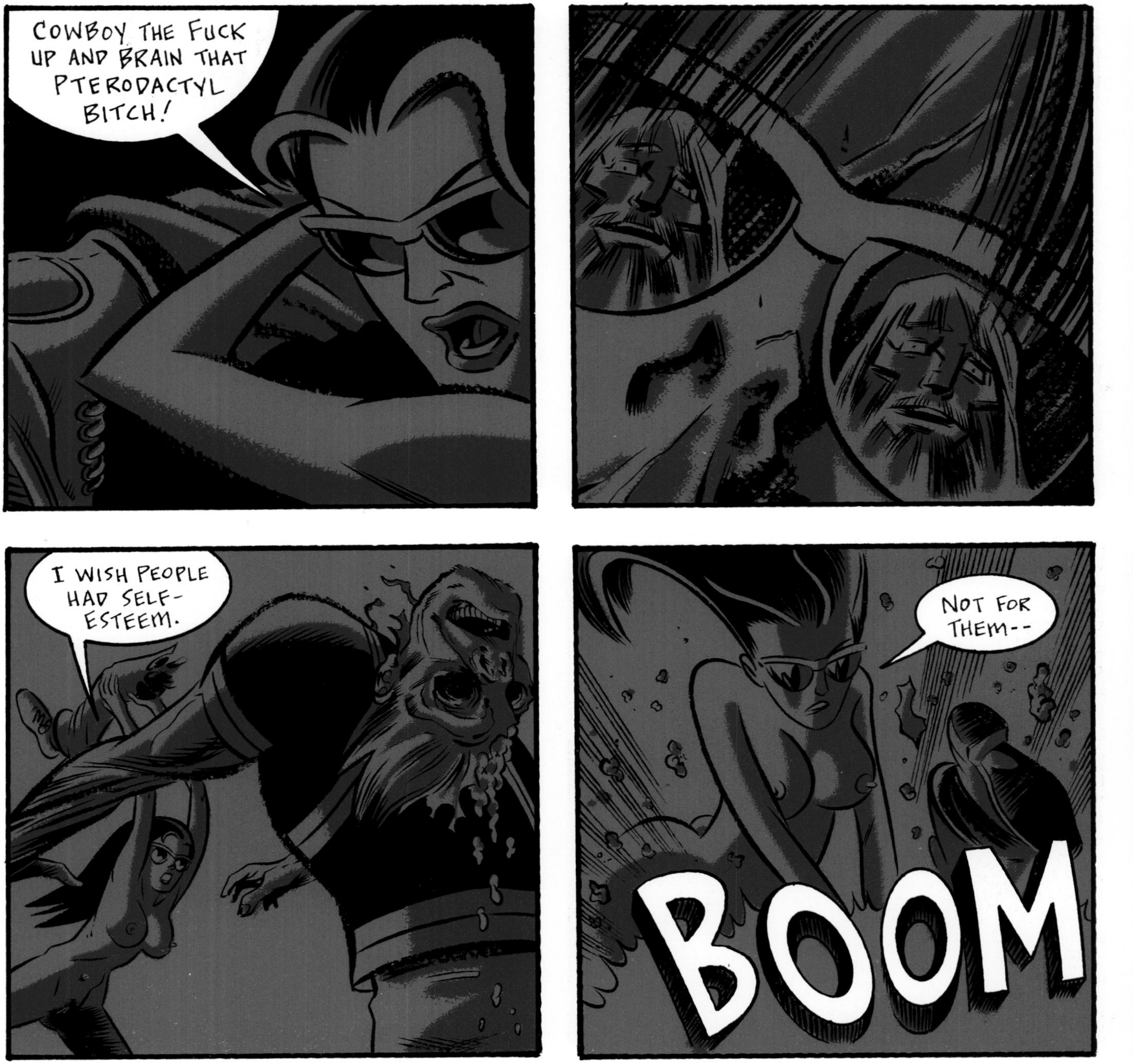
COWBOY THE FUCK UP AND BRAIN THAT PTERODACTYL BITCH!
I WISH PEOPLE HAD SELF-ESTEEM.
NOT FOR THEM--
BOOM

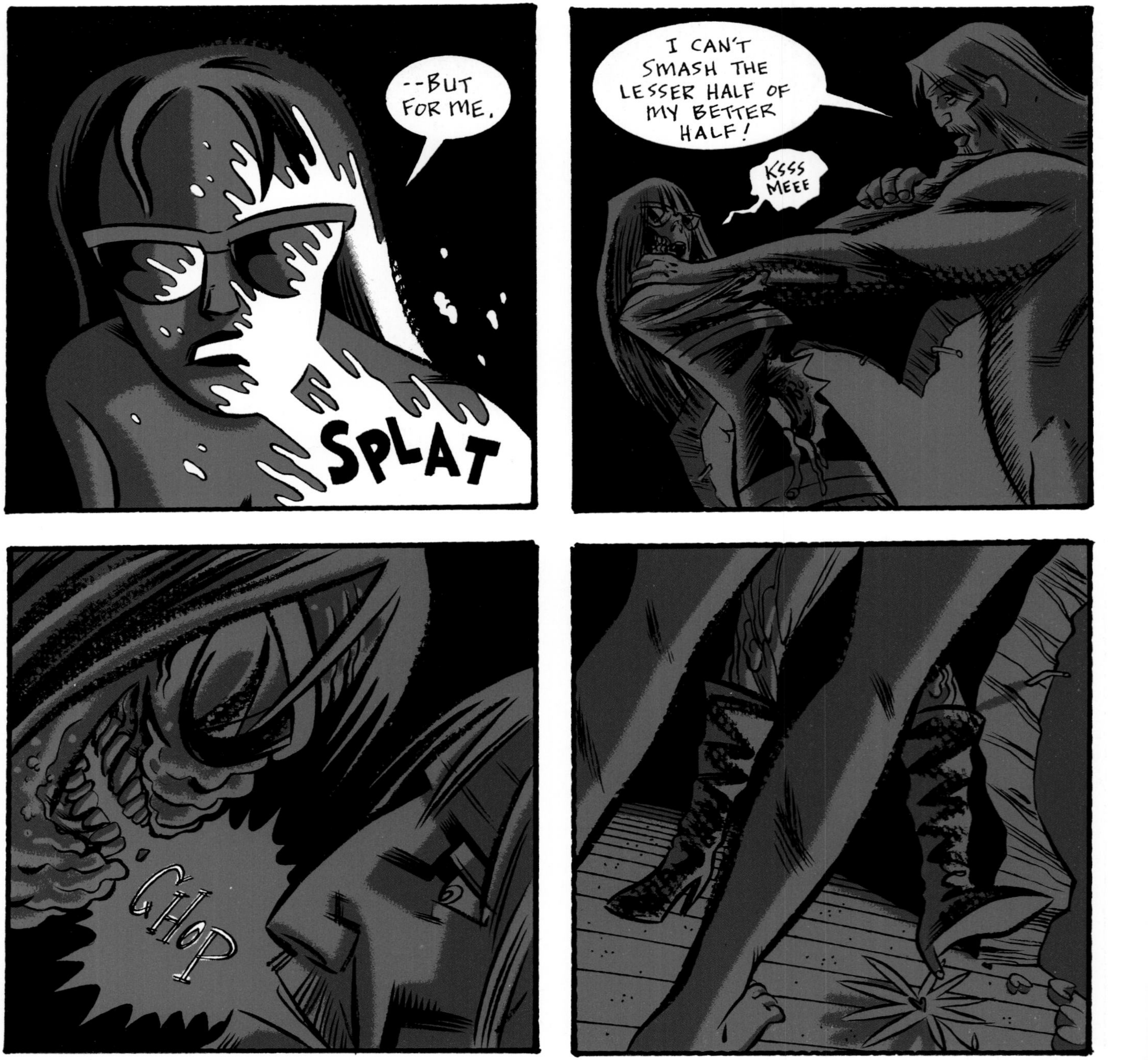
--BUT FOR ME.
SPLAT
I CAN'T SMASH THE LESSER HALF OF MY BETTER HALF!
KSSS MEEE
CHOP

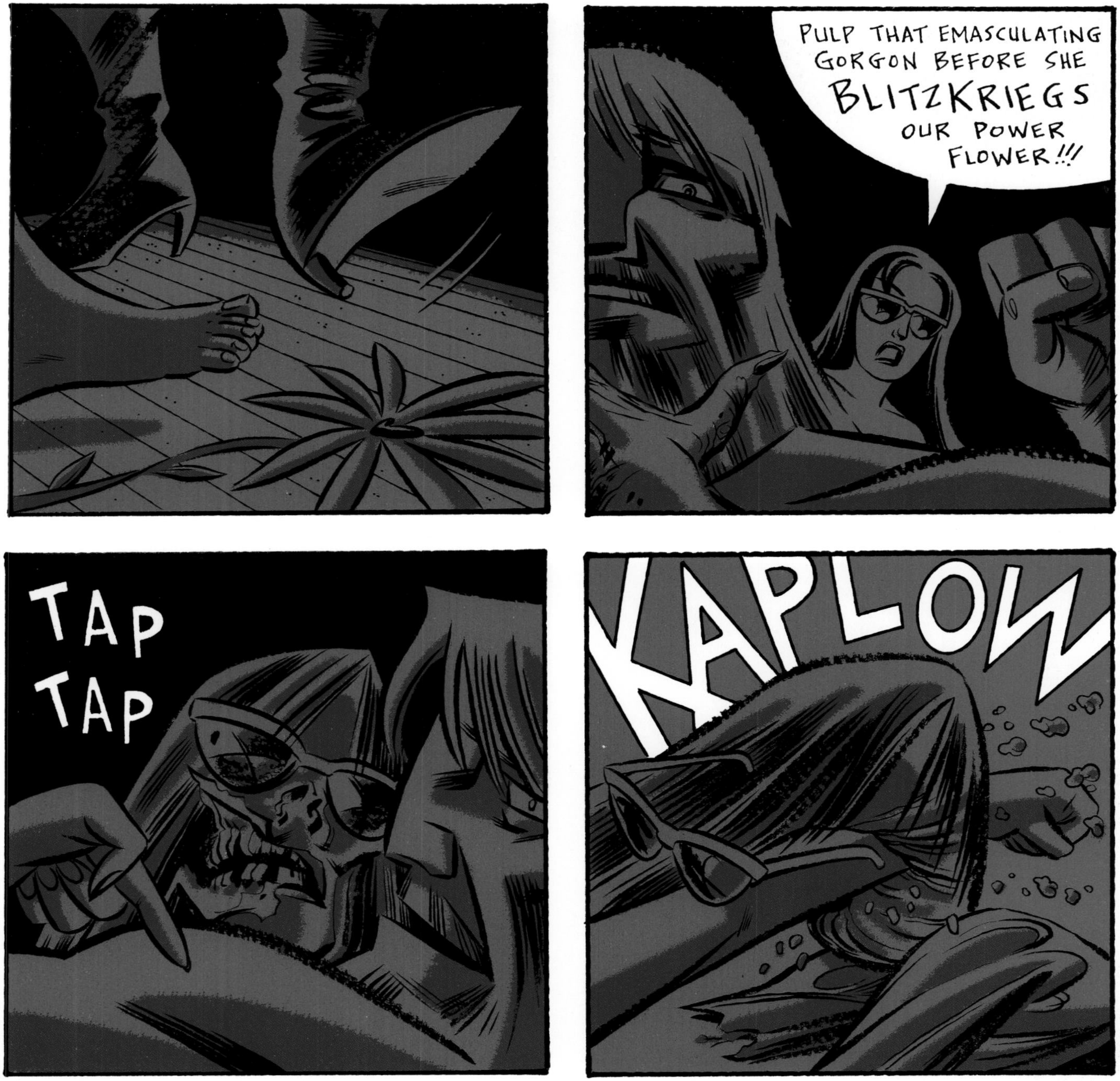
PULP THAT EMASCULATING GORGON BEFORE SHE BLITZKRIEGS OUR POWER FLOWER!!!
TAP TAP
KAPLOW

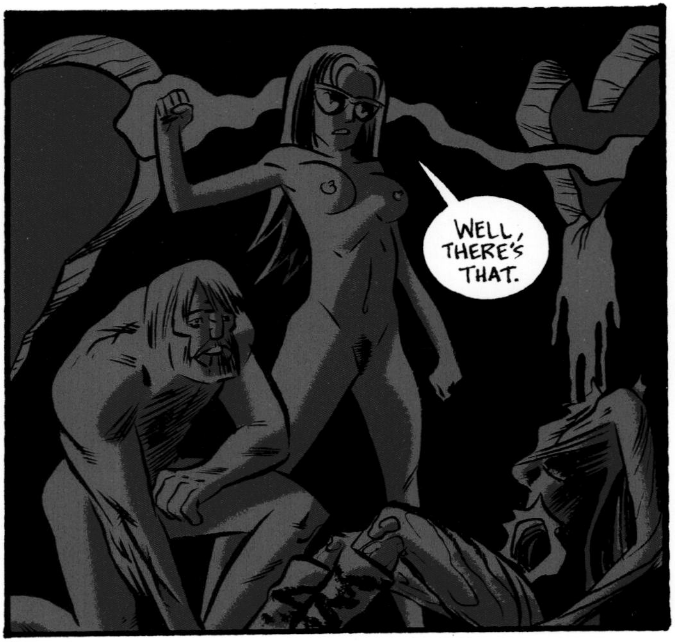
WELL, THERE'S THAT.

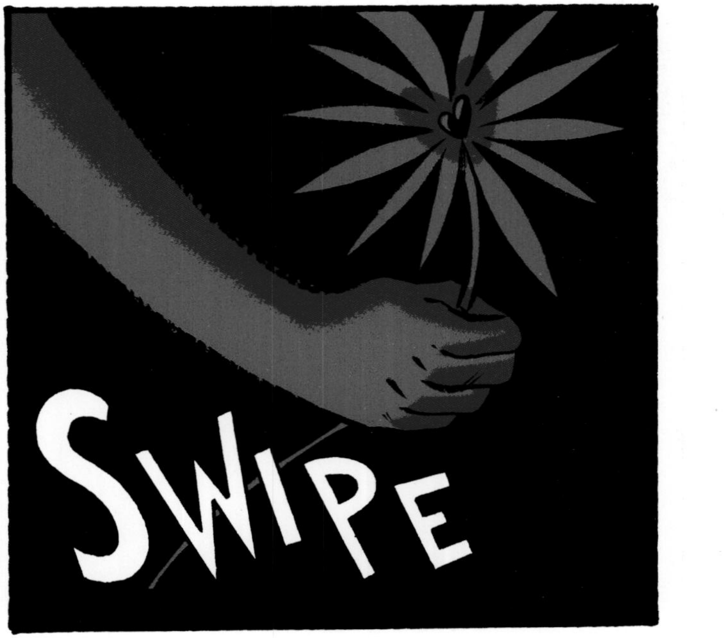
SWIPE

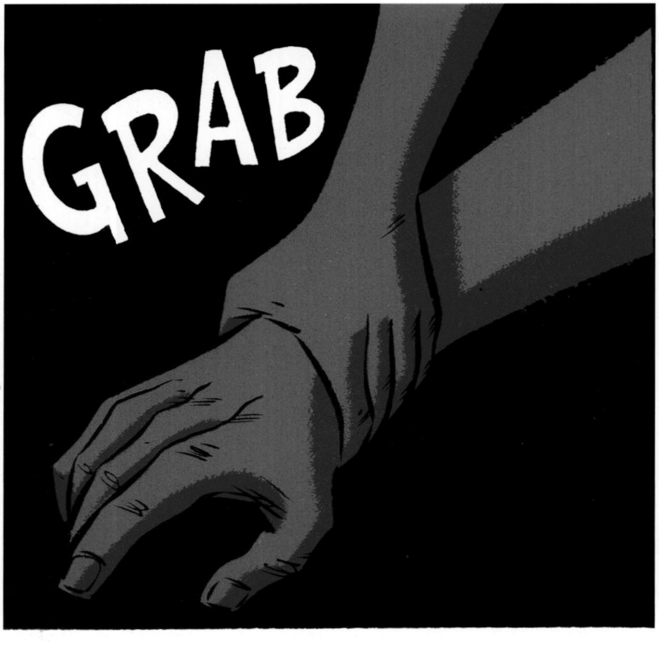
GRAB

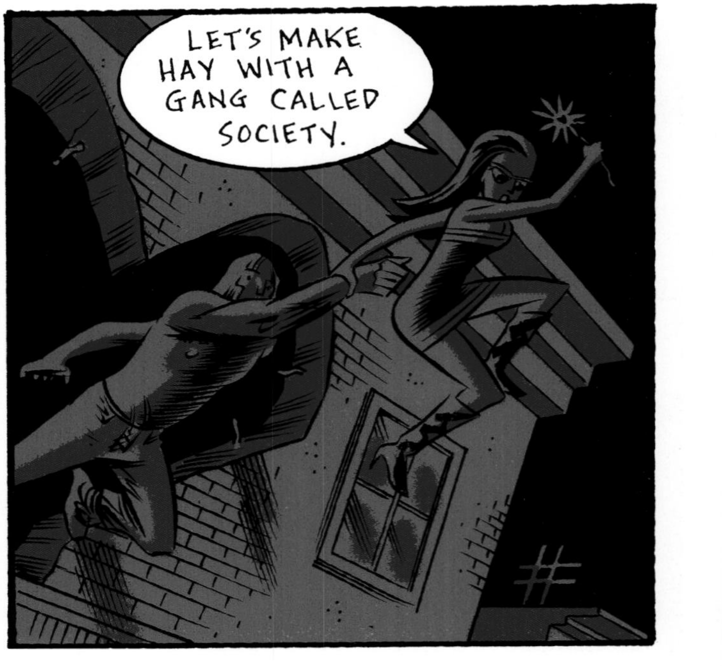
LET'S MAKE HAY WITH A GANG CALLED SOCIETY.

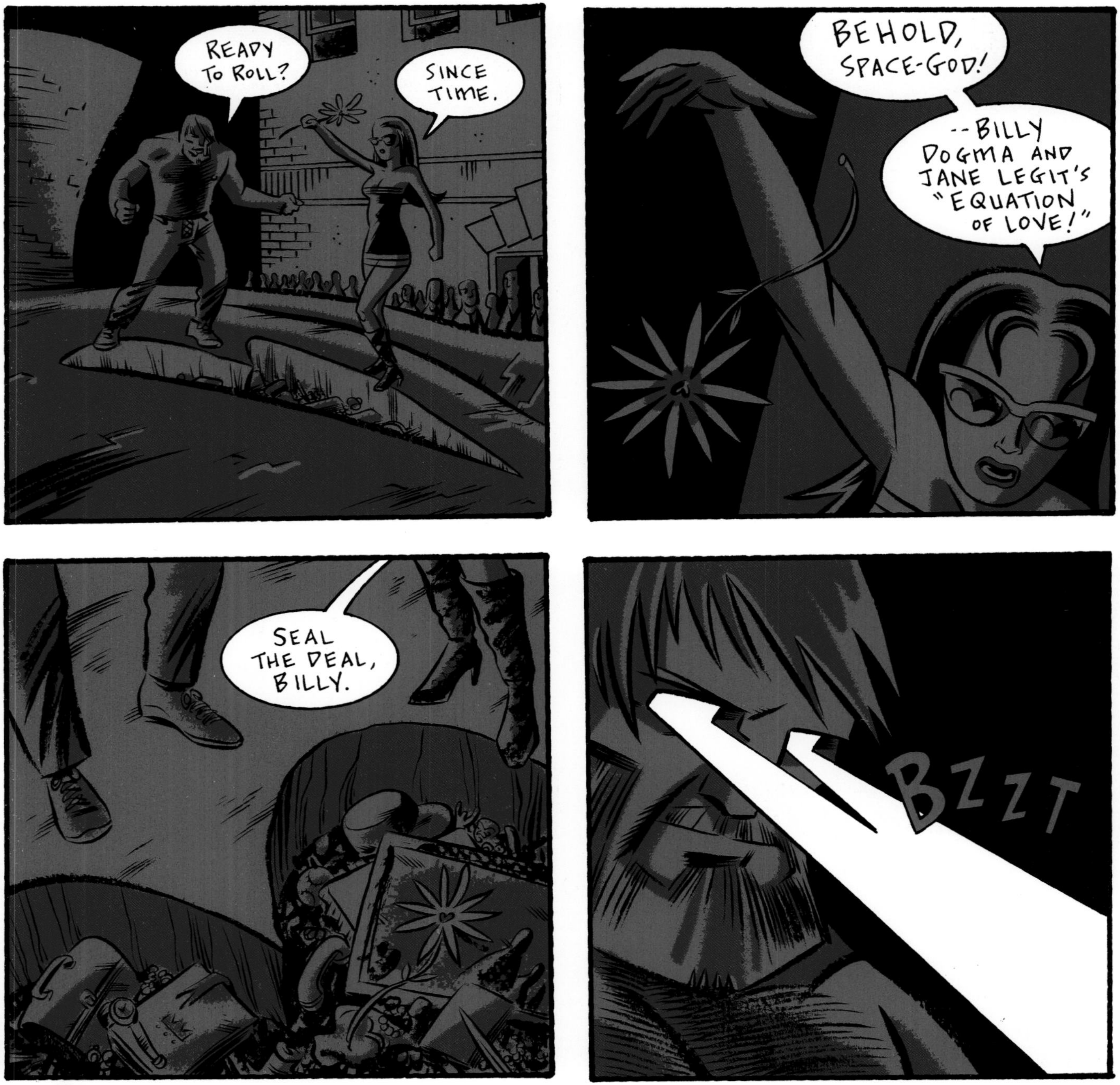
READY TO ROLL?
SINCE TIME.
BEHOLD, SPACE-GOD!
--BILLY DOGMA AND JANE LEGIT'S "EQUATION OF LOVE!"
SEAL THE DEAL, BILLY.
BZZT

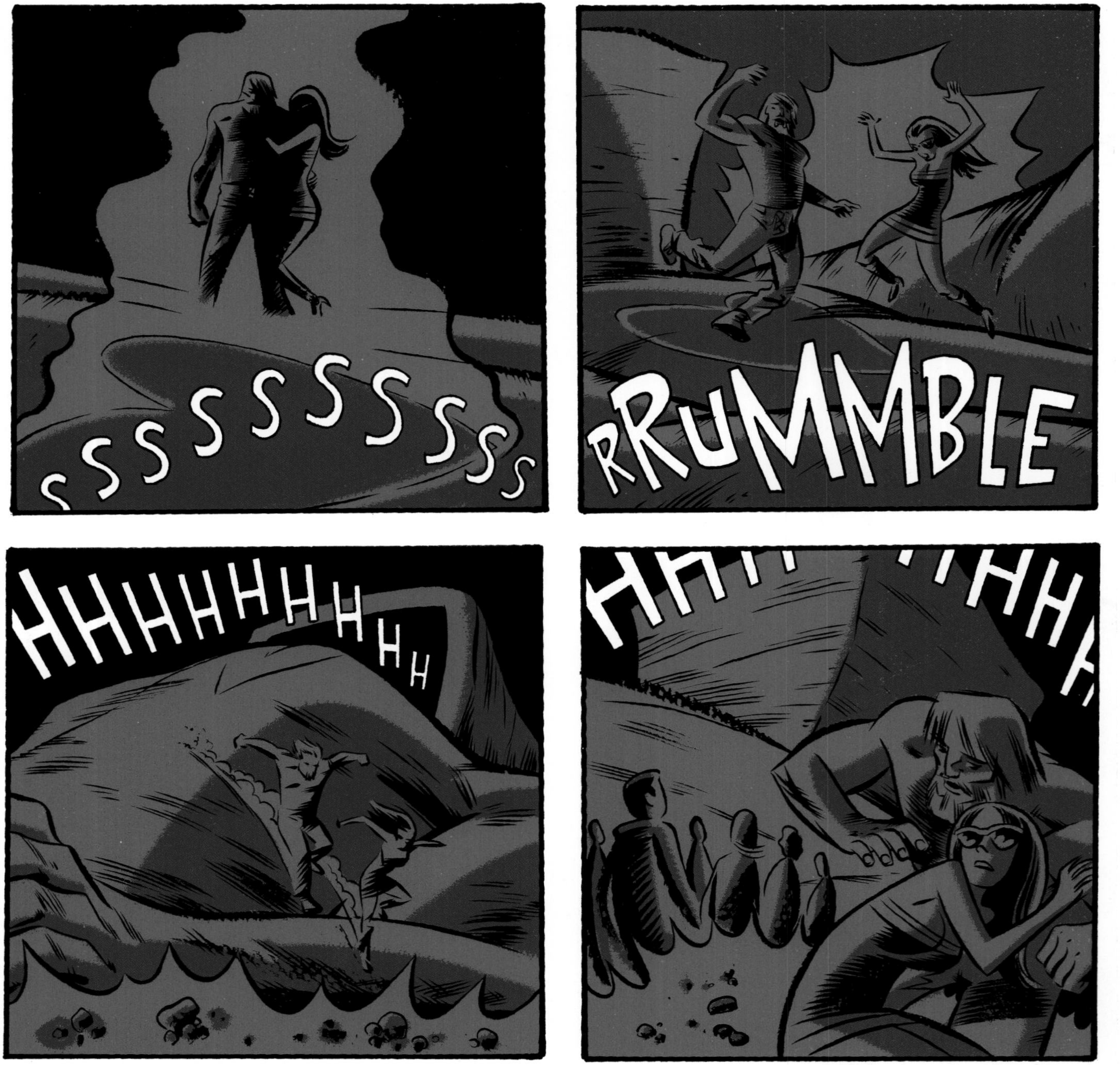
SSSSSSSSSS
RRUMMBLE
HHHHHHHHHH

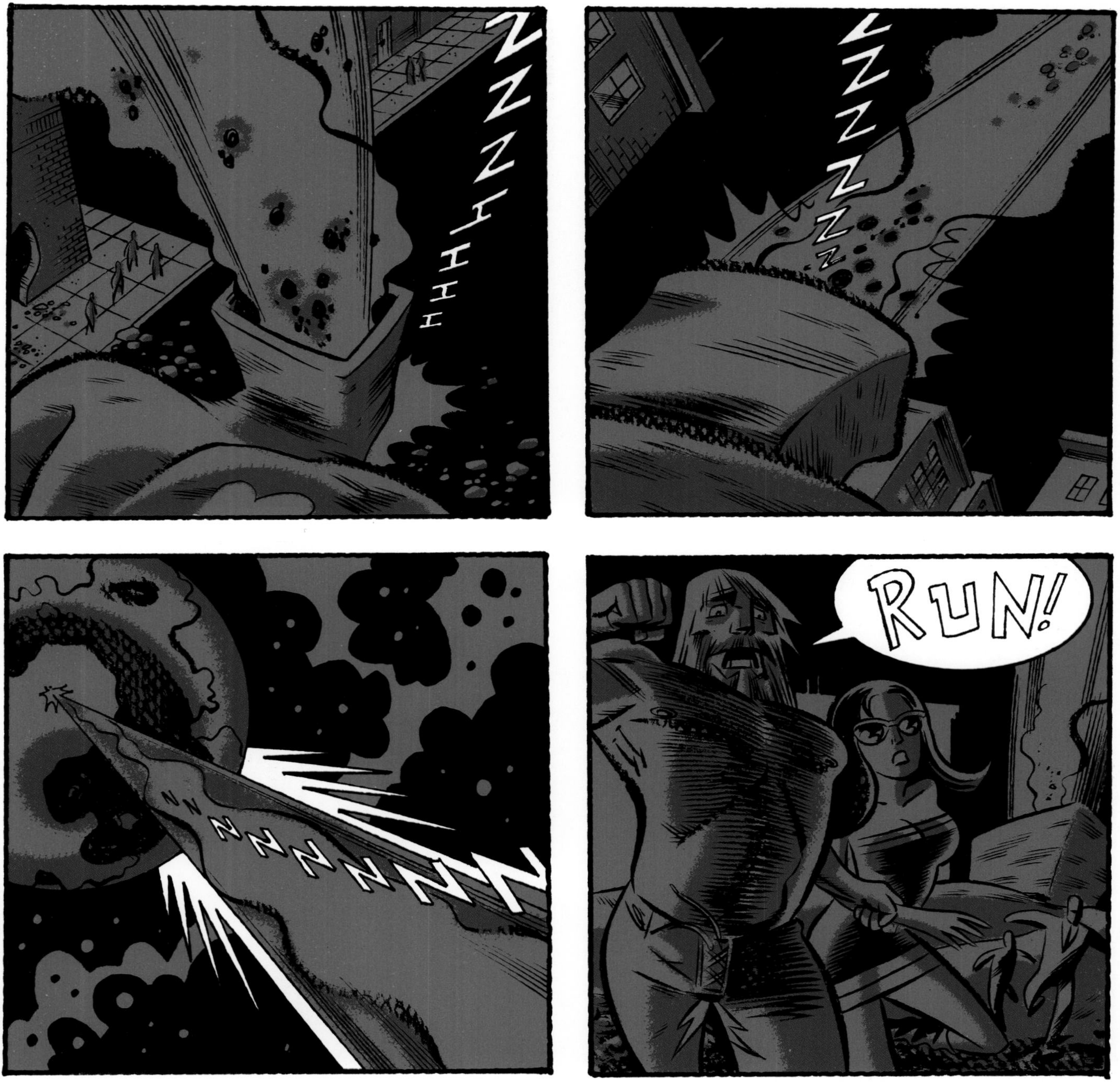
RUN!

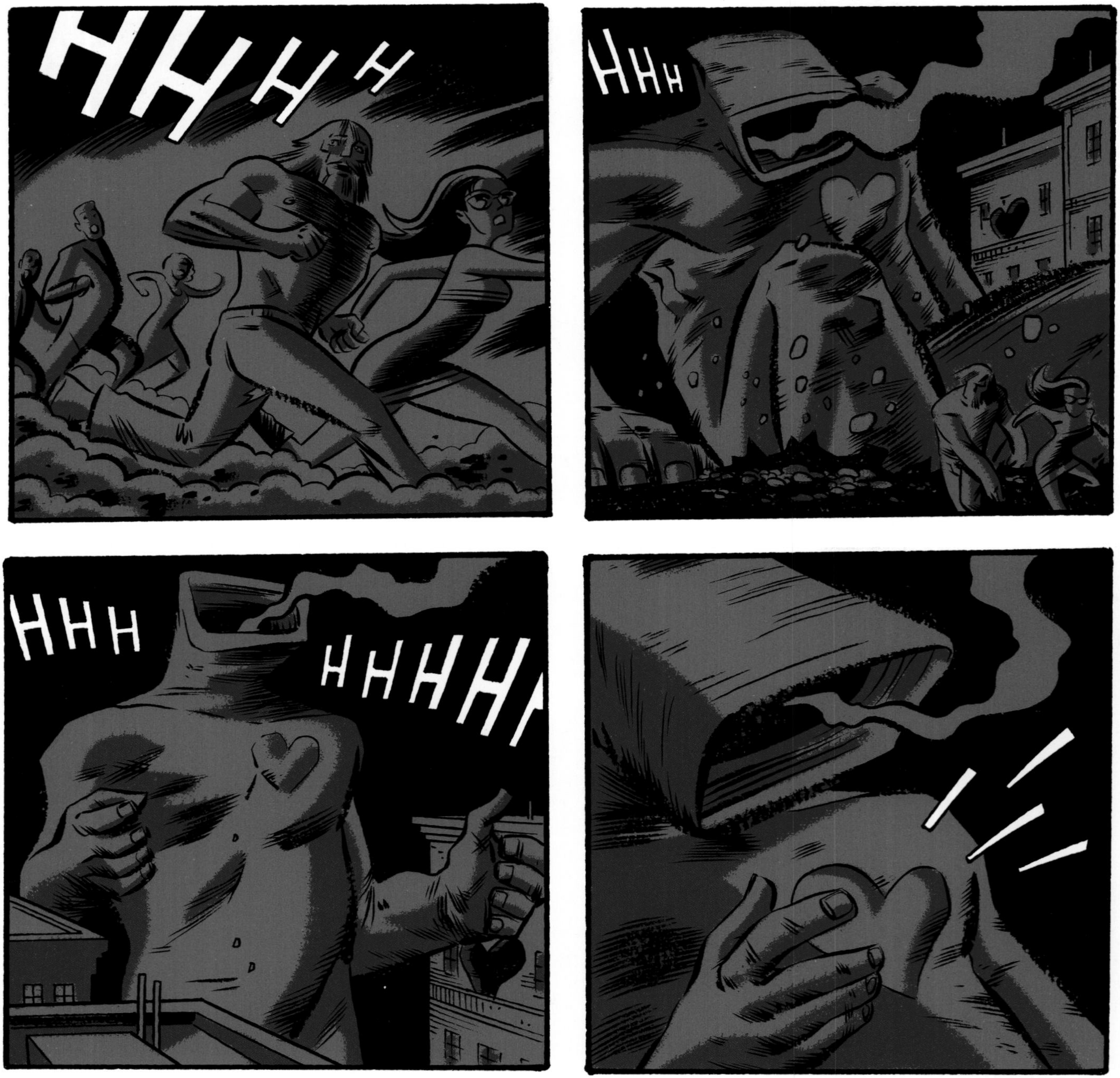
HHHHH
HHH
HHH
HHHHH

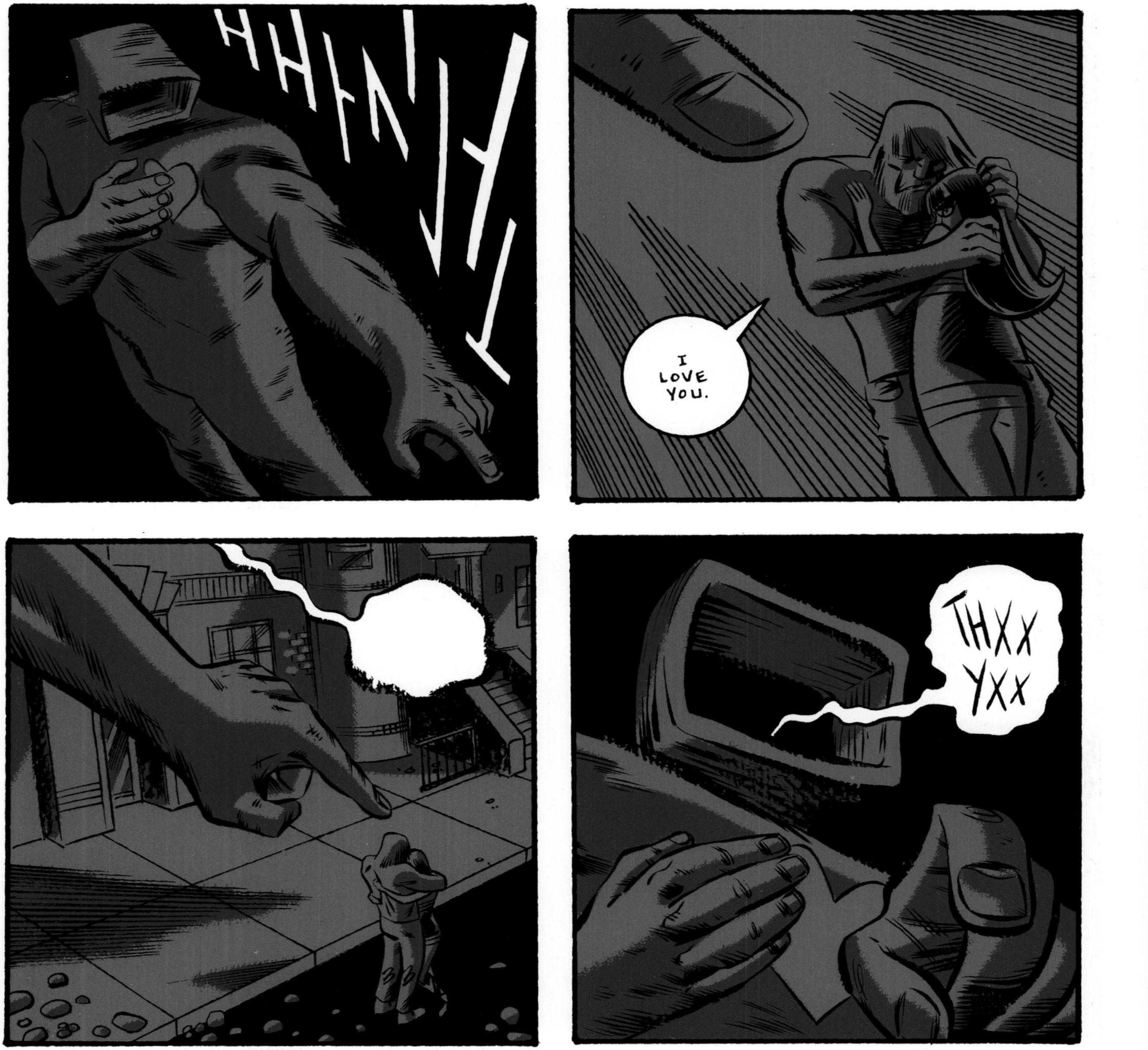
I LOVE YOU.

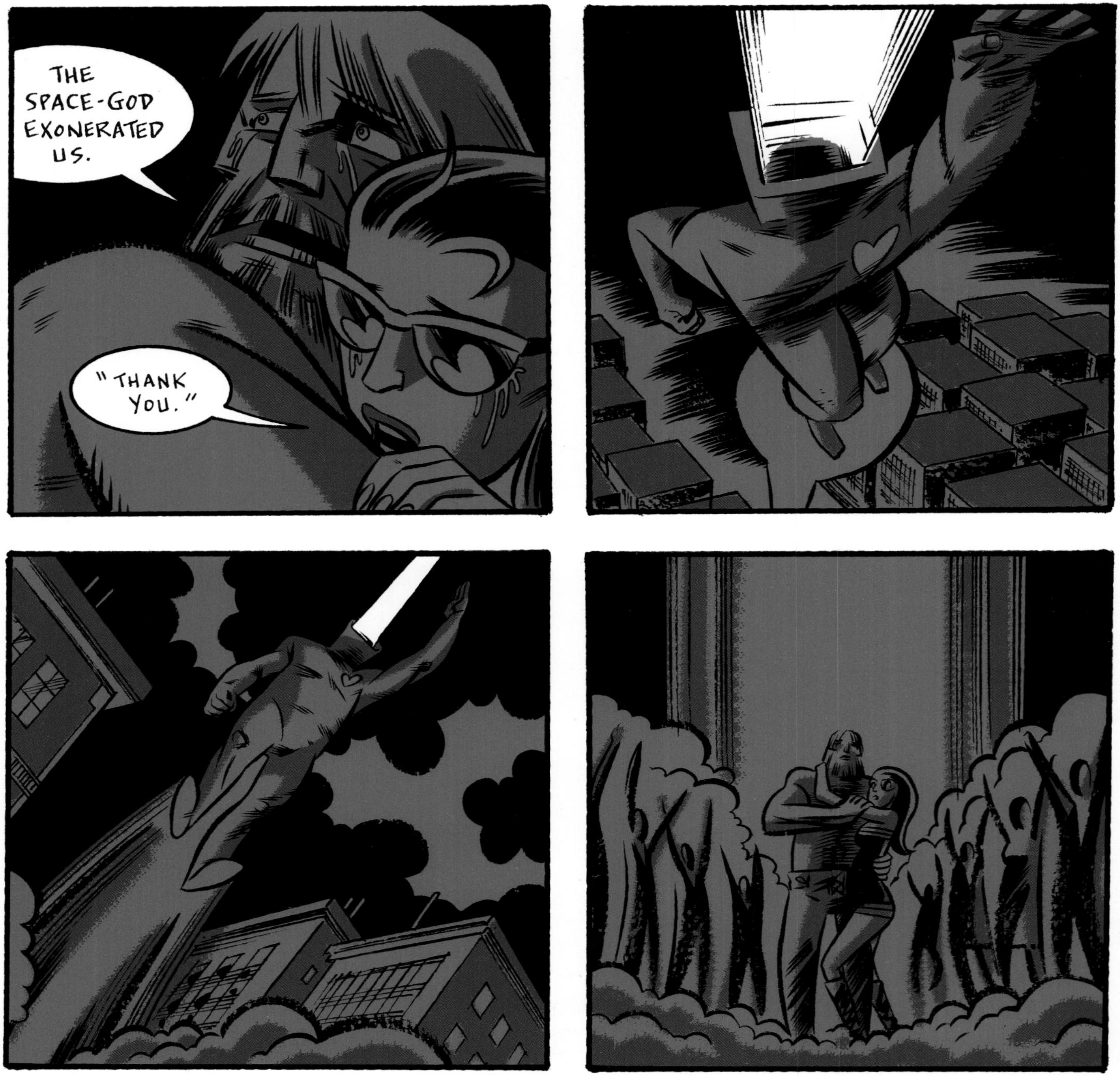
THE SPACE-GOD EXONERATED US.
"THANK YOU."

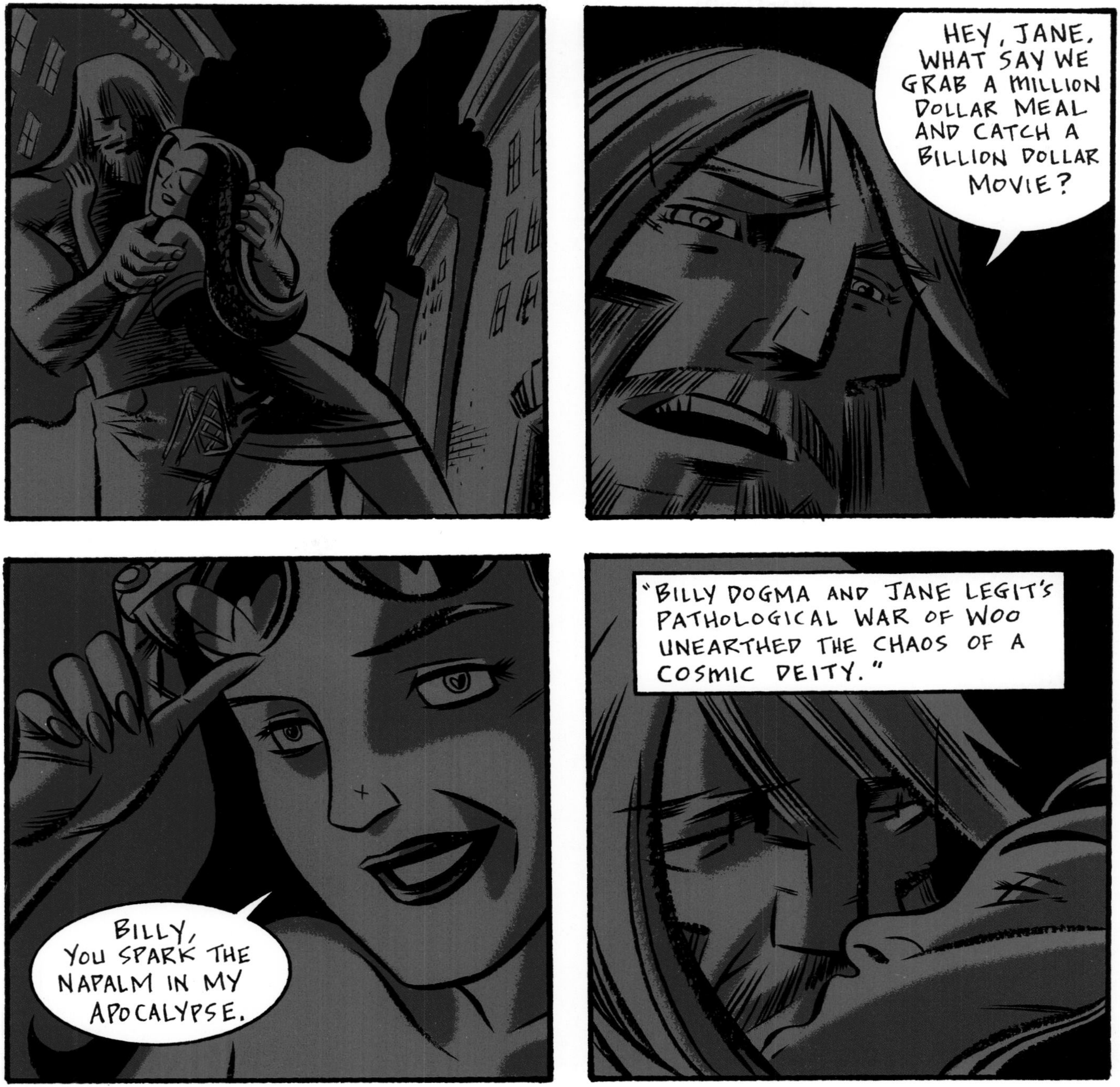
HEY, JANE, WHAT SAY WE GRAB A MILLION DOLLAR MEAL AND CATCH A BILLION DOLLAR MOVIE?
BILLY, YOU SPARK THE NAPALM IN MY APOCALYPSE.
"BILLY DOGMA AND JANE LEGIT'S PATHOLOGICAL WAR OF WOO UNEARTHED THE CHAOS OF A COSMIC DEITY."

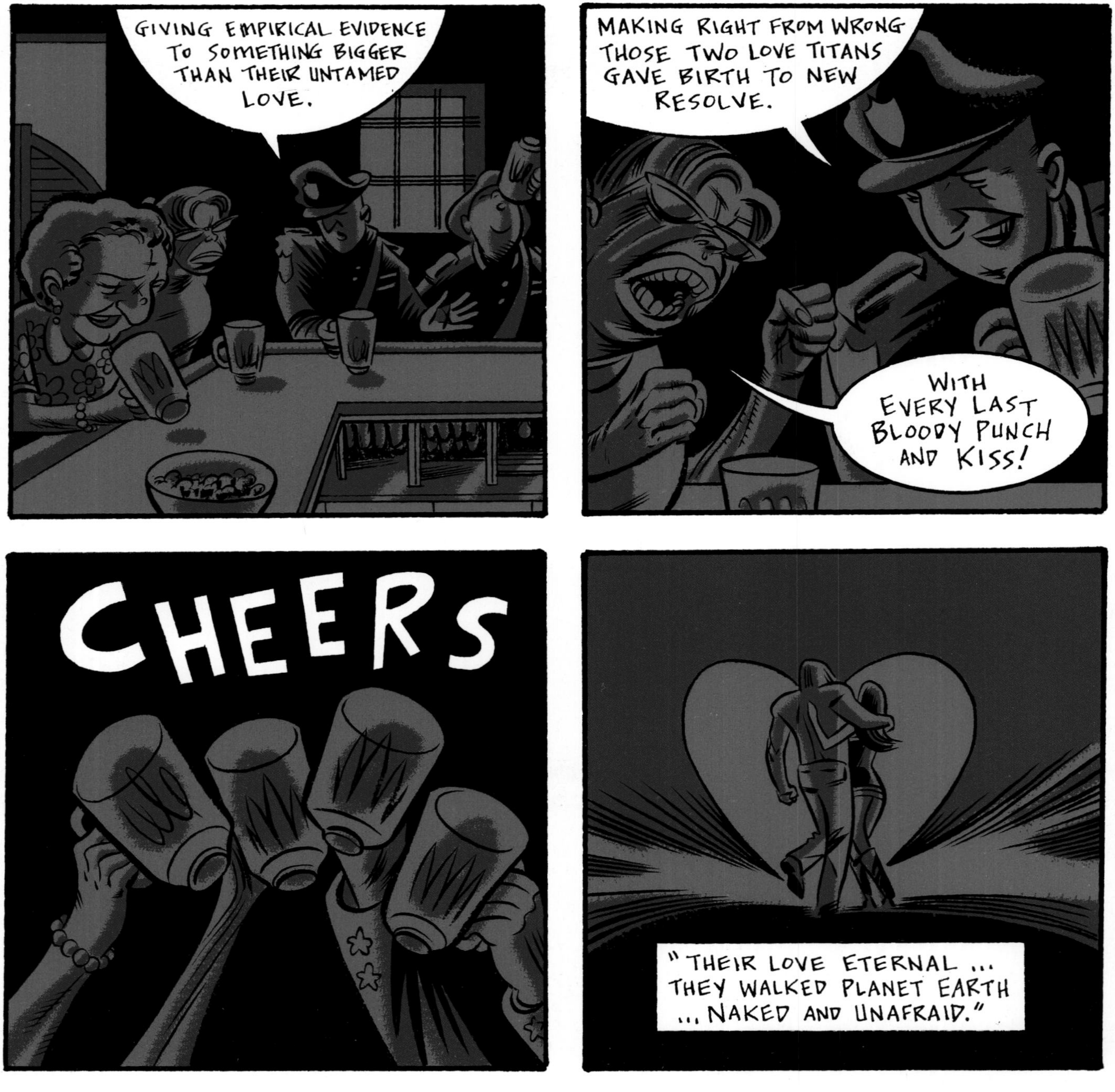
GIVING EMPIRICAL EVIDENCE TO SOMETHING BIGGER THAN THEIR UNTAMED LOVE.
MAKING RIGHT FROM WRONG THOSE TWO LOVE TITANS GAVE BIRTH TO NEW RESOLVE.
WITH EVERY LAST BLOODY PUNCH AND KISS!
CHEERS
"THEIR LOVE ETERNAL ... THEY WALKED PLANET EARTH ... NAKED AND UNAFRAID."

PART TWO: "FEAR, MY

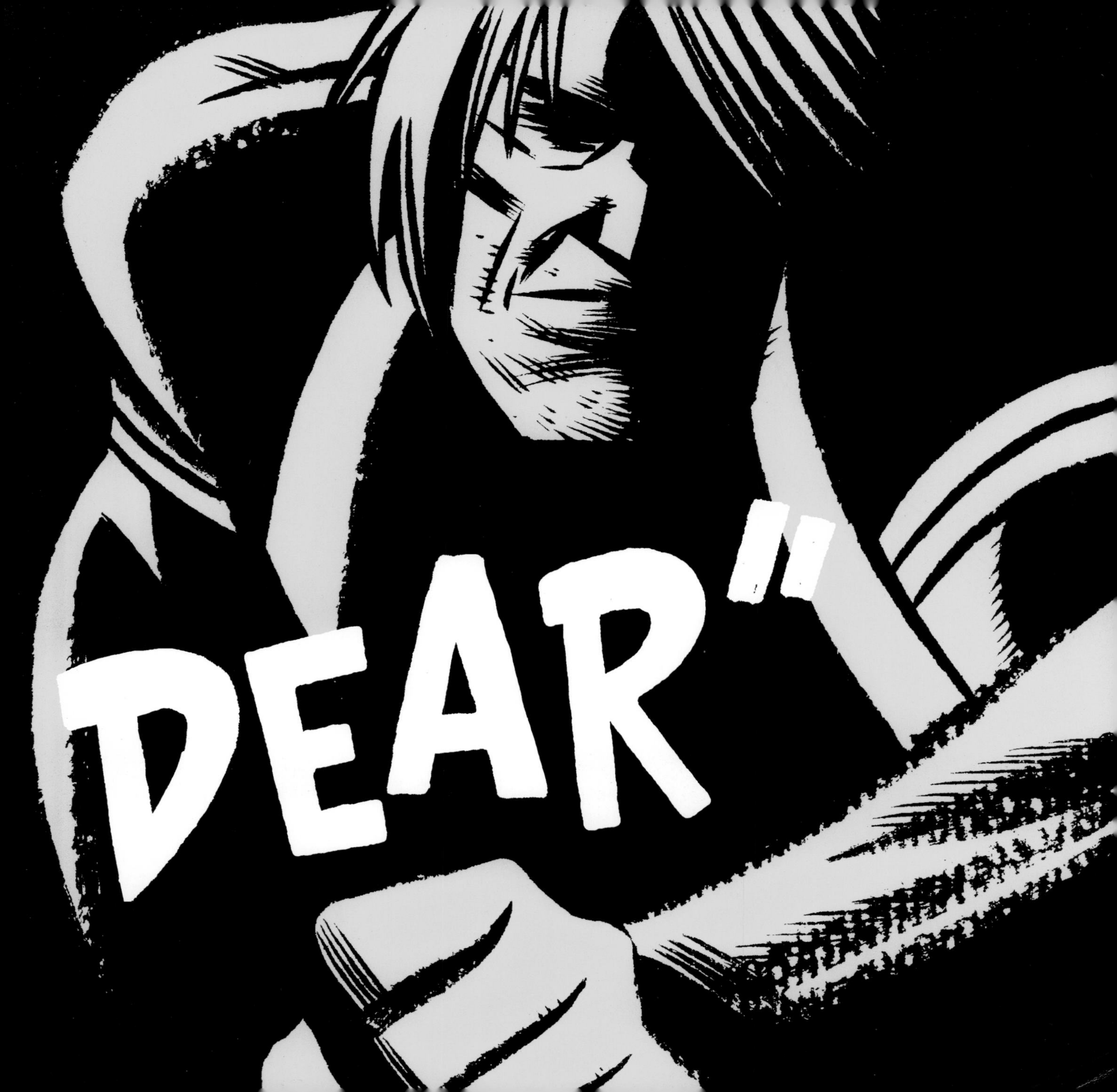
DEAR"

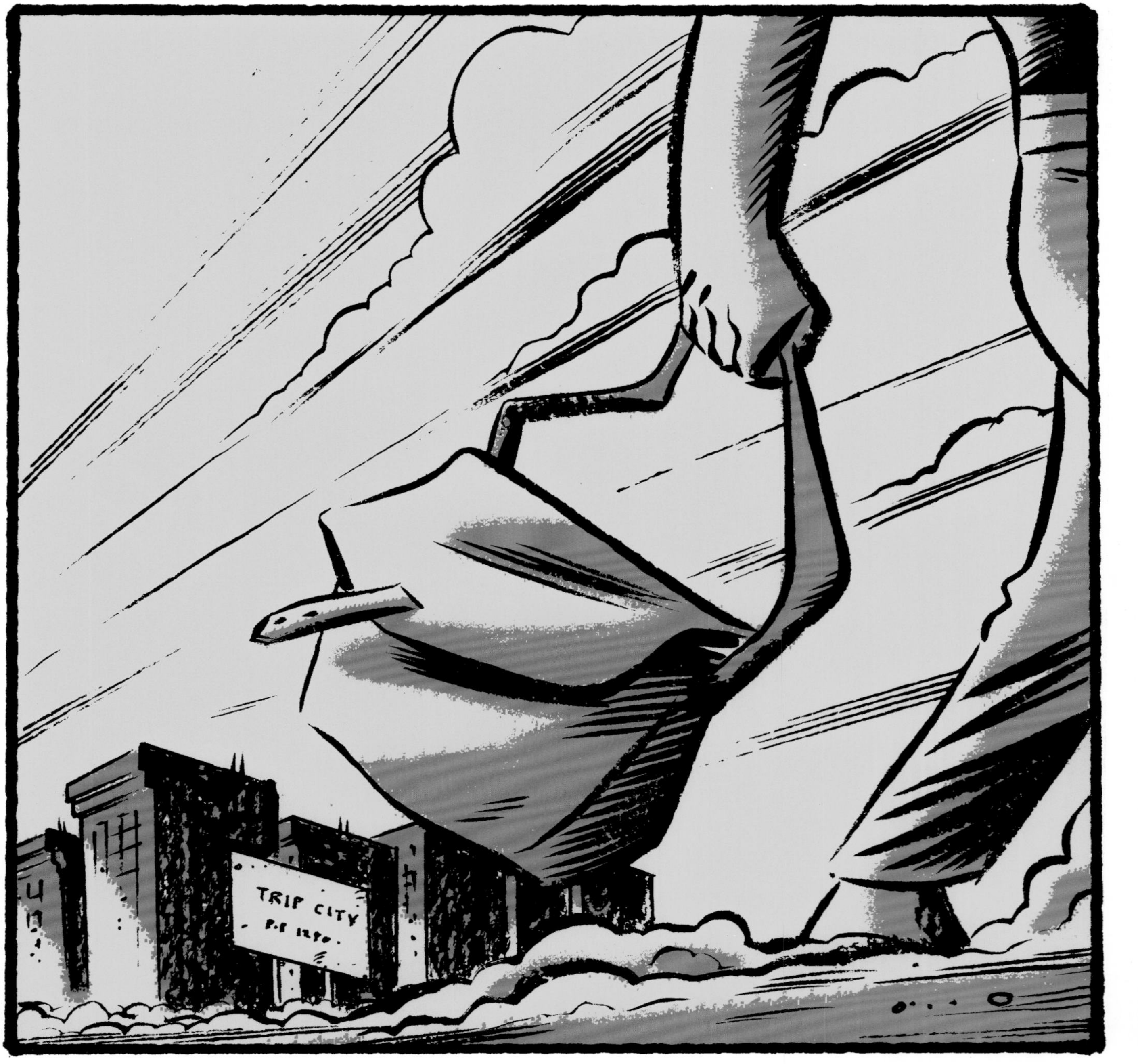
TRIP CITY

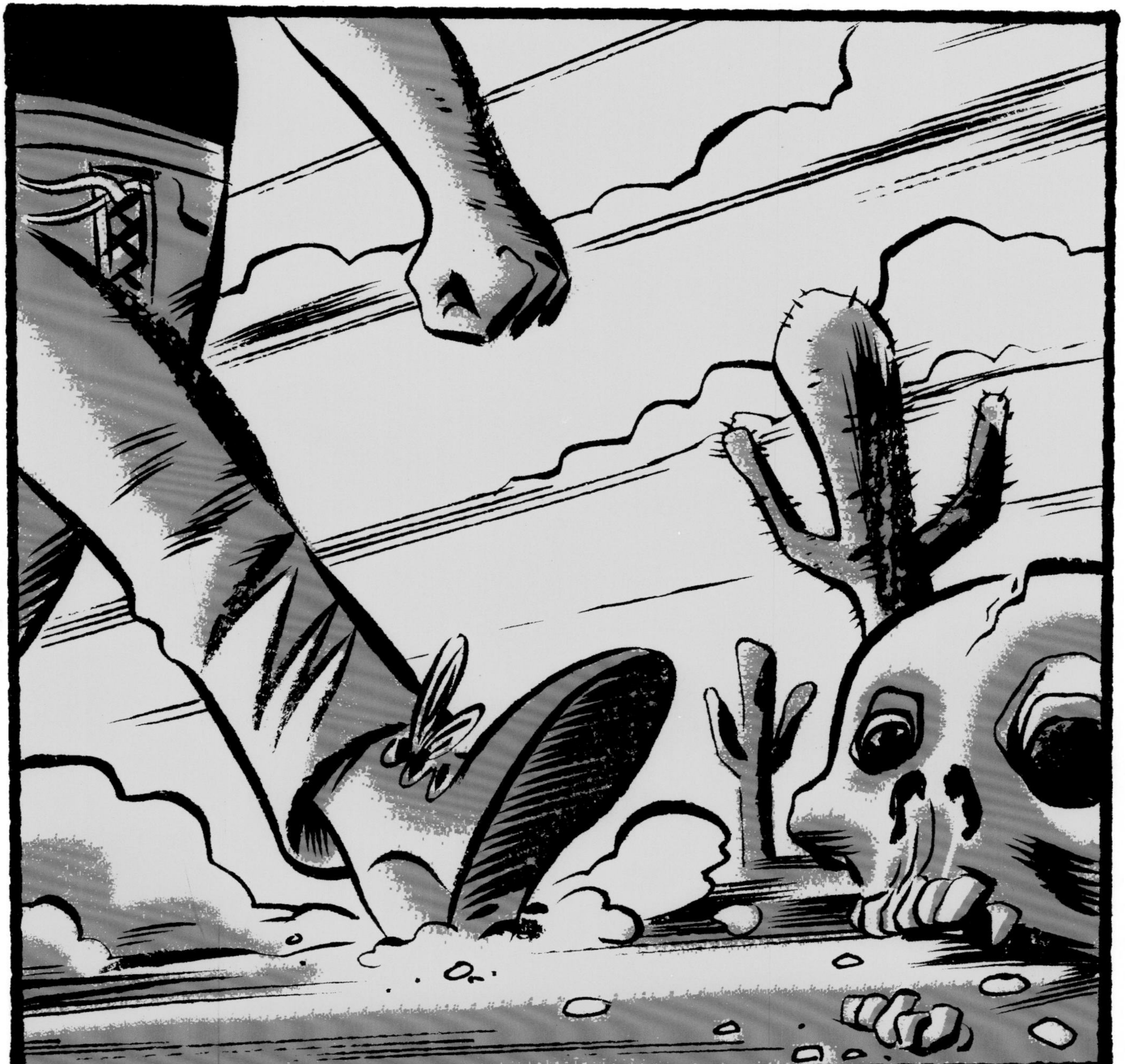

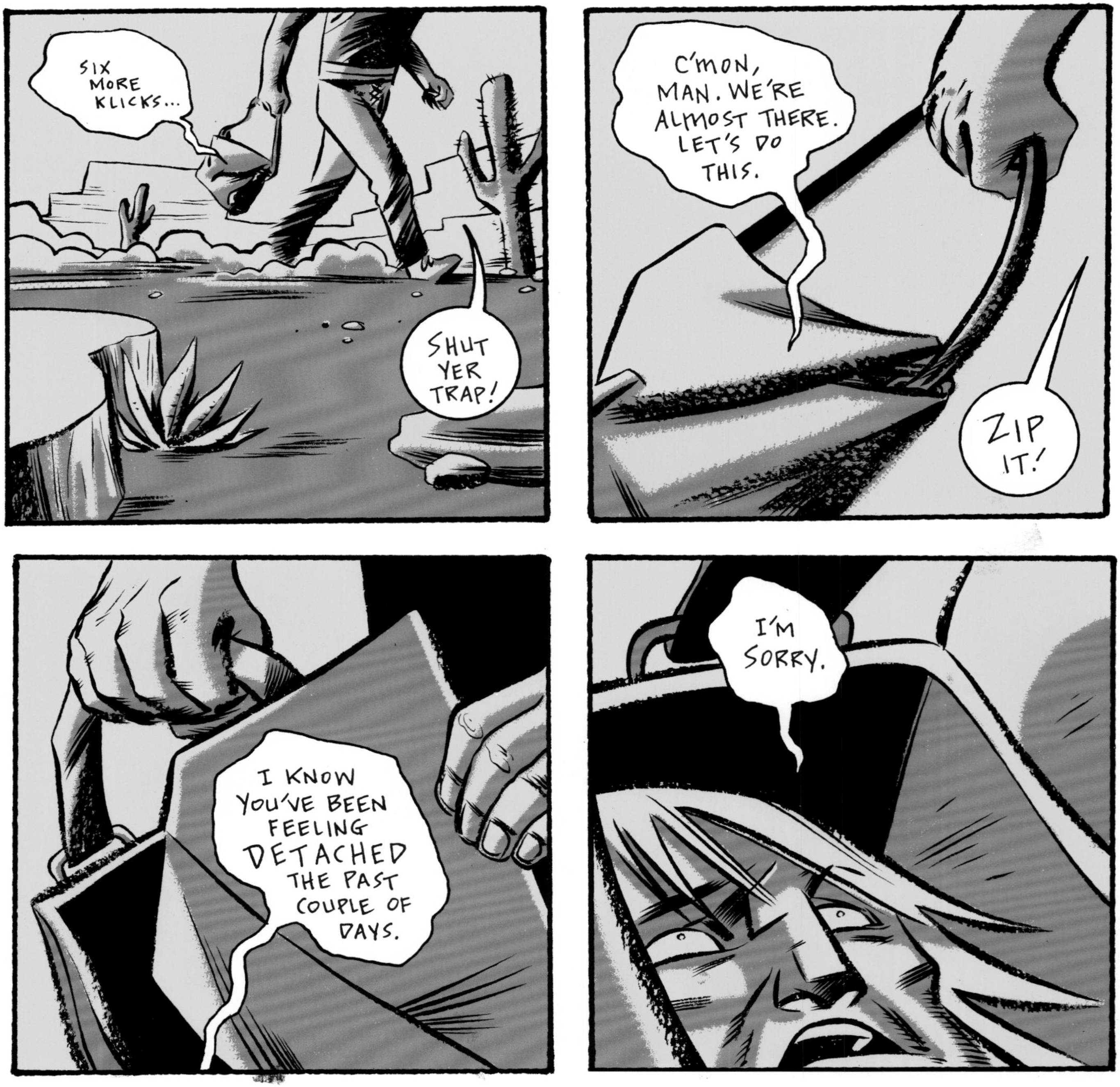
SIX MORE KLICKS...
SHUT YER TRAP!
C'MON, MAN. WE'RE ALMOST THERE. LET'S DO THIS.
ZIP IT!
I KNOW YOU'VE BEEN FEELING DETACHED THE PAST COUPLE OF DAYS.
I'M SORRY.

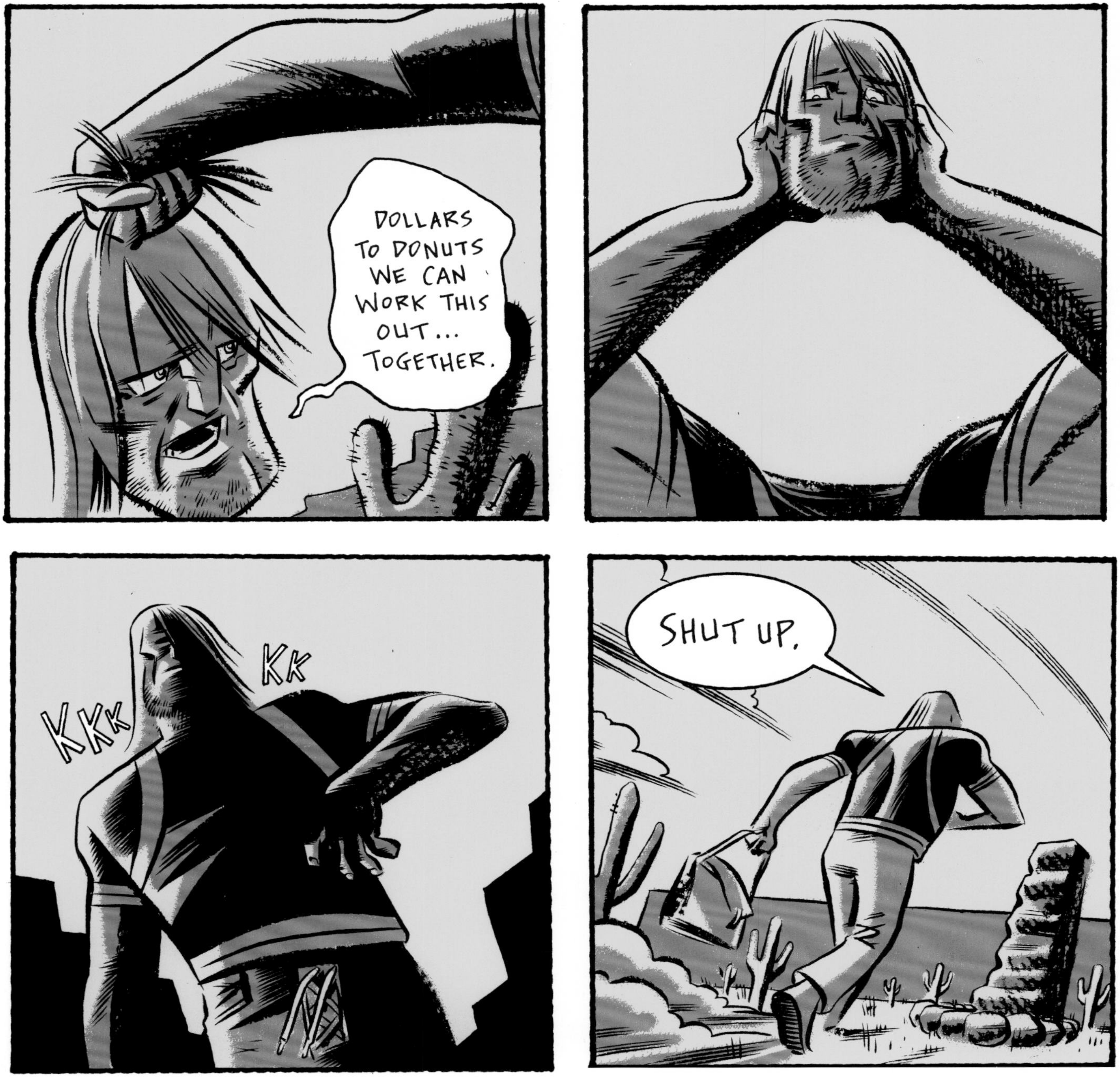
DOLLARS TO DONUTS WE CAN WORK THIS OUT... TOGETHER.
KKK
KK
SHUT UP.

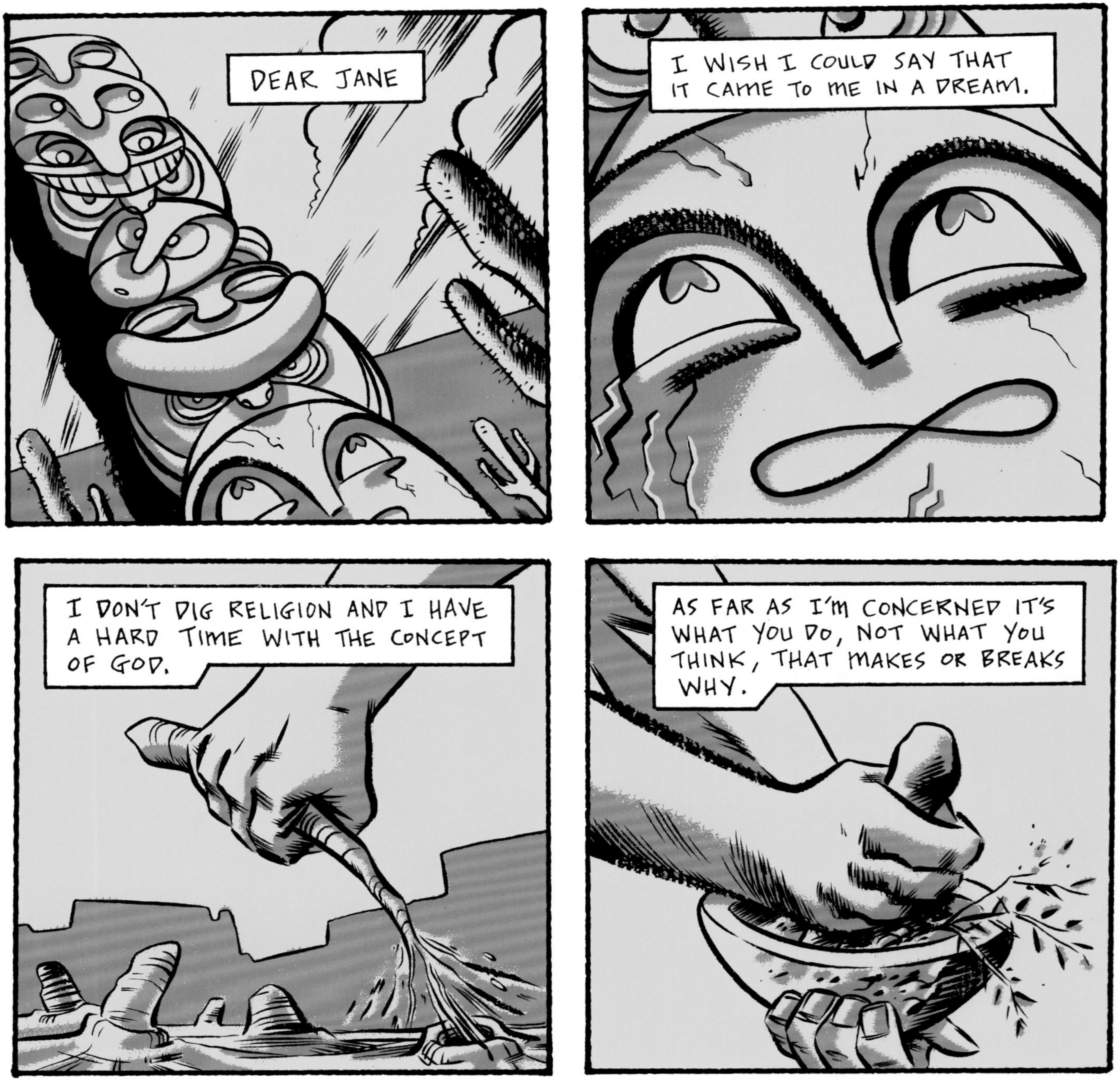
DEAR JANE
I WISH I COULD SAY THAT IT CAME TO ME IN A DREAM.
I DON'T DIG RELIGION AND I HAVE A HARD TIME WITH THE CONCEPT OF GOD.
AS FAR AS I'M CONCERNED IT'S WHAT YOU DO, NOT WHAT YOU THINK, THAT MAKES OR BREAKS WHY.

AND, BECAUSE I HOUSE A CONSCIENCE THAT CAN'T BURY THE BIG QUESTIONS...

...I HAD TO SPLIT DODGE SO I CAN MAKE PEACE WITH THE BUGS IN MY BRAIN.

BZZT

FWOOSH

SCRIPTURE STATES THERE ARE SEVEN DEADLY SINS.

I DISCOVERED AN EIGHTH.

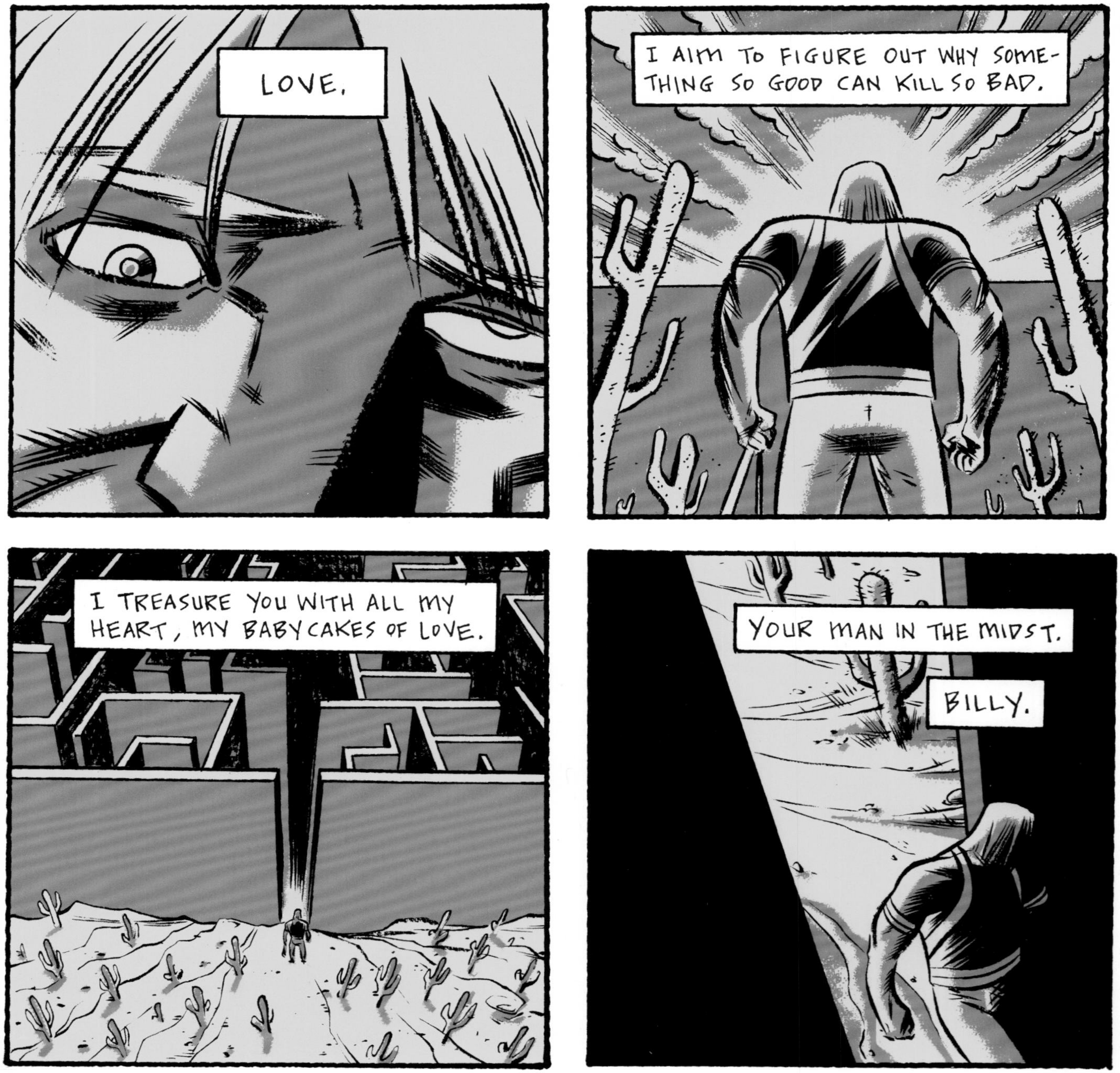
LOVE.
I AIM TO FIGURE OUT WHY SOMETHING SO GOOD CAN KILL SO BAD.
I TREASURE YOU WITH ALL MY HEART, MY BABYCAKES OF LOVE.
YOUR MAN IN THE MIDST.
BILLY.

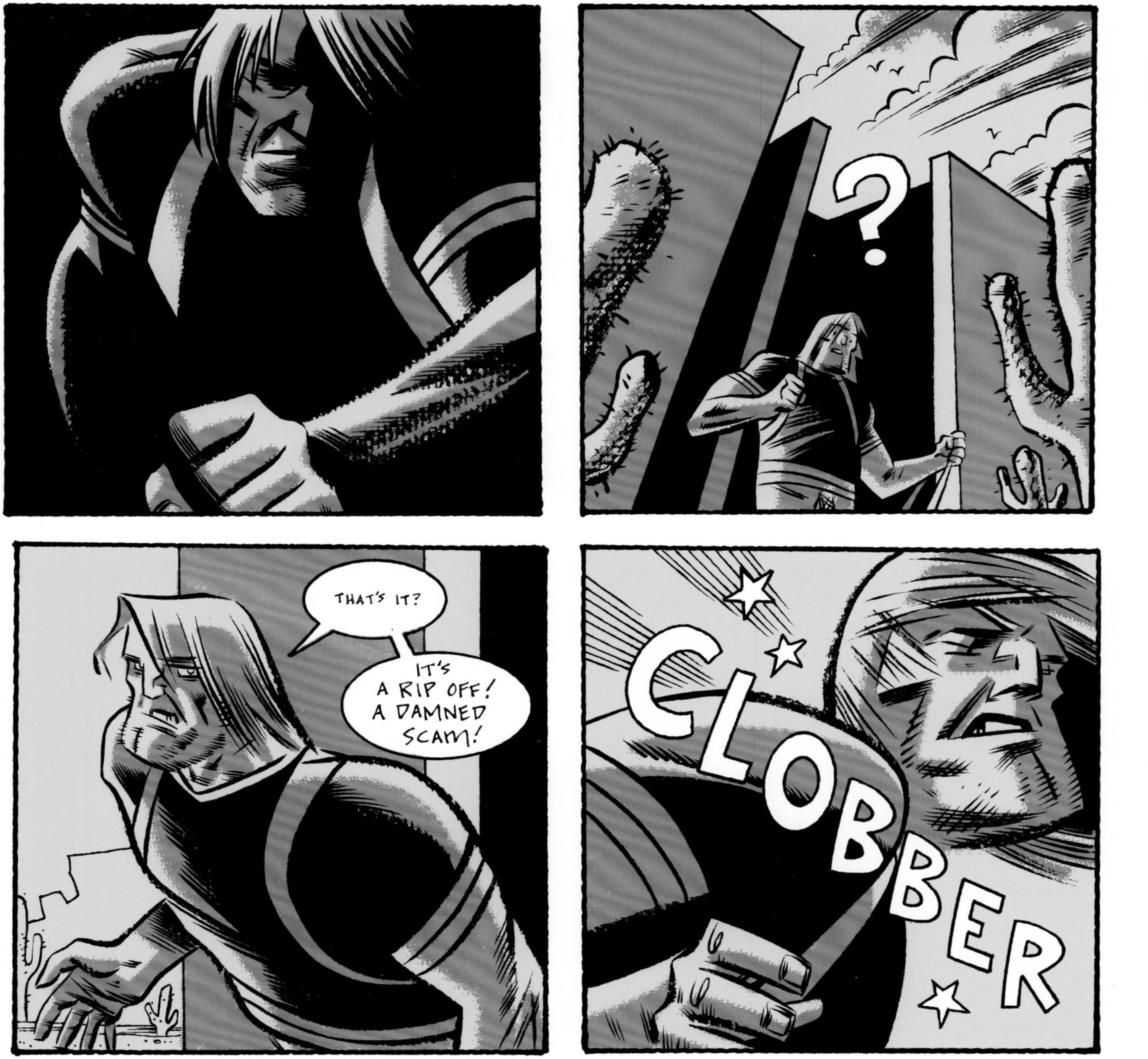
?
THAT'S IT?
IT'S A RIP OFF! A DAMNED SCAM!
CLOBBER

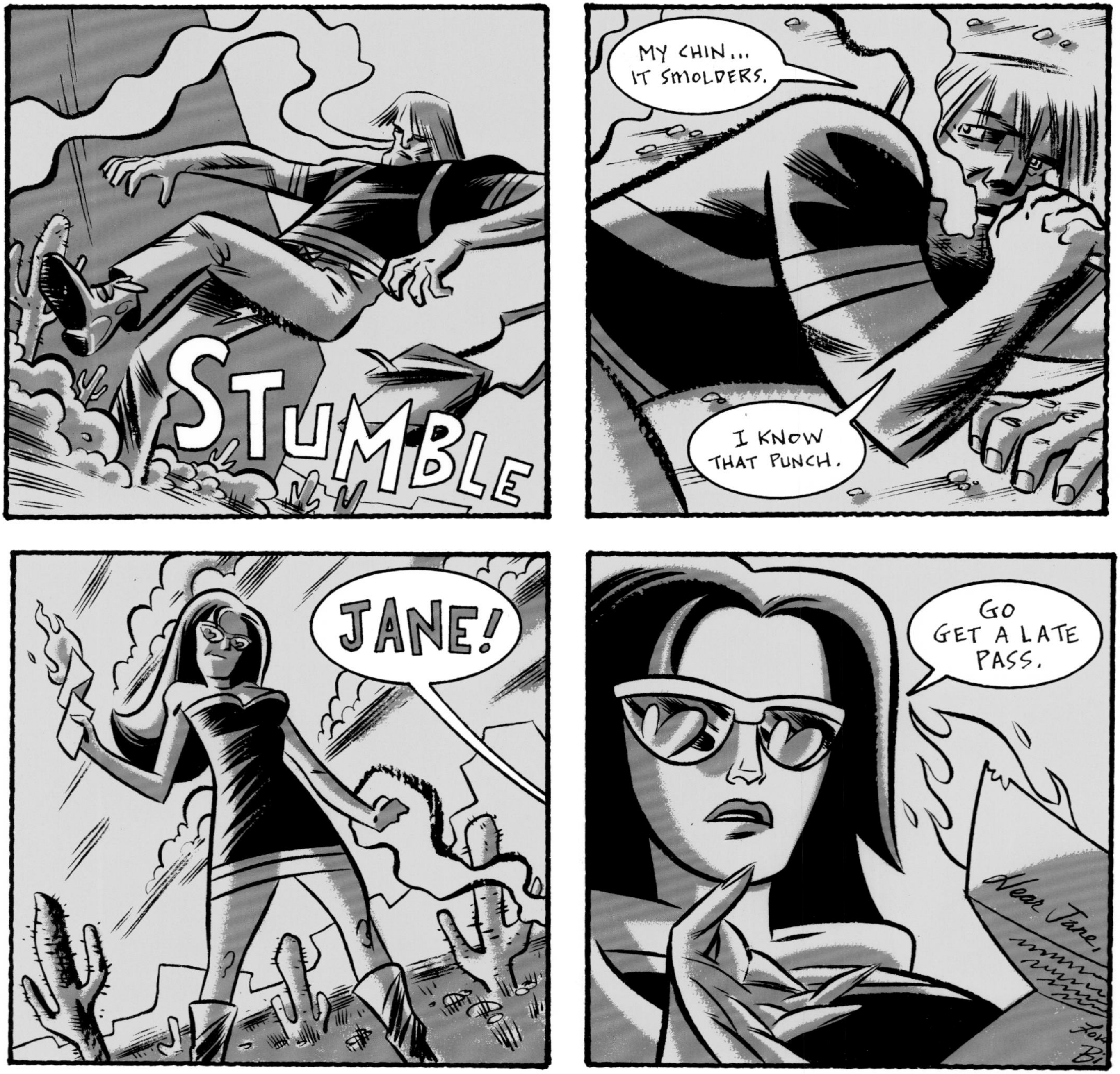
STUMBLE
MY CHIN... IT SMOLDERS.
I KNOW THAT PUNCH.
JANE!
GO GET A LATE PASS.
Dear Jane,

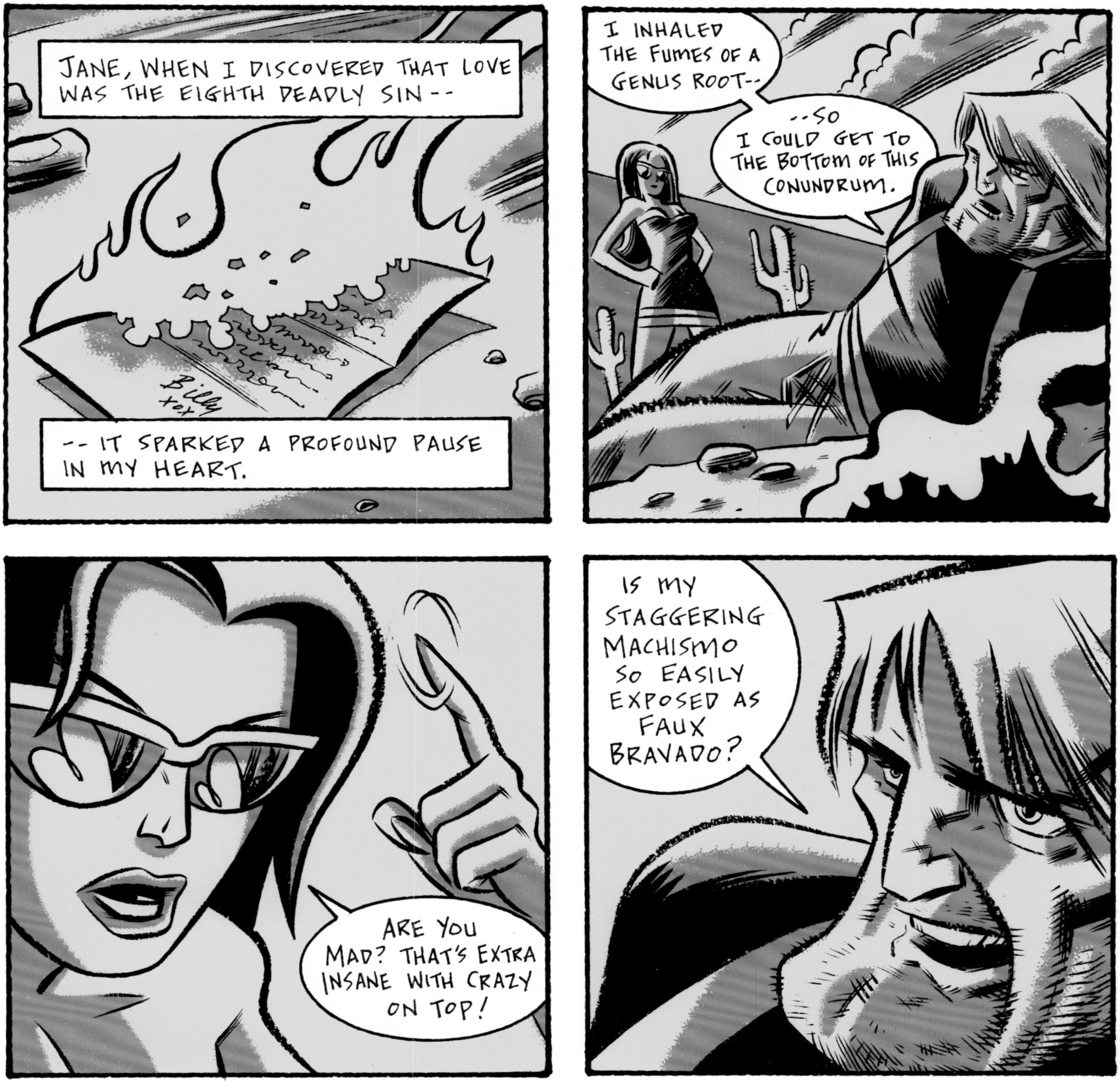
JANE, WHEN I DISCOVERED THAT LOVE WAS THE EIGHTH DEADLY SIN --
-- IT SPARKED A PROFOUND PAUSE IN MY HEART.
I INHALED THE FUMES OF A GENUS ROOT--
--SO I COULD GET TO THE BOTTOM OF THIS CONUNDRUM.
ARE YOU MAD? THAT'S EXTRA INSANE WITH CRAZY ON TOP!
IS MY STAGGERING MACHISMO SO EASILY EXPOSED AS FAUX BRAVADO?

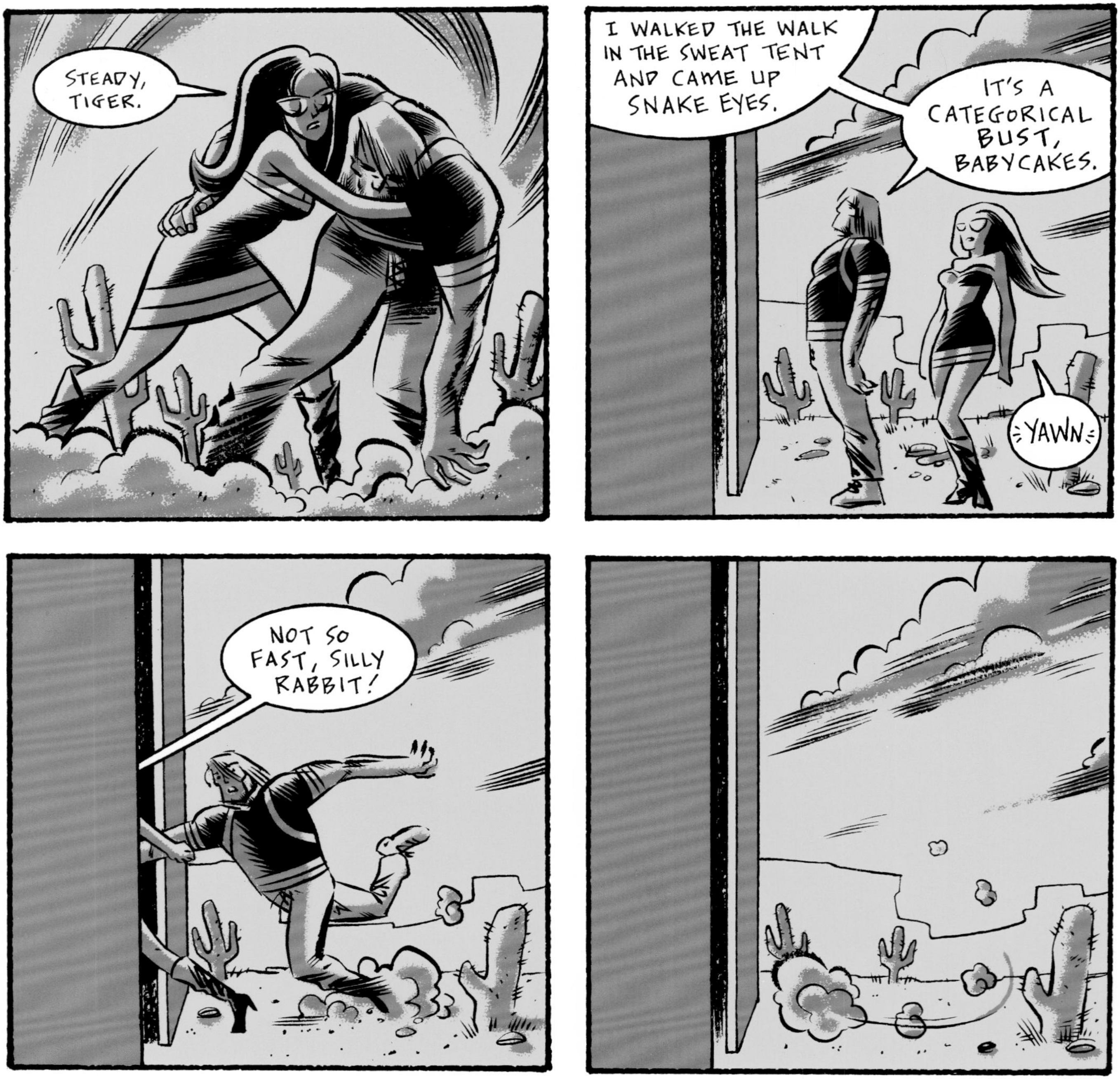
STEADY, TIGER.
I WALKED THE WALK IN THE SWEAT TENT AND CAME UP SNAKE EYES.
IT'S A CATEGORICAL BUST, BABYCAKES.
YAWN
NOT SO FAST, SILLY RABBIT!

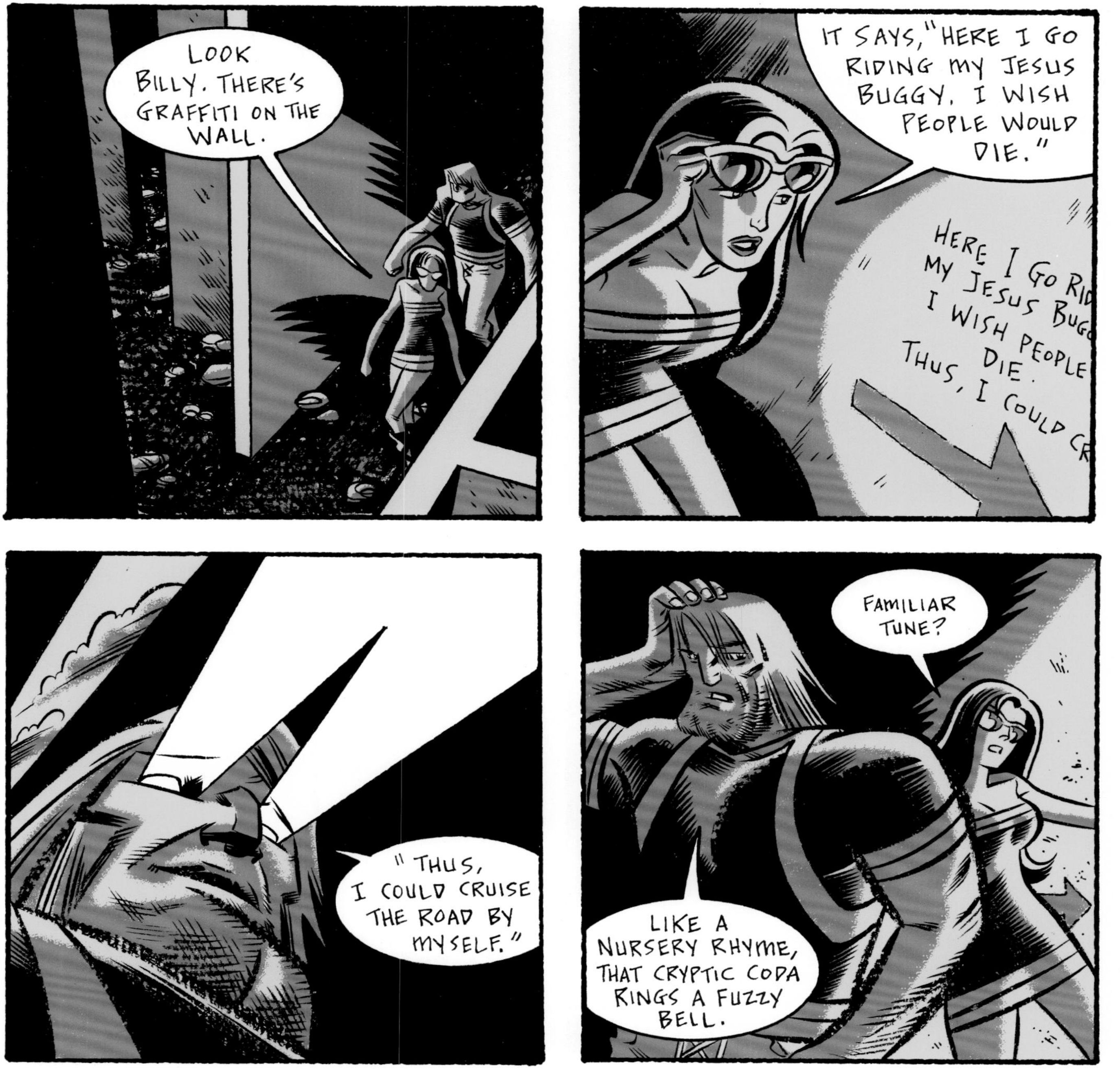
LOOK BILLY. THERE'S GRAFFITI ON THE WALL.
IT SAYS, "HERE I GO RIDING MY JESUS BUGGY. I WISH PEOPLE WOULD DIE."
HERE I GO RID
MY JESUS BUG
I WISH PEOPLE
DIE.
THUS, I COULD CR
"THUS, I COULD CRUISE THE ROAD BY MYSELF."
FAMILIAR TUNE?
LIKE A NURSERY RHYME, THAT CRYPTIC CODA RINGS A FUZZY BELL.

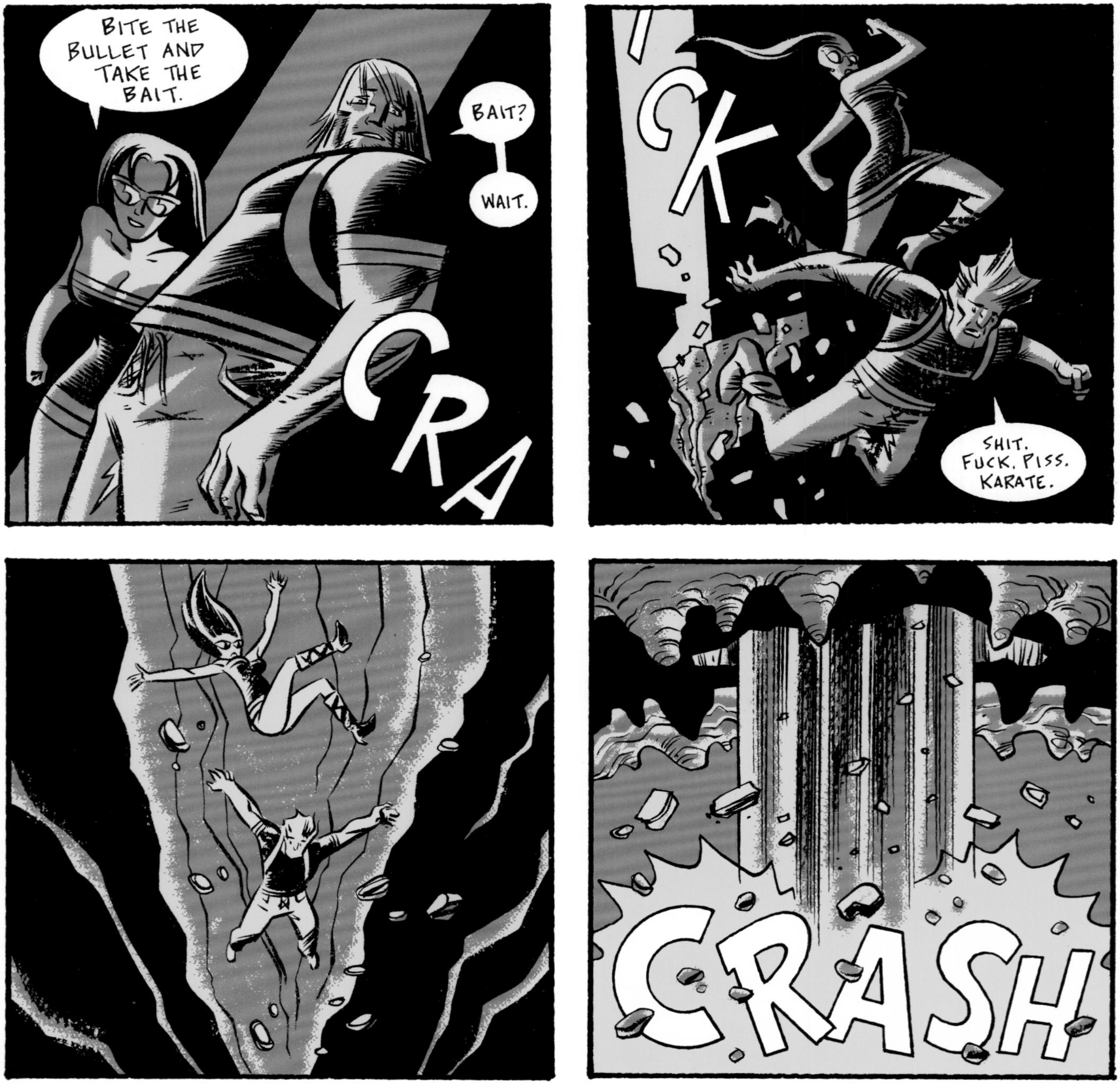
BITE THE BULLET AND TAKE THE BAIT.
BAIT?
WAIT.
CRA
CK
SHIT. FUCK. PISS. KARATE.
CRASH

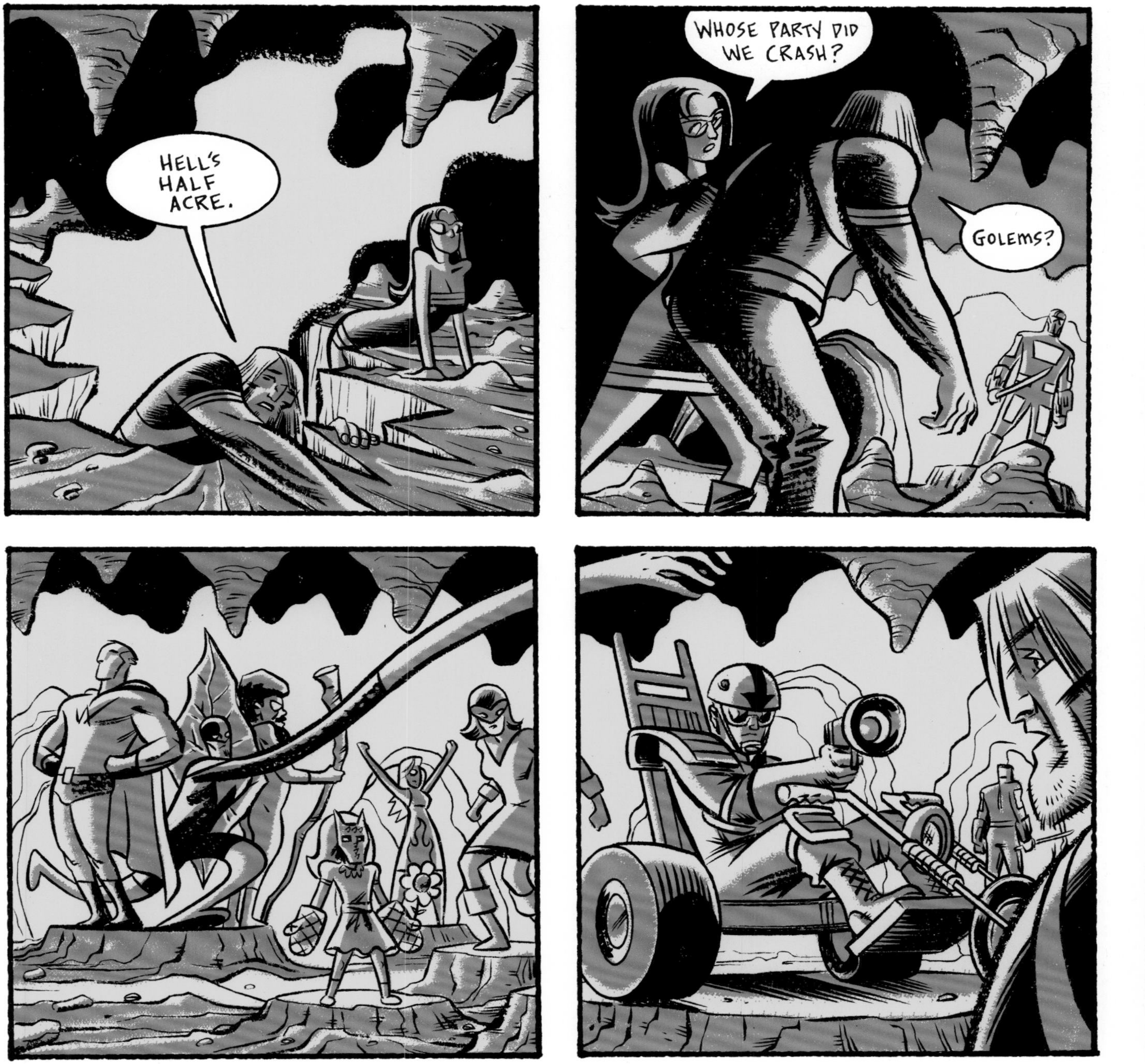
HELL'S HALF ACRE.
WHOSE PARTY DID WE CRASH?
GOLEMS?

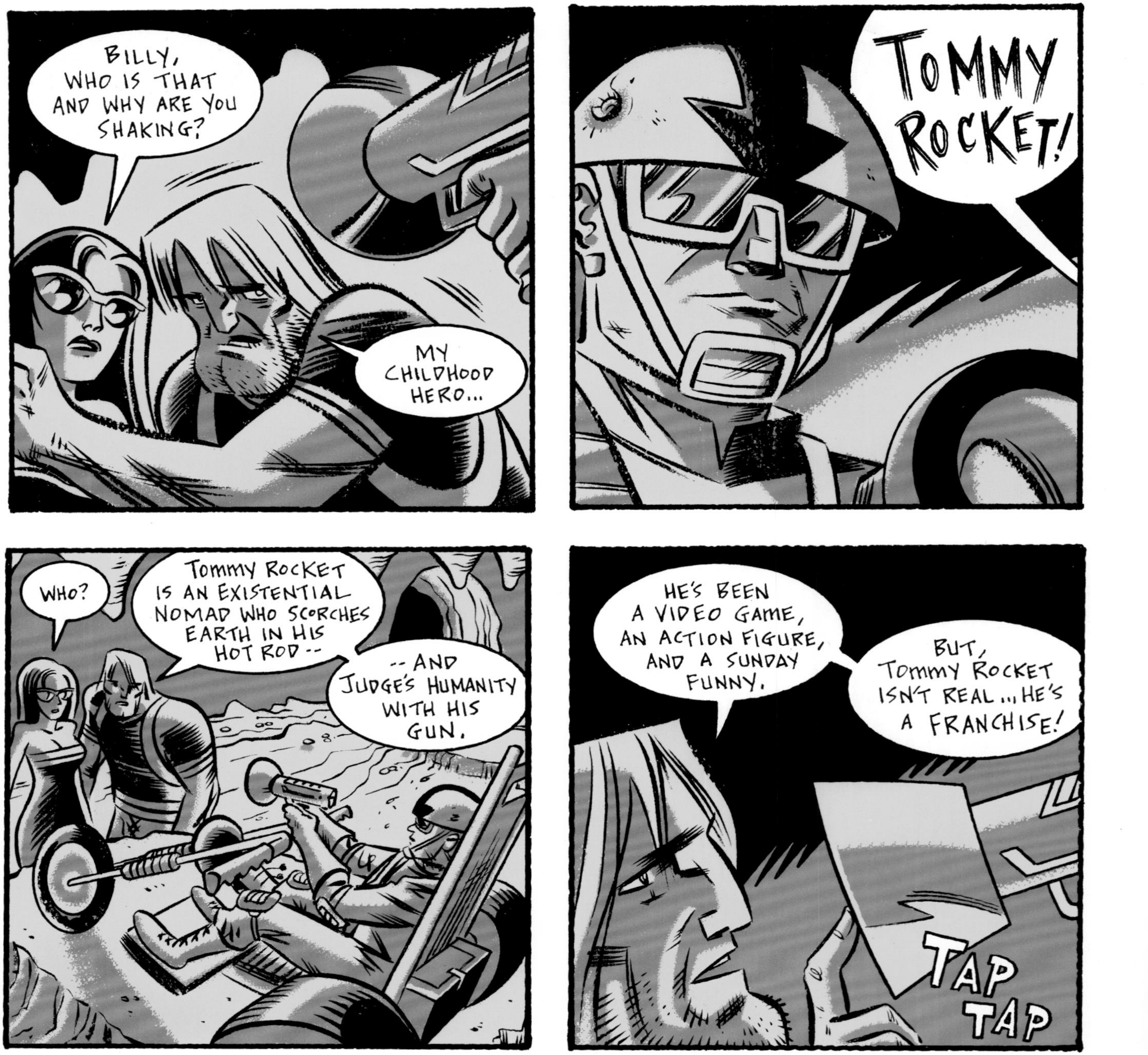
BILLY, WHO IS THAT AND WHY ARE YOU SHAKING?
MY CHILDHOOD HERO...
TOMMY ROCKET!
WHO?
Tommy Rocket IS AN EXISTENTIAL NOMAD WHO SCORCHES EARTH IN HIS HOT ROD --
-- AND JUDGE'S HUMANITY WITH HIS GUN.
HE'S BEEN A VIDEO GAME, AN ACTION FIGURE, AND A SUNDAY FUNNY.
BUT, Tommy Rocket ISN'T REAL... HE'S A FRANCHISE!
TAP TAP

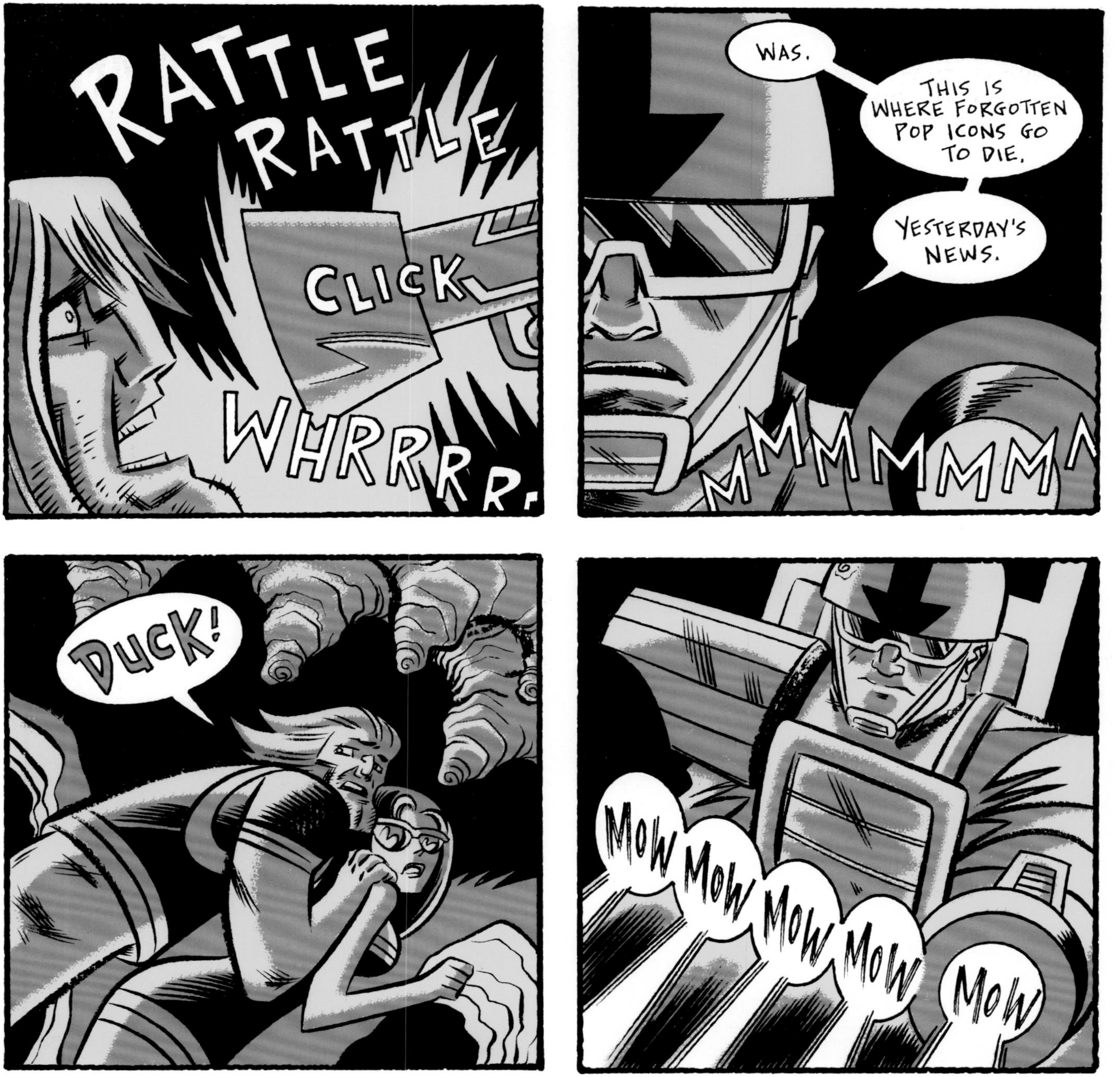
RATTLE RATTLE
CLICK
WHRRRRR
WAS.
THIS IS WHERE FORGOTTEN POP ICONS GO TO DIE.
YESTERDAY'S NEWS.
MMMMMMMM
DUCK!
MOW MOW MOW MOW MOW

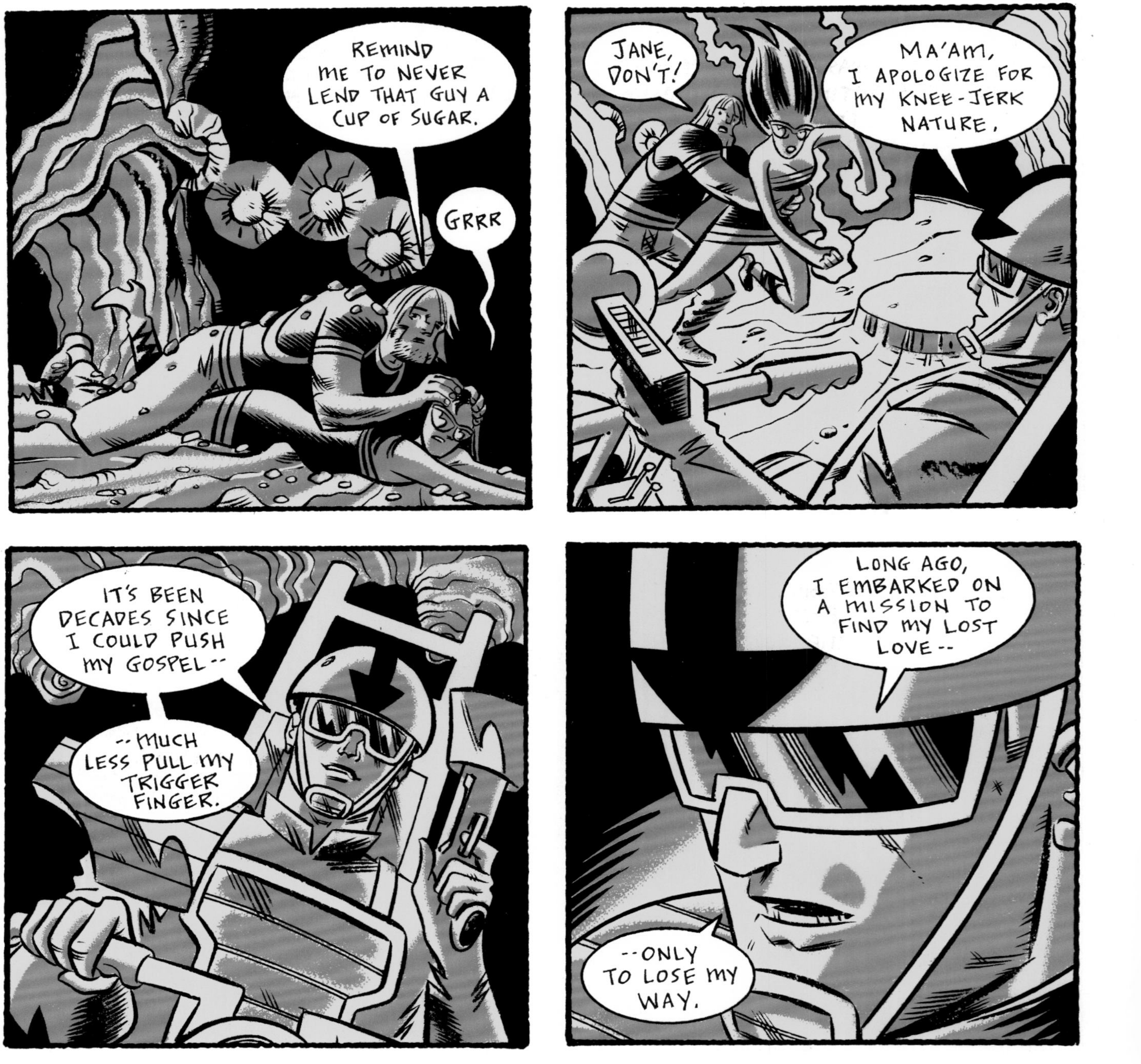
REMIND ME TO NEVER LEND THAT GUY A CUP OF SUGAR.
GRRR
JANE, DON'T!
MA'AM, I APOLOGIZE FOR MY KNEE-JERK NATURE,
IT'S BEEN DECADES SINCE I COULD PUSH MY GOSPEL--
--MUCH LESS PULL MY TRIGGER FINGER.
LONG AGO, I EMBARKED ON A MISSION TO FIND MY LOST LOVE--
--ONLY TO LOSE MY WAY.

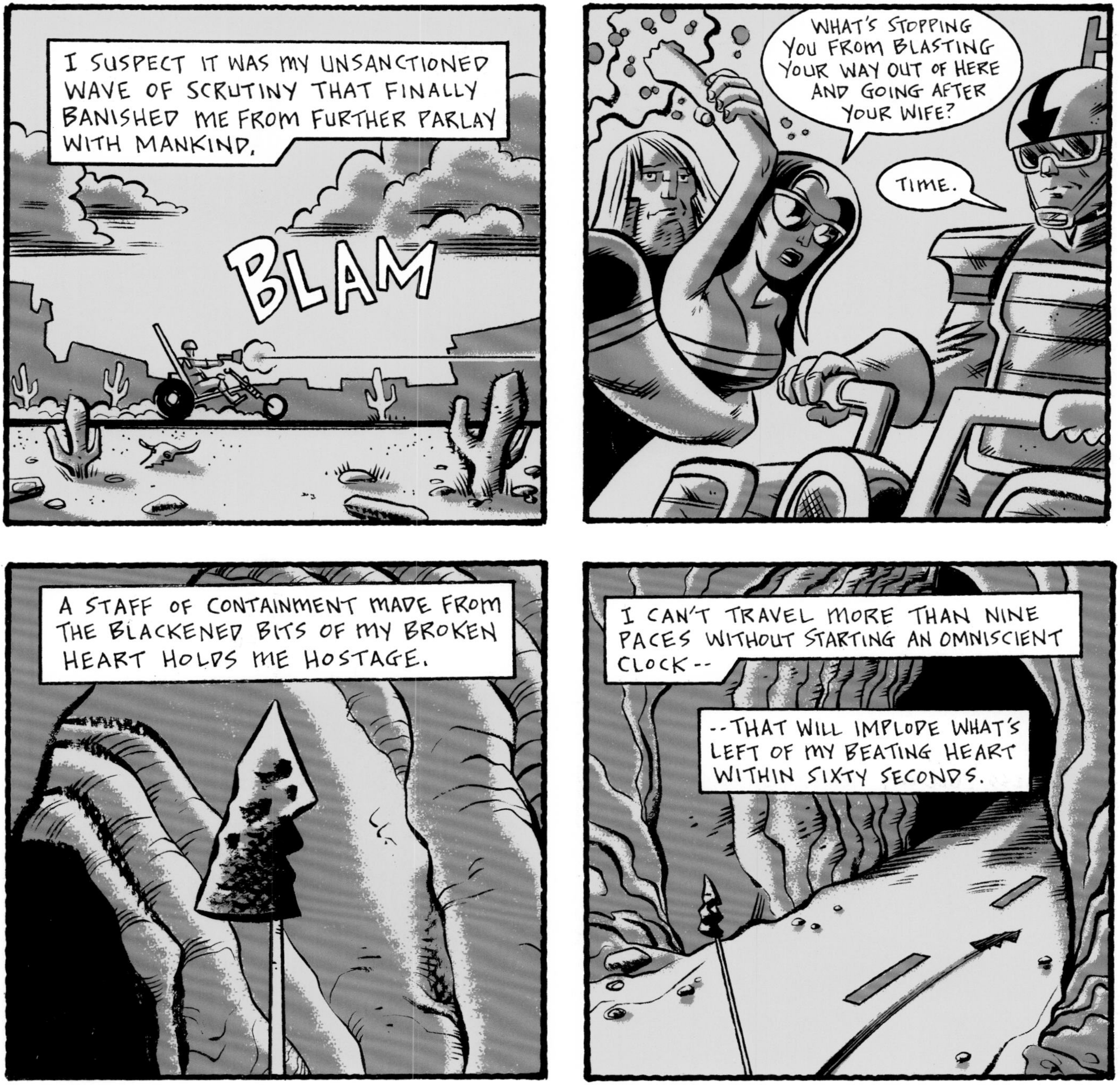
I SUSPECT IT WAS MY UNSANCTIONED WAVE OF SCRUTINY THAT FINALLY BANISHED ME FROM FURTHER PARLAY WITH MANKIND.
BLAM
WHAT'S STOPPING YOU FROM BLASTING YOUR WAY OUT OF HERE AND GOING AFTER YOUR WIFE?
TIME.
A STAFF OF CONTAINMENT MADE FROM THE BLACKENED BITS OF MY BROKEN HEART HOLDS ME HOSTAGE.
I CAN'T TRAVEL MORE THAN NINE PACES WITHOUT STARTING AN OMNISCIENT CLOCK--
--THAT WILL IMPLODE WHAT'S LEFT OF MY BEATING HEART WITHIN SIXTY SECONDS.

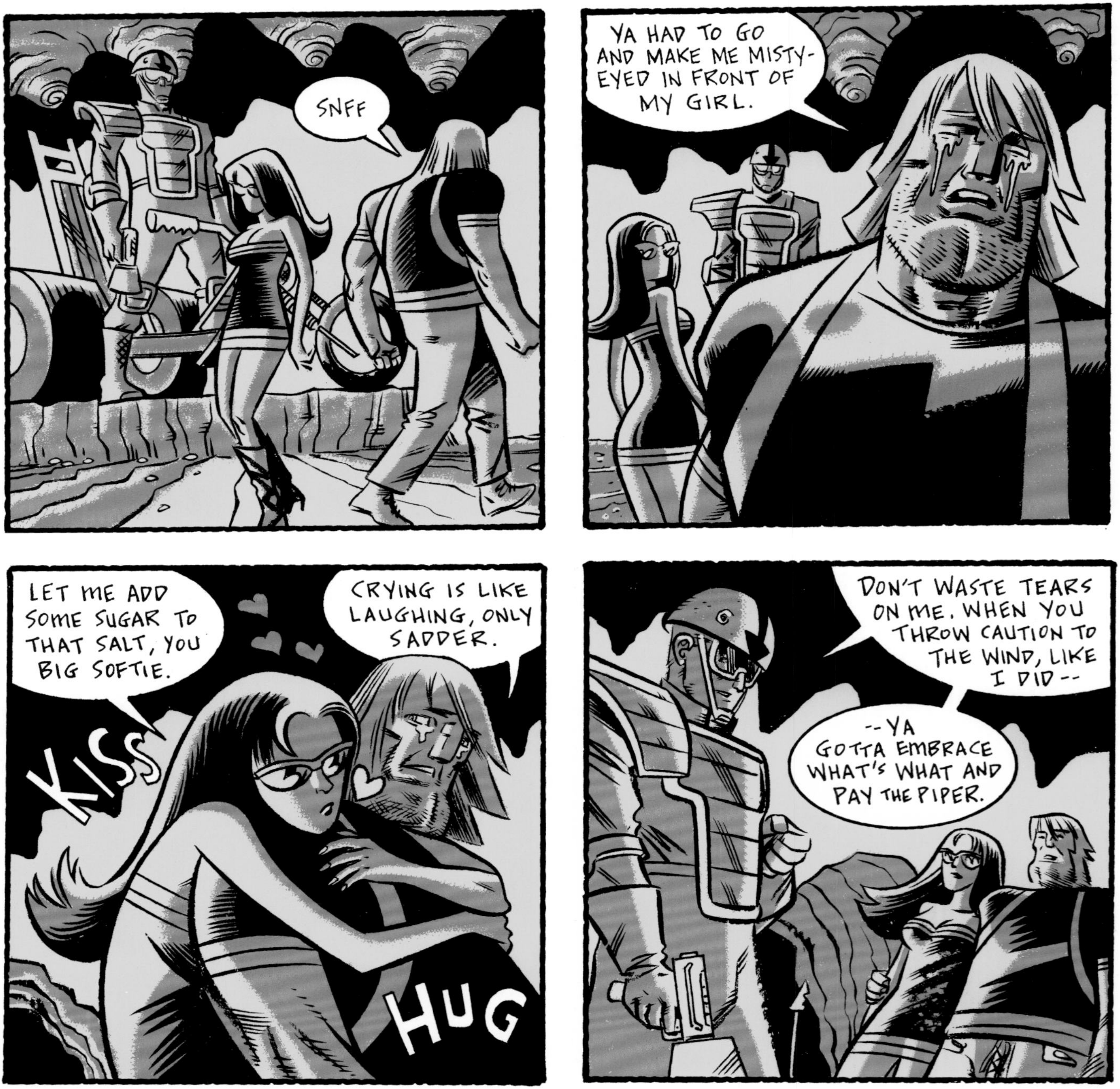
SNFF
YA HAD TO GO AND MAKE ME MISTY-EYED IN FRONT OF MY GIRL.
LET ME ADD SOME SUGAR TO THAT SALT, YOU BIG SOFTIE.
CRYING IS LIKE LAUGHING, ONLY SADDER.
KISS
HUG
DON'T WASTE TEARS ON ME. WHEN YOU THROW CAUTION TO THE WIND, LIKE I DID --
-- YA GOTTA EMBRACE WHAT'S WHAT AND PAY THE PIPER.

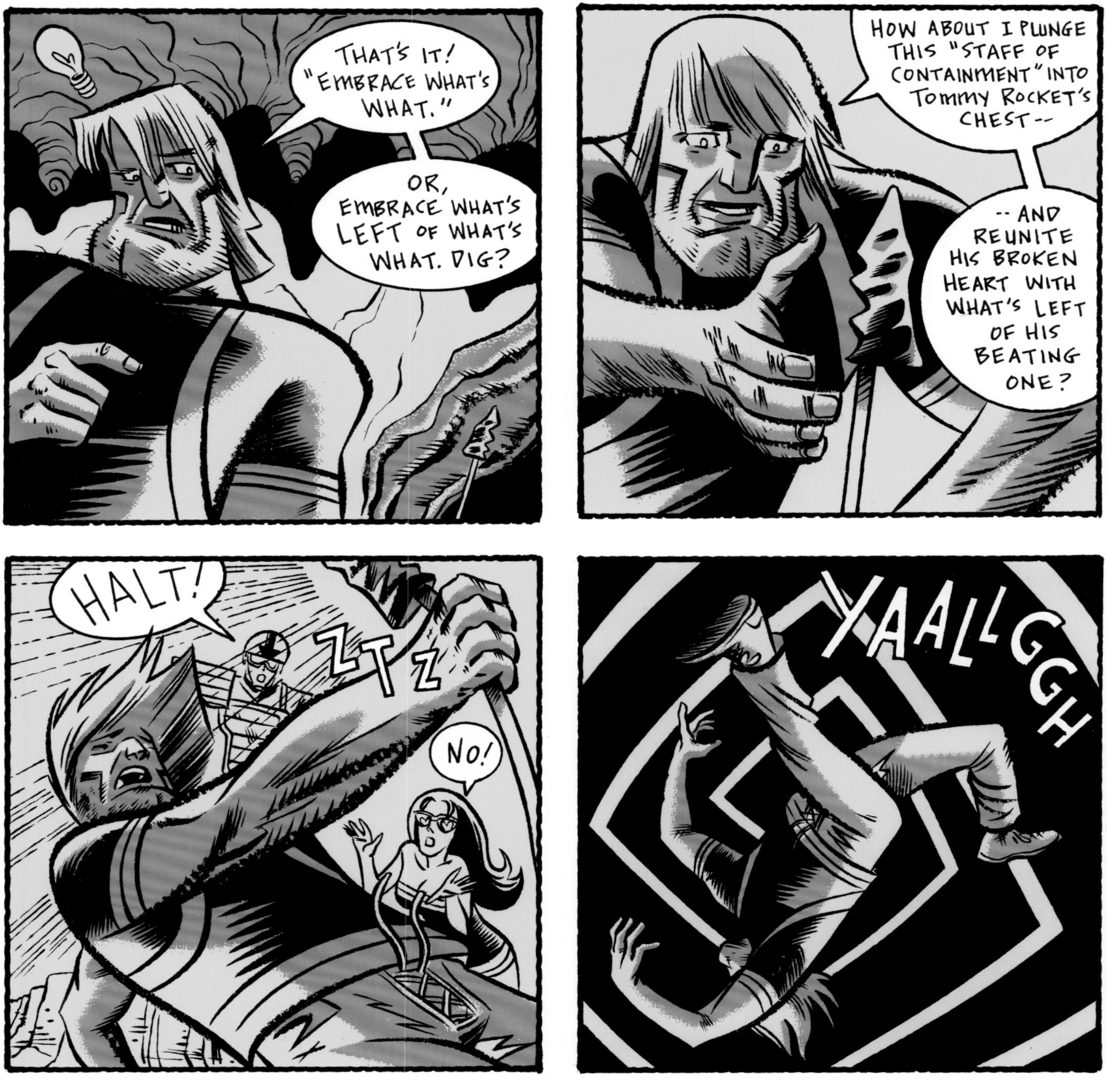
THAT'S IT! "EMBRACE WHAT'S WHAT."
OR, EMBRACE WHAT'S LEFT OF WHAT'S WHAT. DIG?
HOW ABOUT I PLUNGE THIS "STAFF OF CONTAINMENT" INTO TOMMY ROCKET'S CHEST --
-- AND REUNITE HIS BROKEN HEART WITH WHAT'S LEFT OF HIS BEATING ONE?
HALT!
ZZZ
NO!
YAALLGGH

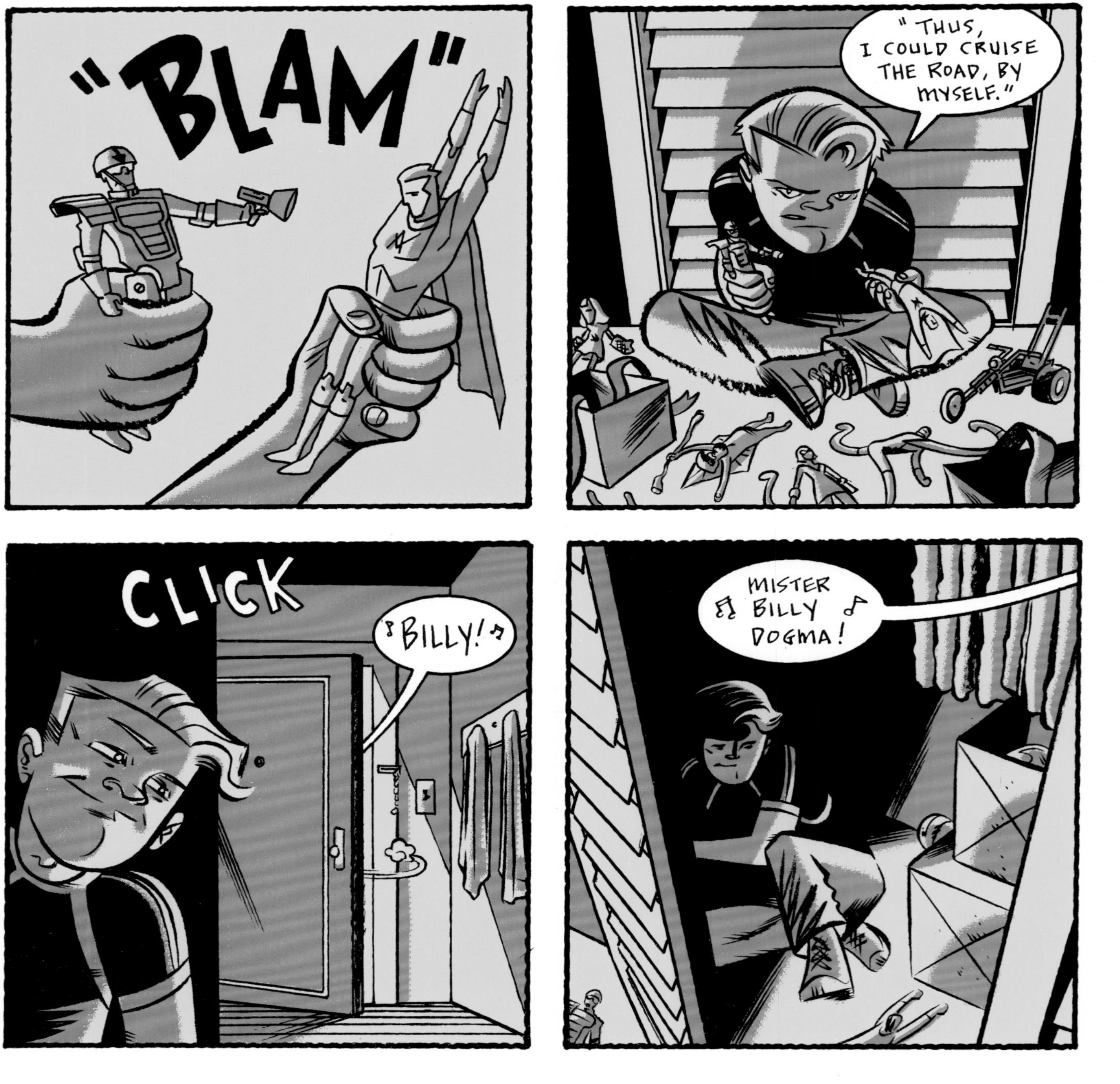
"BLAM"
"THUS, I COULD CRUISE THE ROAD, BY MYSELF."
CLICK
BILLY!
MISTER BILLY DOGMA!

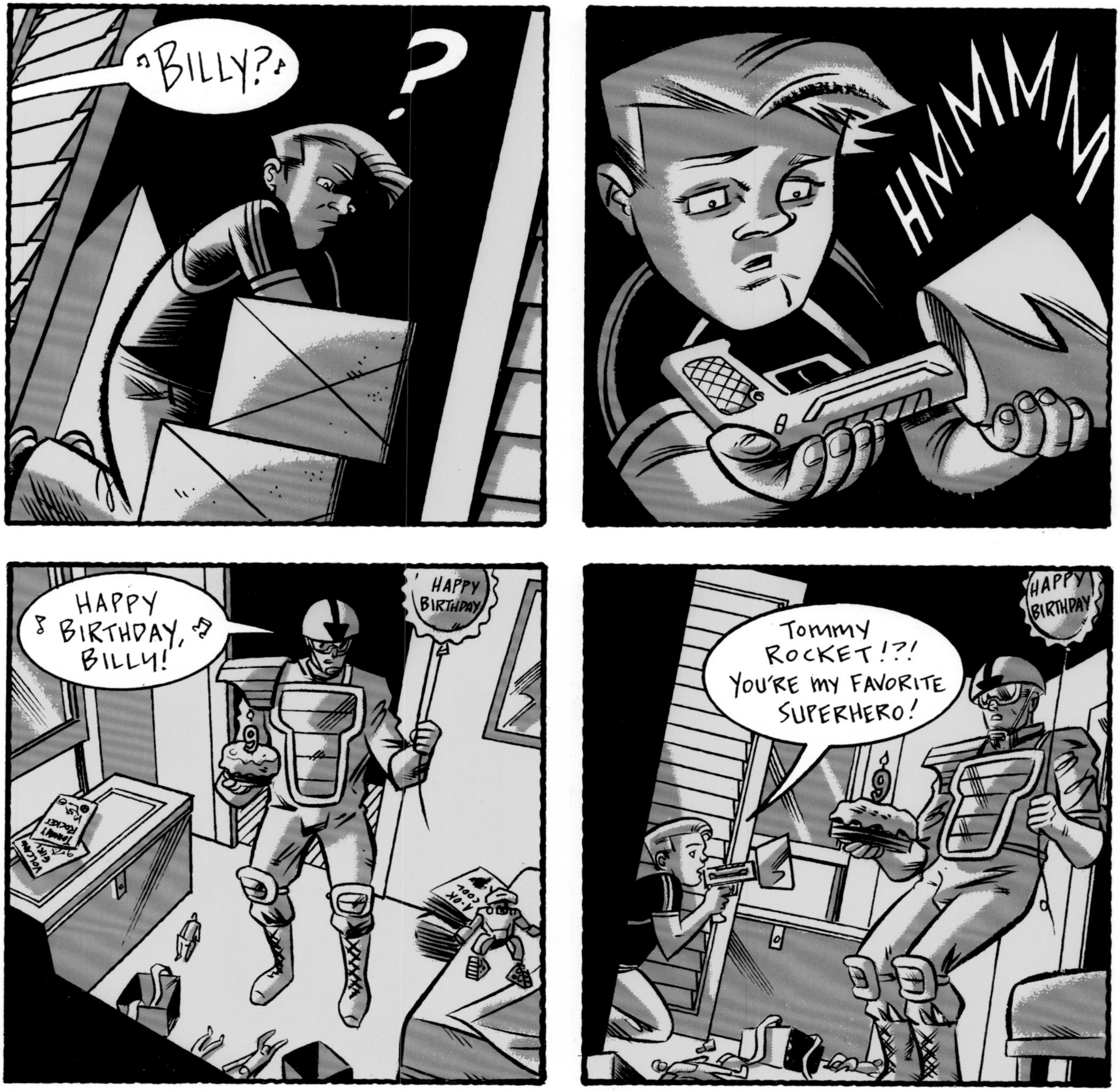
BILLY?
?
HMMMM
HAPPY BIRTHDAY, BILLY!
HAPPY BIRTHDAY
HAPPY BIRTHDAY
TOMMY ROCKET!?! YOU'RE MY FAVORITE SUPERHERO!

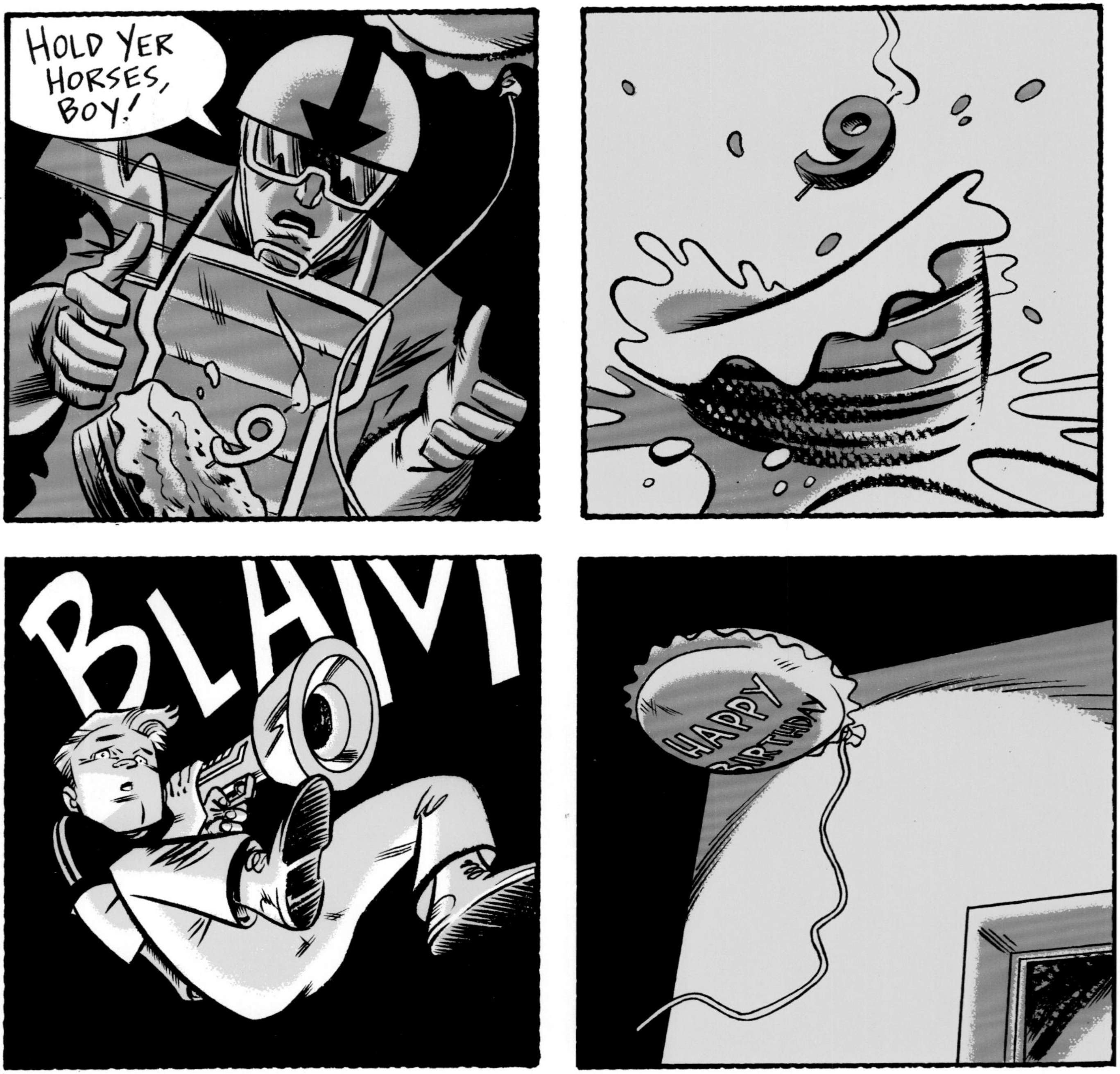
HOLD YER HORSES, BOY!
BLAM
HAPPY BIRTHDAY

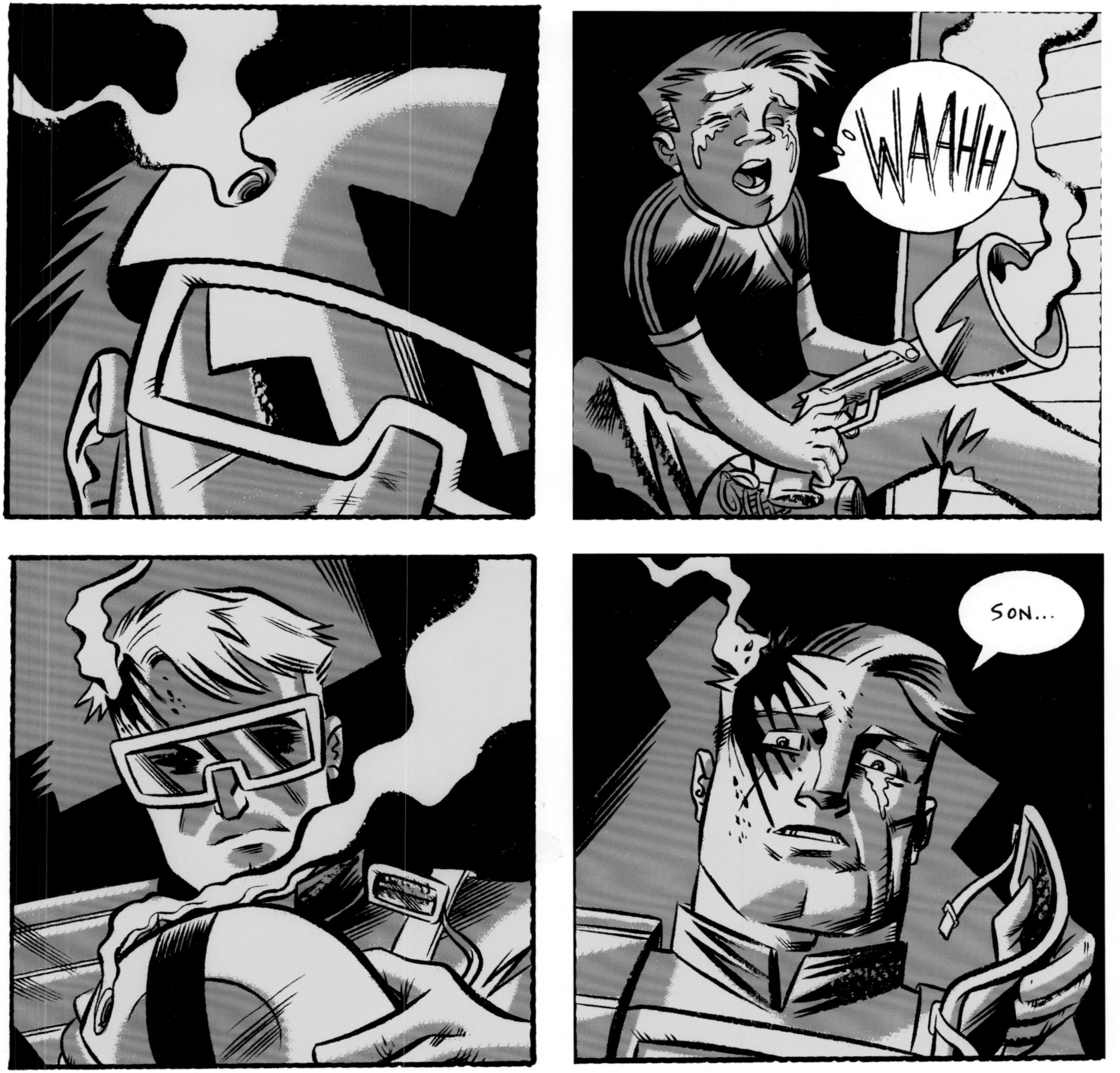
WAAHH
SON...

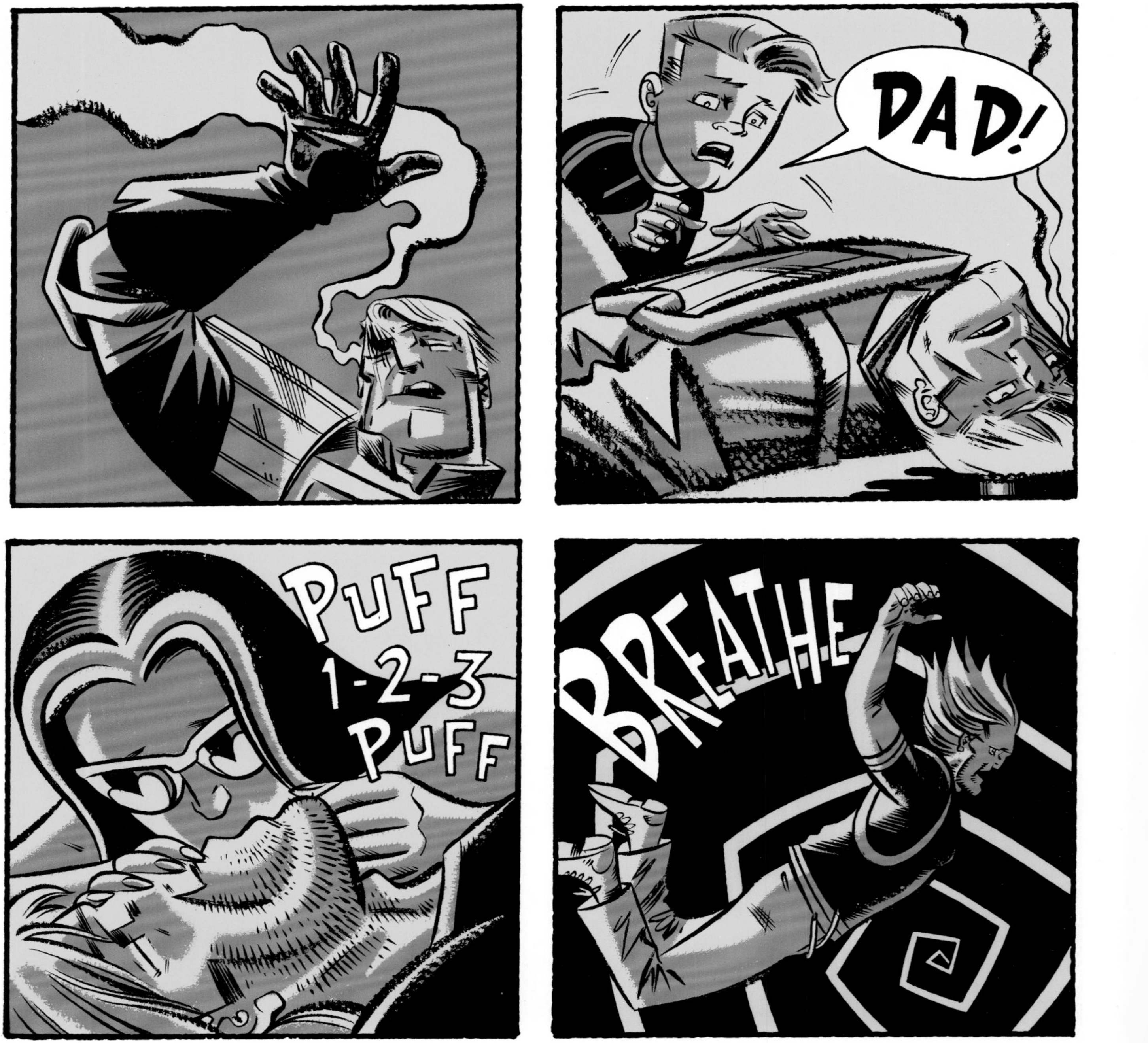
DAD!
PUFF
1-2-3
PUFF
BREATHE

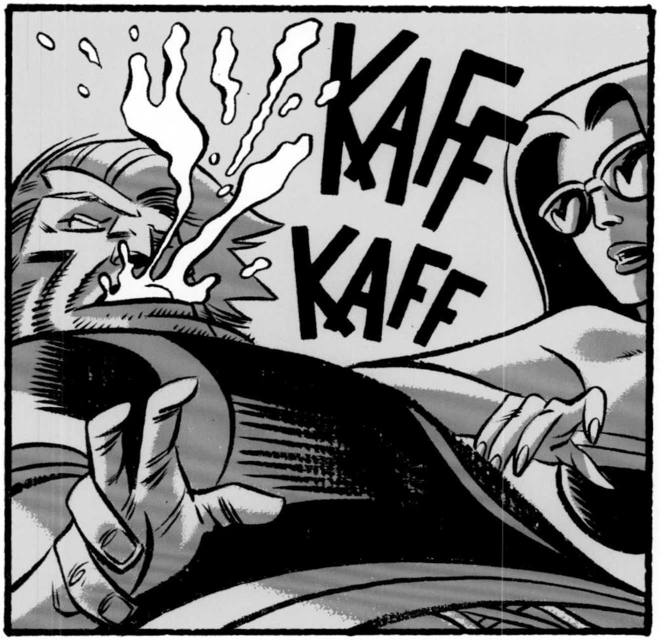
KAFF
KAFF

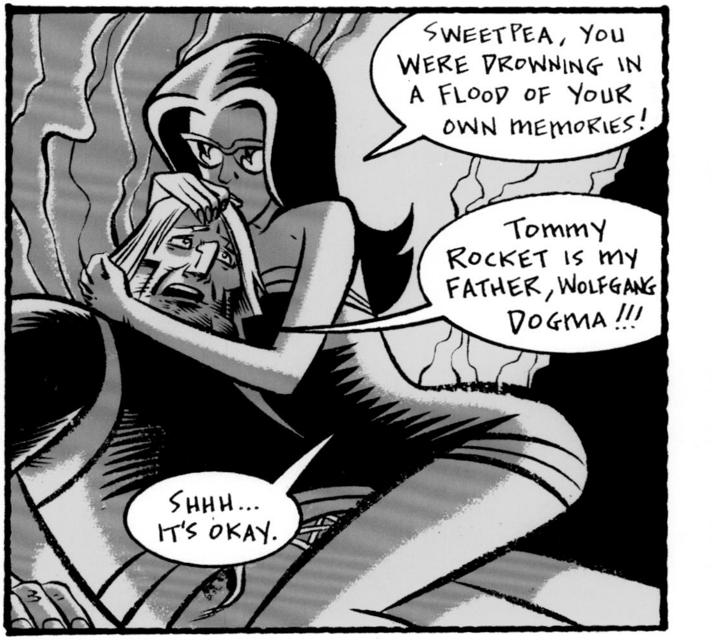
SWEETPEA, YOU WERE DROWNING IN A FLOOD OF YOUR OWN MEMORIES!
Tommy ROCKET IS MY FATHER, WOLFGANG DOGMA!!!
SHHH... IT'S OKAY.

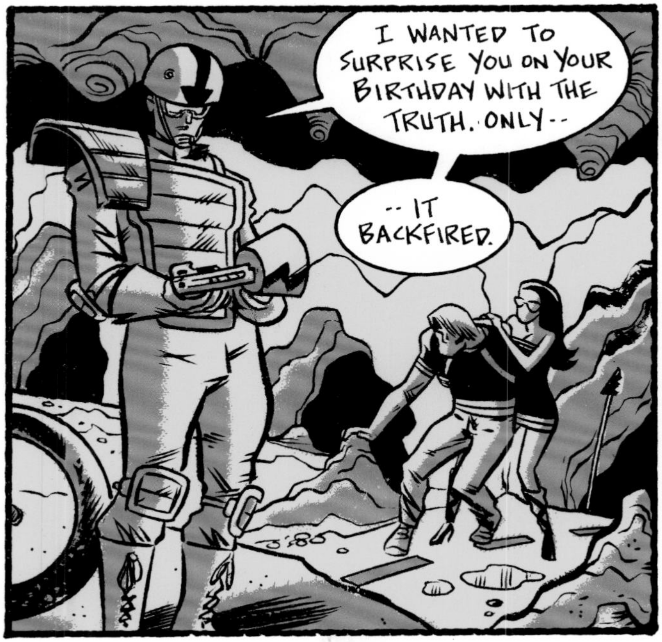
I WANTED TO SURPRISE YOU ON YOUR BIRTHDAY WITH THE TRUTH. ONLY--
--IT BACKFIRED.

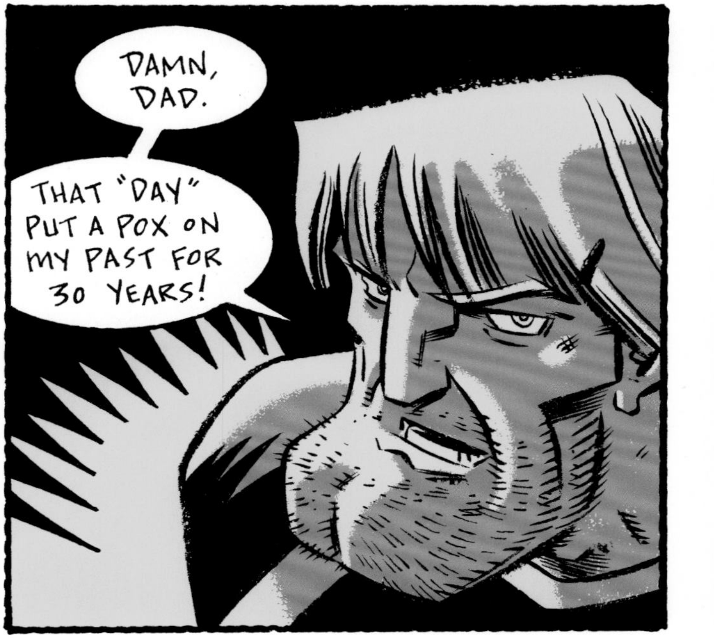
DAMN, DAD.
THAT "DAY" PUT A POX ON MY PAST FOR 30 YEARS!

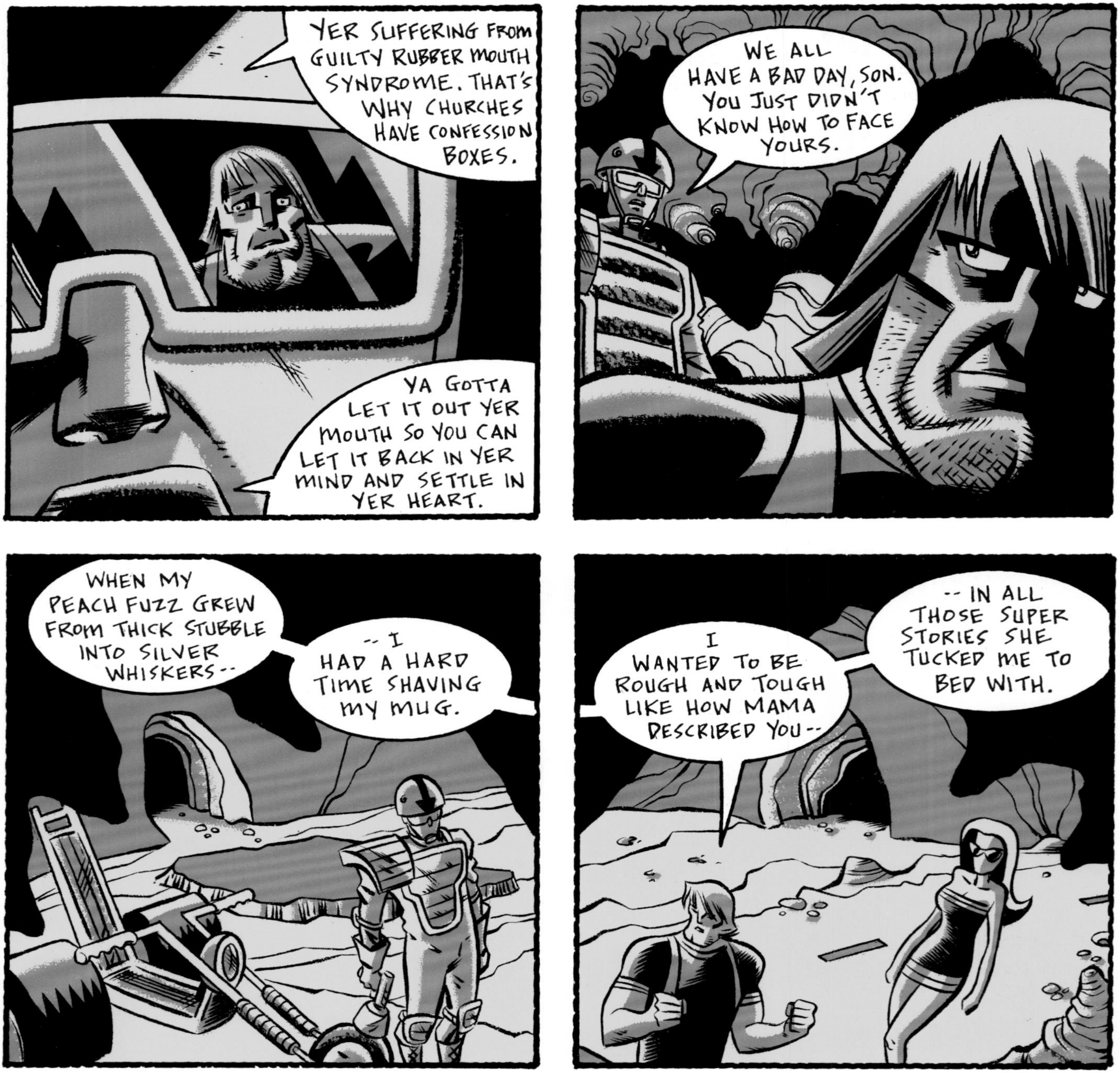
YER SUFFERING FROM GUILTY RUBBER MOUTH SYNDROME. THAT'S WHY CHURCHES HAVE CONFESSION BOXES.
YA GOTTA LET IT OUT YER MOUTH SO YOU CAN LET IT BACK IN YER MIND AND SETTLE IN YER HEART.
WE ALL HAVE A BAD DAY, SON. YOU JUST DIDN'T KNOW HOW TO FACE YOURS.
WHEN MY PEACH FUZZ GREW FROM THICK STUBBLE INTO SILVER WHISKERS--
--I HAD A HARD TIME SHAVING MY MUG.
I WANTED TO BE ROUGH AND TOUGH LIKE HOW MAMA DESCRIBED YOU--
--IN ALL THOSE SUPER STORIES SHE TUCKED ME TO BED WITH.

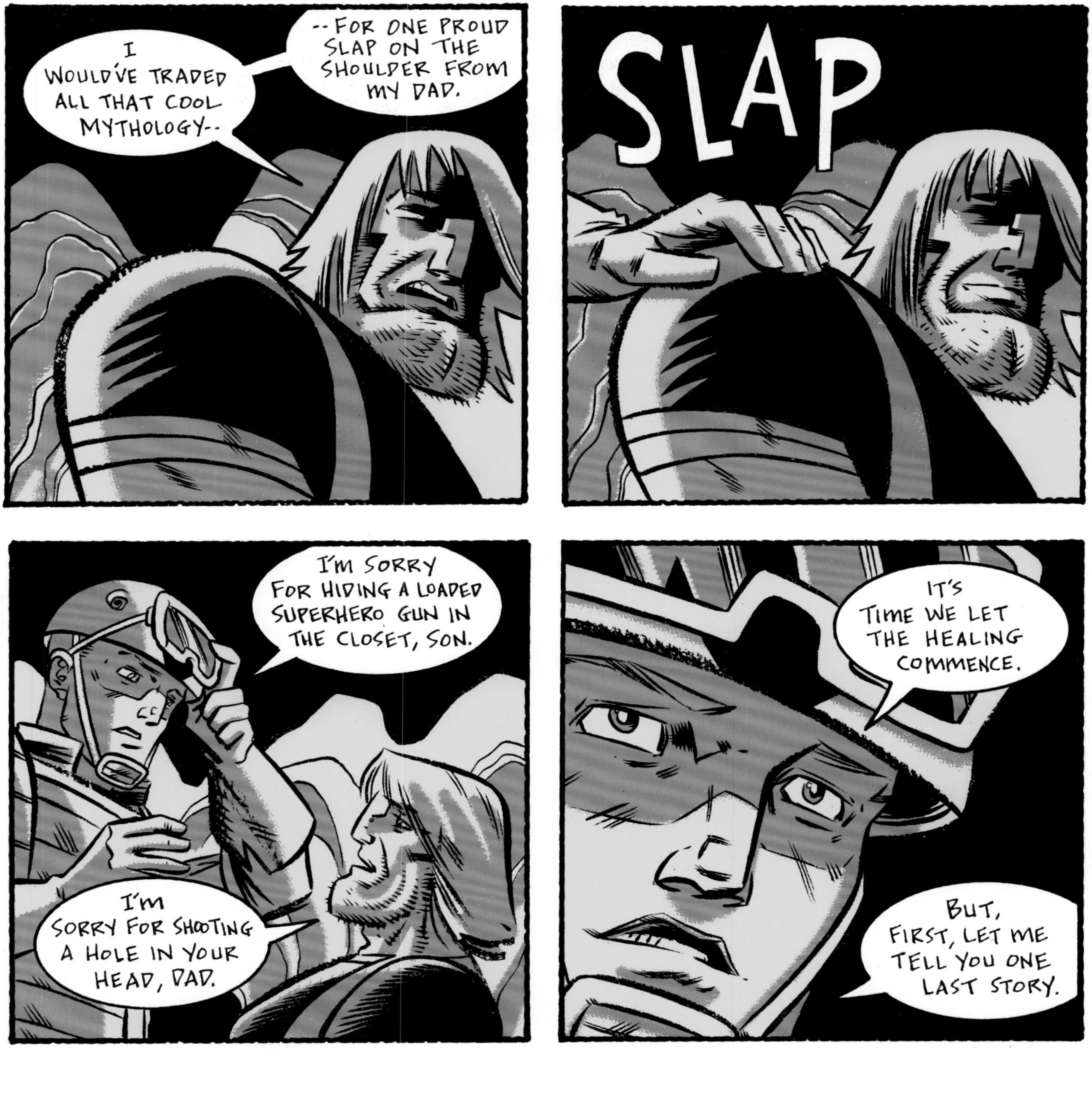
I WOULD'VE TRADED ALL THAT COOL MYTHOLOGY--
--FOR ONE PROUD SLAP ON THE SHOULDER FROM MY DAD.
SLAP
I'M SORRY FOR HIDING A LOADED SUPERHERO GUN IN THE CLOSET, SON.
I'M SORRY FOR SHOOTING A HOLE IN YOUR HEAD, DAD.
IT'S TIME WE LET THE HEALING COMMENCE.
BUT, FIRST, LET ME TELL YOU ONE LAST STORY.

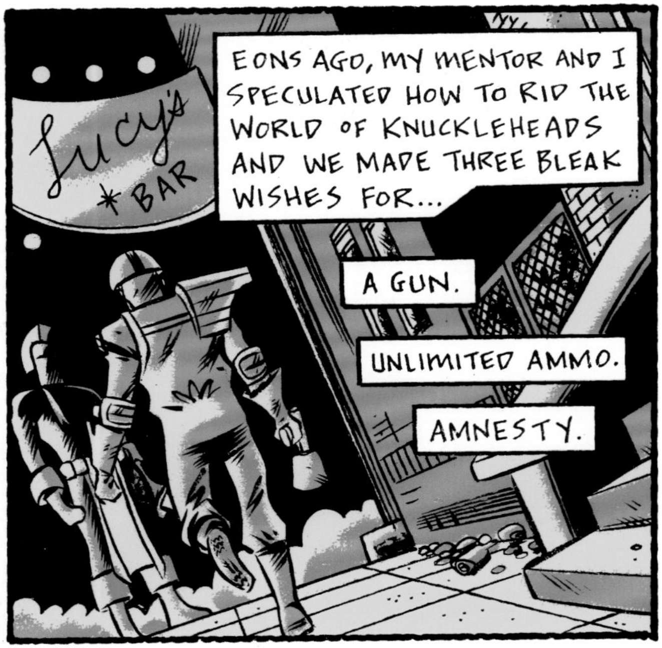
EONS AGO, MY MENTOR AND I SPECULATED HOW TO RID THE WORLD OF KNUCKLEHEADS AND WE MADE THREE BLEAK WISHES FOR...
Lucy's
BAR
A GUN.
UNLIMITED AMMO.
AMNESTY.

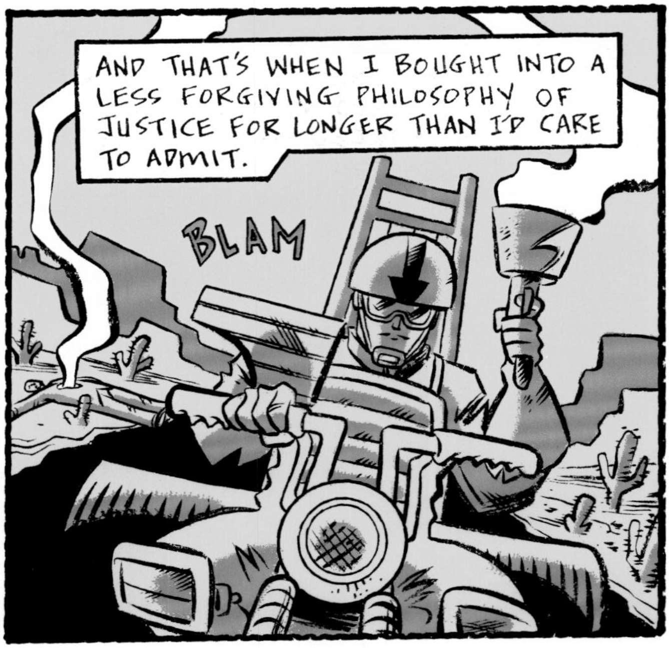
AND THAT'S WHEN I BOUGHT INTO A LESS FORGIVING PHILOSOPHY OF JUSTICE FOR LONGER THAN I'D CARE TO ADMIT.
BLAM

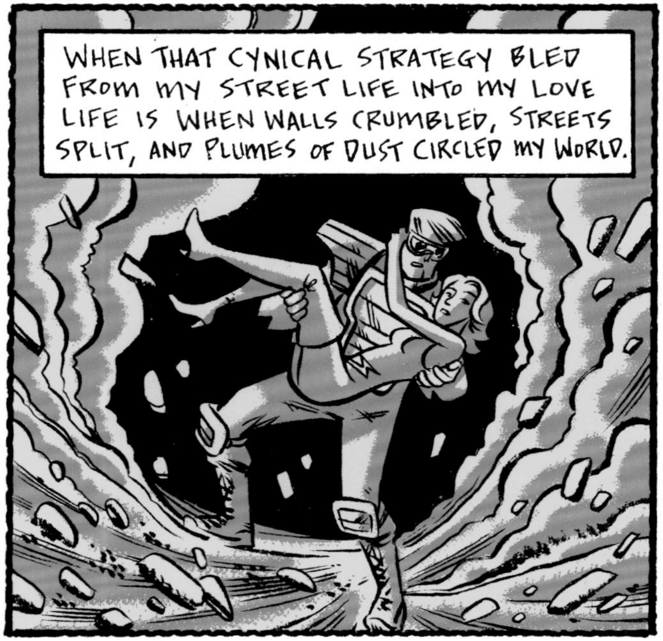
WHEN THAT CYNICAL STRATEGY BLED FROM MY STREET LIFE INTO MY LOVE LIFE IS WHEN WALLS CRUMBLED, STREETS SPLIT, AND PLUMES OF DUST CIRCLED MY WORLD.

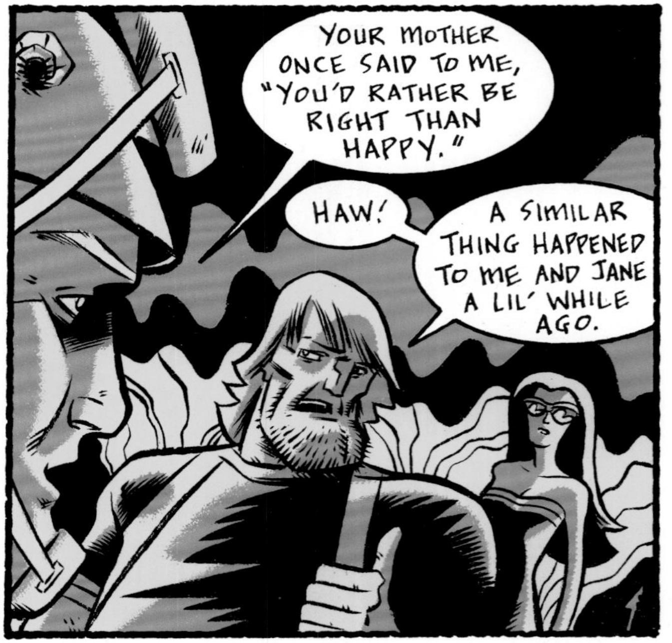
YOUR MOTHER ONCE SAID TO ME, "YOU'D RATHER BE RIGHT THAN HAPPY."
HAW!
A SIMILAR THING HAPPENED TO ME AND JANE A LIL' WHILE AGO.

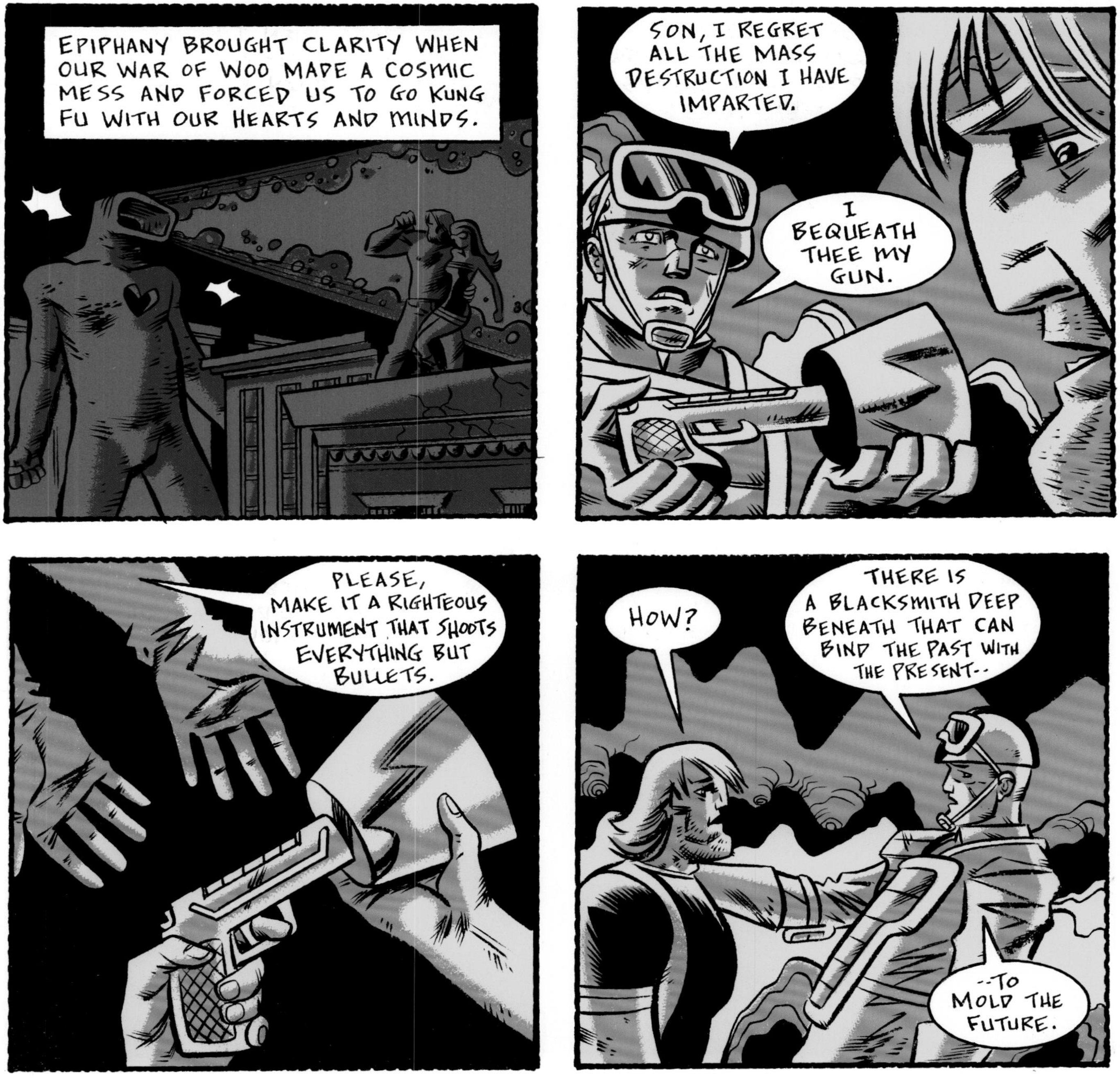
EPIPHANY BROUGHT CLARITY WHEN OUR WAR OF WOO MADE A COSMIC MESS AND FORCED US TO GO KUNG FU WITH OUR HEARTS AND MINDS.
SON, I REGRET ALL THE MASS DESTRUCTION I HAVE IMPARTED.
I BEQUEATH THEE MY GUN.
PLEASE, MAKE IT A RIGHTEOUS INSTRUMENT THAT SHOOTS EVERYTHING BUT BULLETS.
HOW?
THERE IS A BLACKSMITH DEEP BENEATH THAT CAN BIND THE PAST WITH THE PRESENT--
--TO MOLD THE FUTURE.

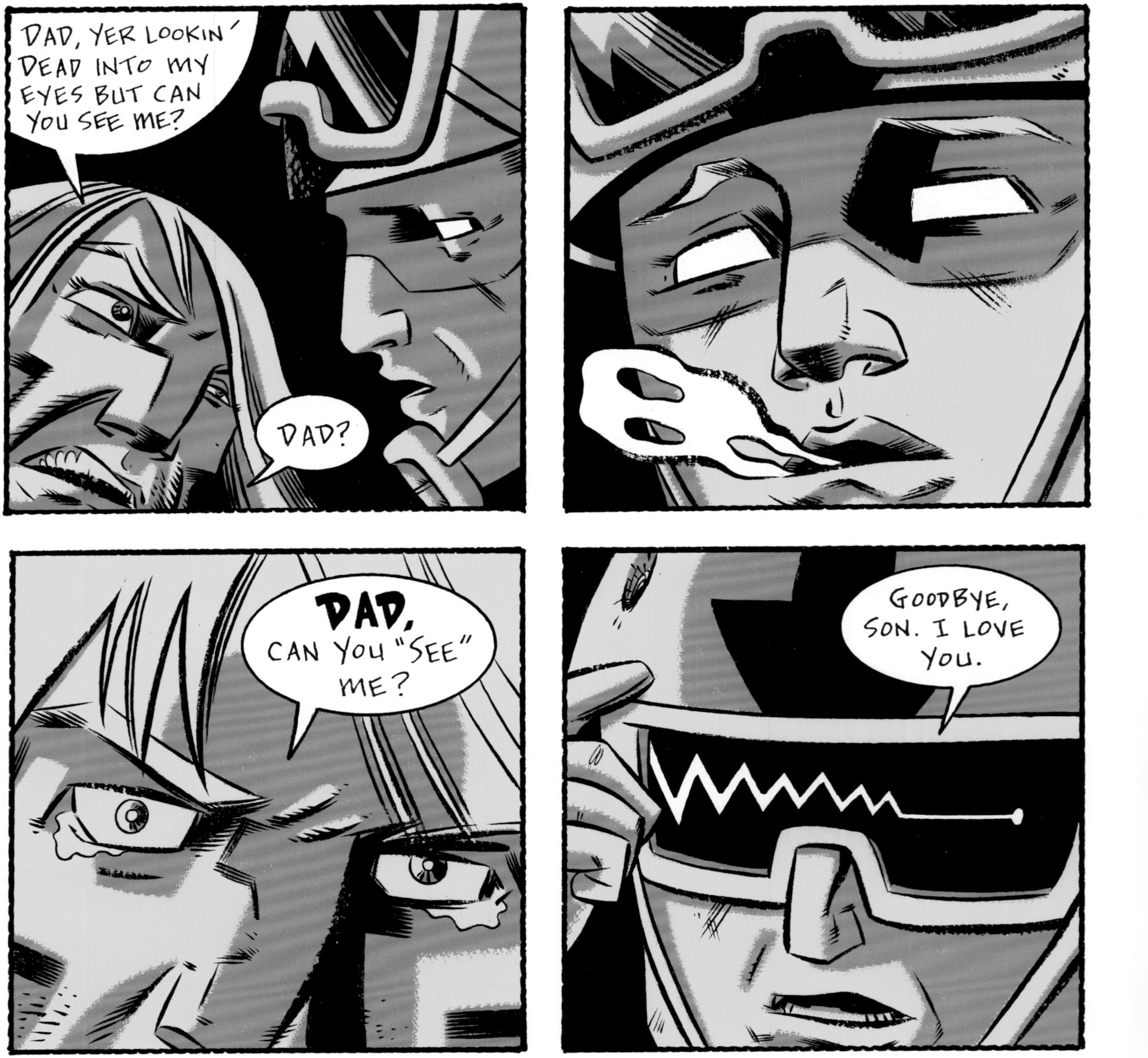
DAD, YER LOOKIN' DEAD INTO MY EYES BUT CAN YOU SEE ME?
DAD?
DAD, CAN YOU "SEE" ME?
GOODBYE, SON. I LOVE YOU.

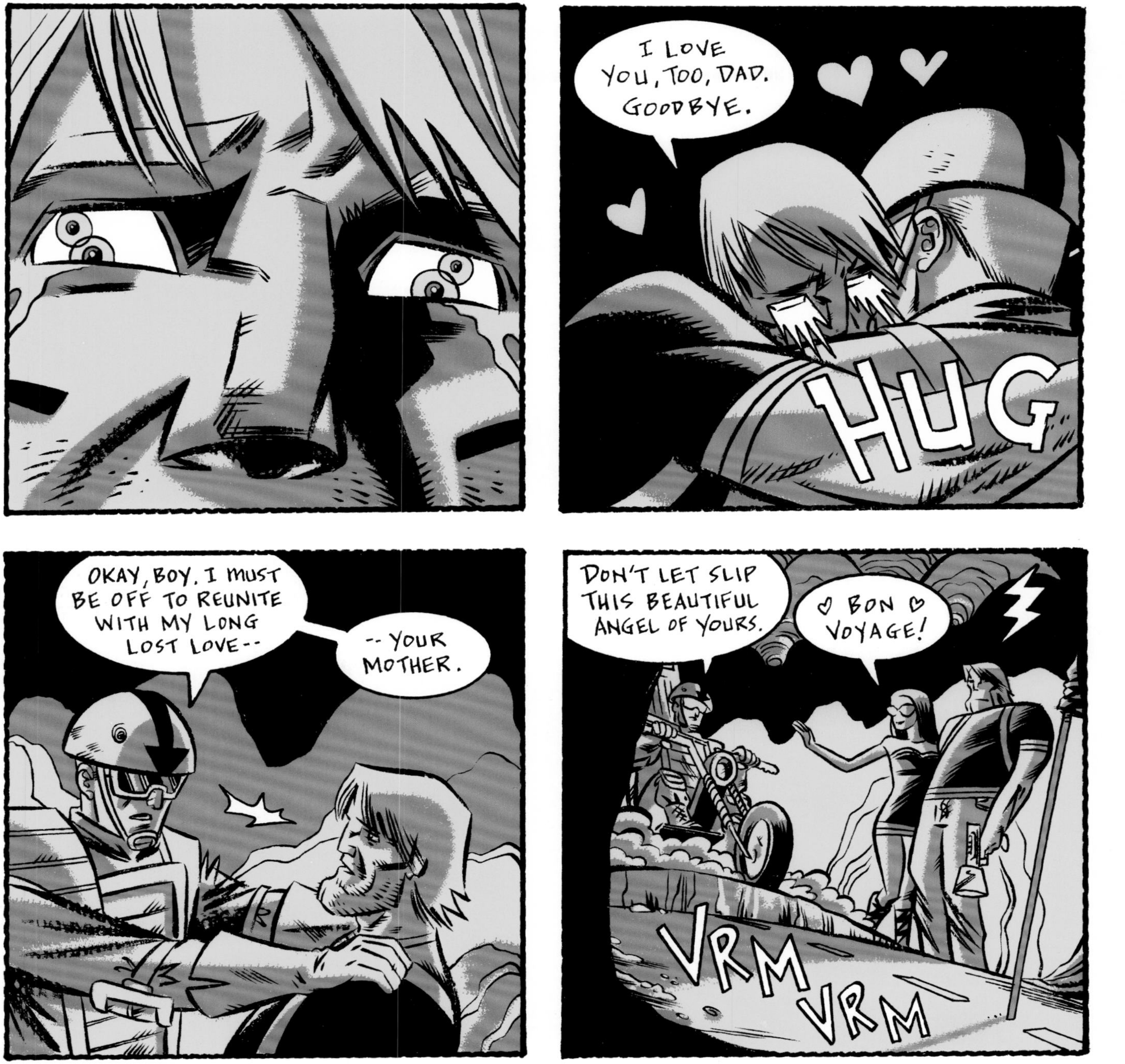
I LOVE YOU, TOO, DAD. GOODBYE.
HUG
OKAY, BOY. I MUST BE OFF TO REUNITE WITH MY LONG LOST LOVE--
-- YOUR MOTHER.
DON'T LET SLIP THIS BEAUTIFUL ANGEL OF YOURS.
♡ BON ♡ VOYAGE!
VRM VRM

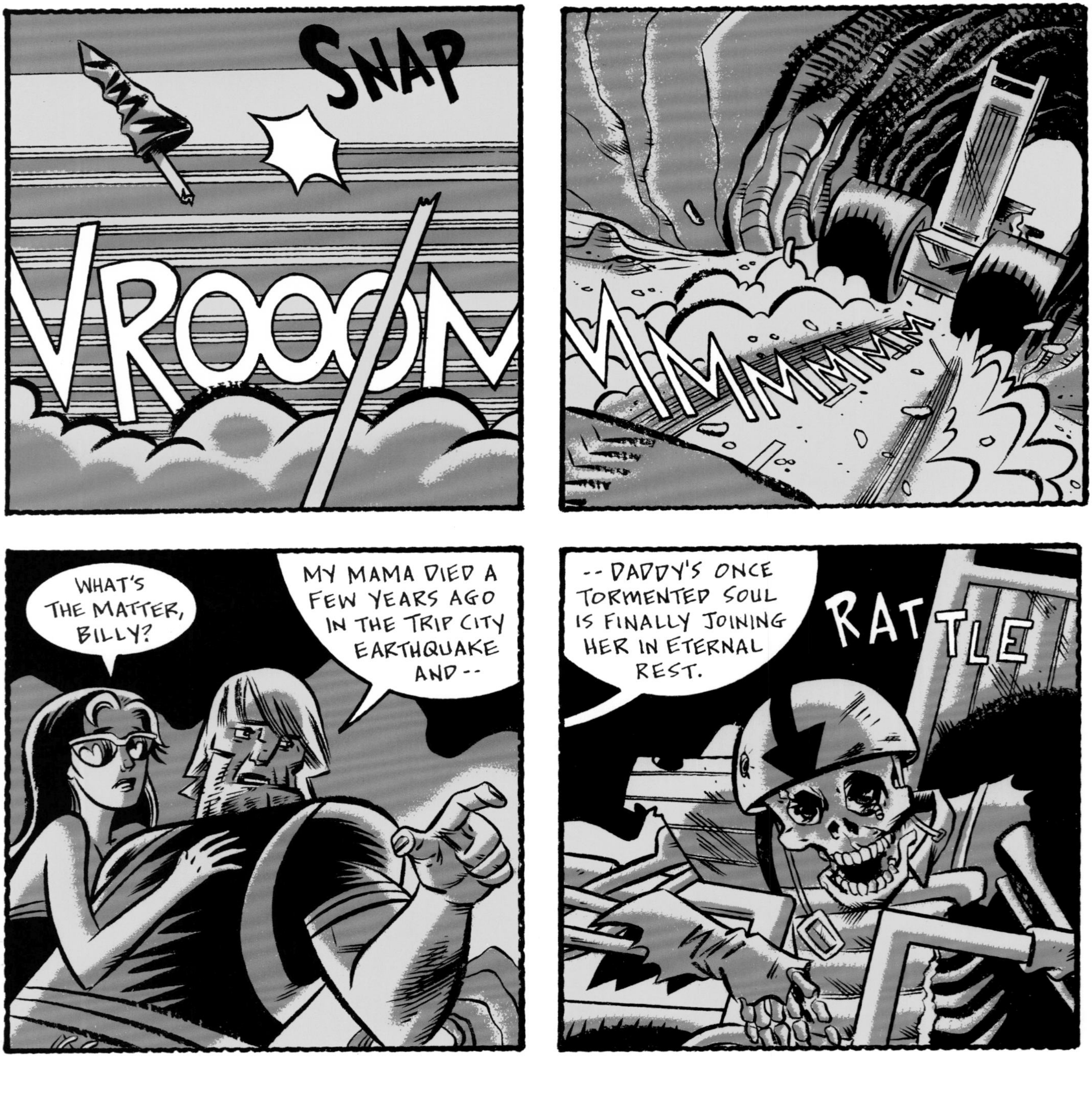
SNAP
VROOOM
MMMMMMM
WHAT'S THE MATTER, BILLY?
MY MAMA DIED A FEW YEARS AGO IN THE TRIP CITY EARTHQUAKE AND--
--DADDY'S ONCE TORMENTED SOUL IS FINALLY JOINING HER IN ETERNAL REST.
RATTLE

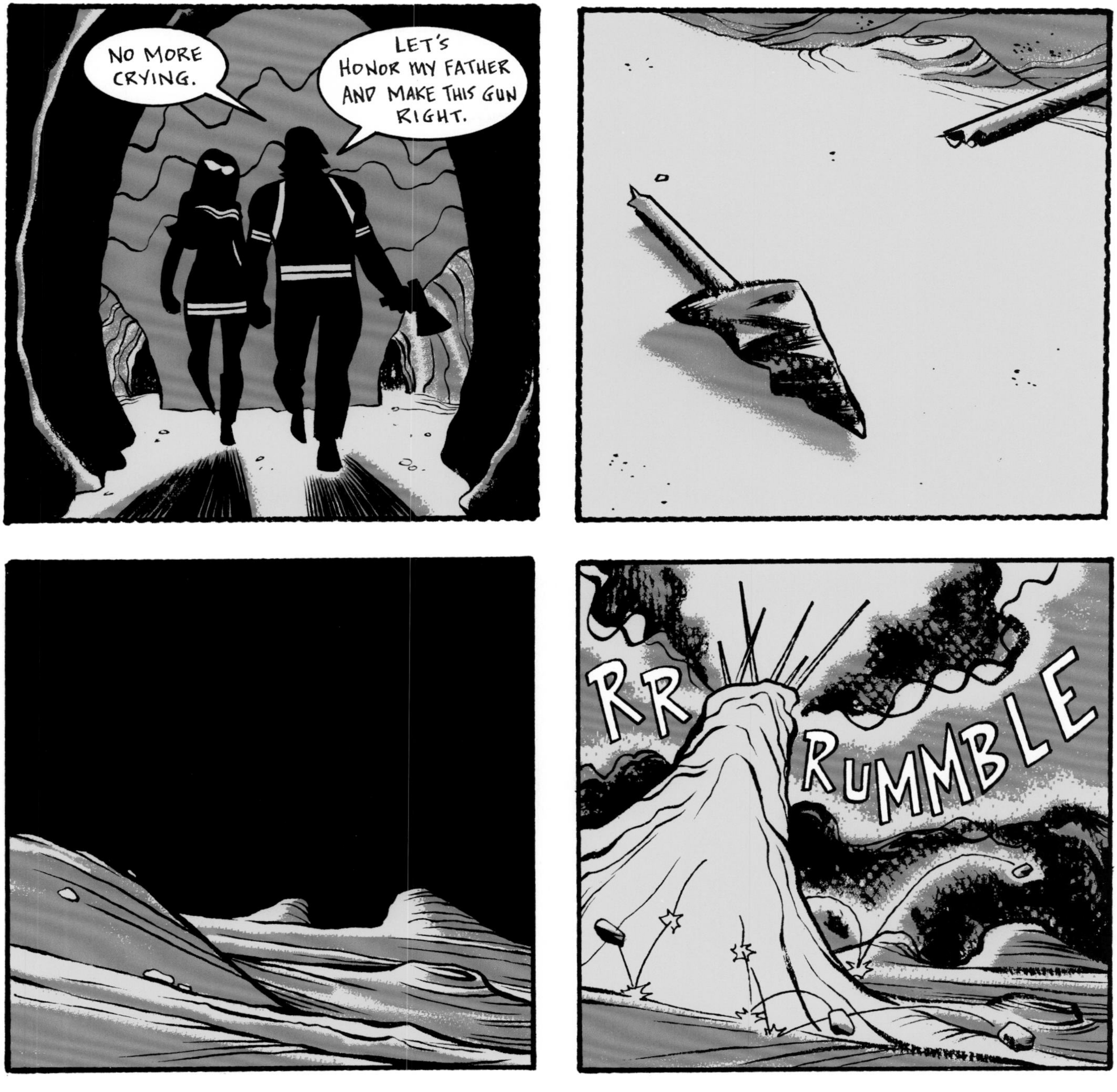

NO MORE CRYING.
LET'S HONOR MY FATHER AND MAKE THIS GUN RIGHT.
RR RUMMBLE

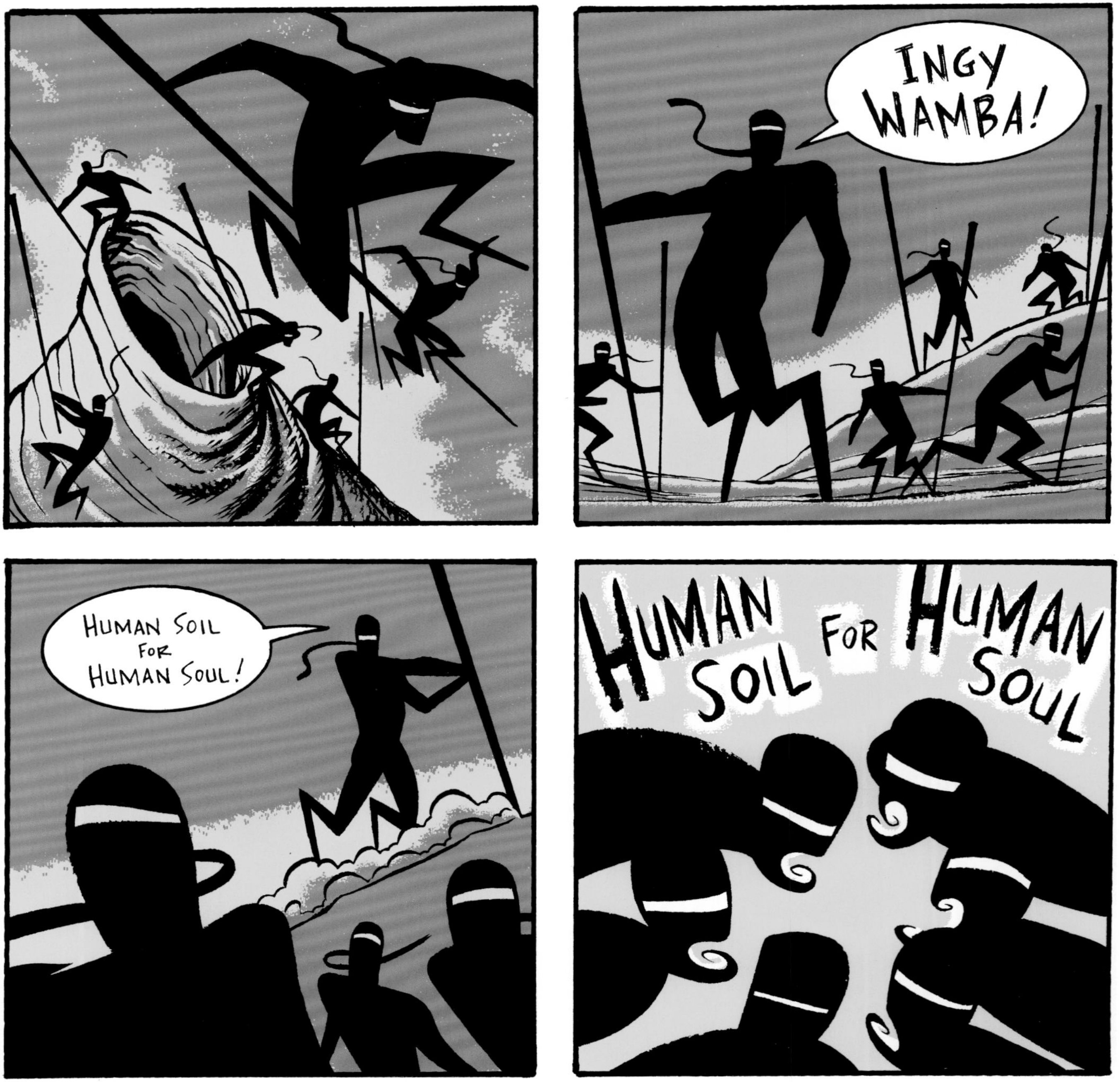
INGY WAMBA!
HUMAN SOIL FOR HUMAN SOUL!
HUMAN SOIL FOR HUMAN SOUL

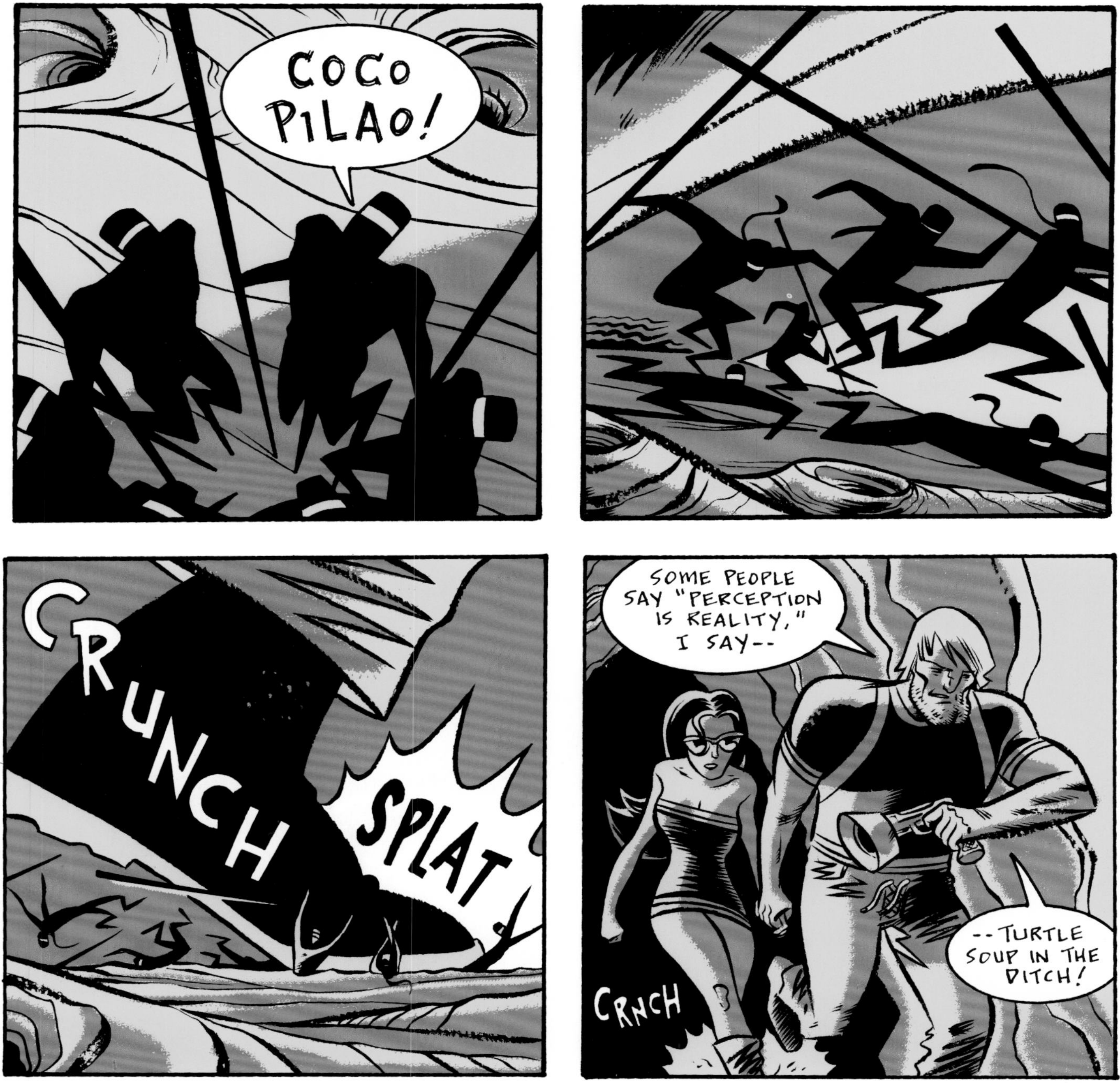
COCO PILAO!
CRUNCH
SPLAT
SOME PEOPLE SAY "PERCEPTION IS REALITY," I SAY--
--TURTLE SOUP IN THE DITCH!
CRNCH

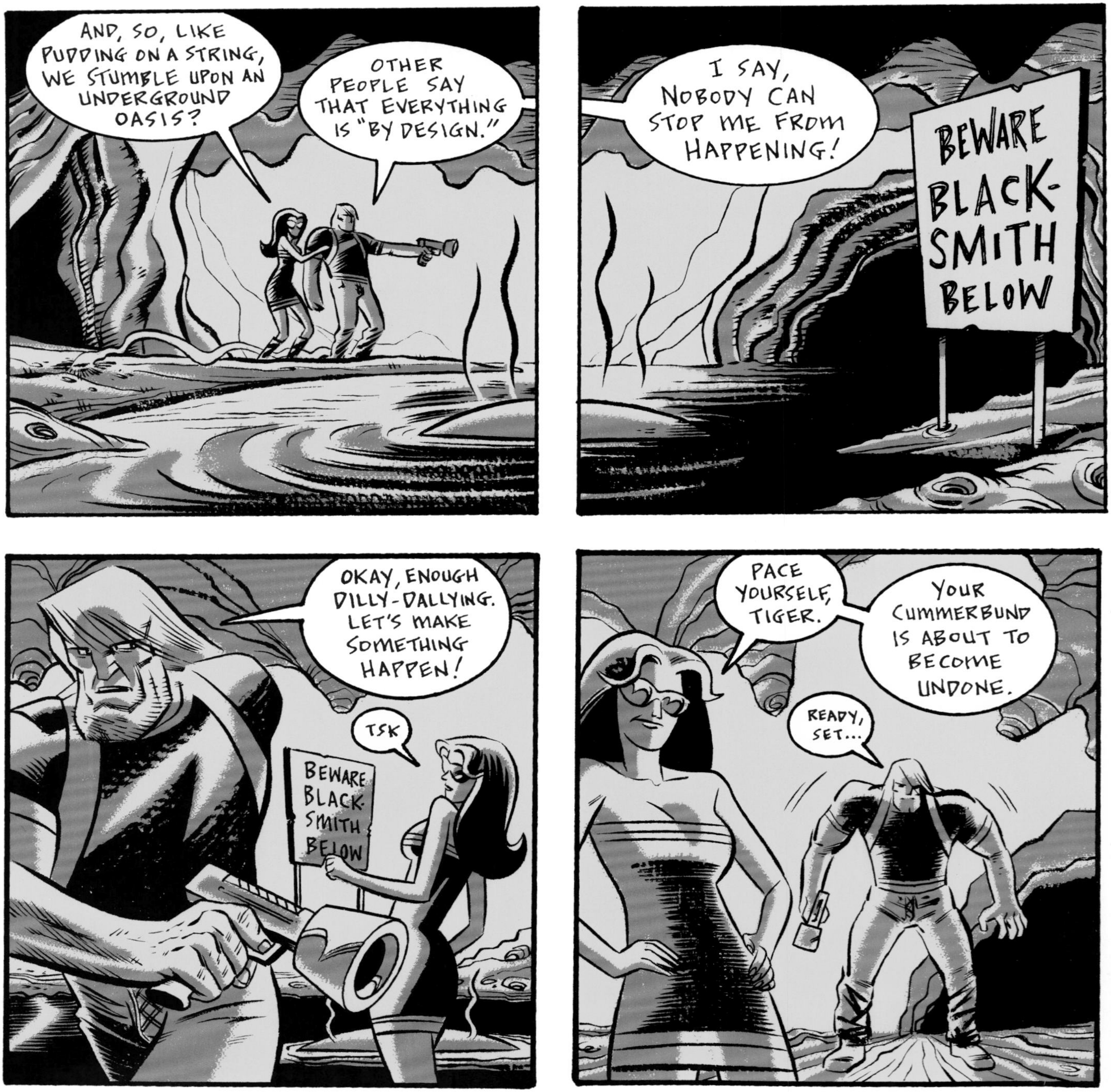
AND, SO, LIKE PUDDING ON A STRING, WE STUMBLE UPON AN UNDERGROUND OASIS?
OTHER PEOPLE SAY THAT EVERYTHING IS "BY DESIGN."
I SAY, NOBODY CAN STOP ME FROM HAPPENING!
BEWARE BLACK-SMITH BELOW
OKAY, ENOUGH DILLY-DALLYING. LET'S MAKE SOMETHING HAPPEN!
TSK
BEWARE BLACK-SMITH BELOW
PACE YOURSELF, TIGER.
YOUR CUMMERBUND IS ABOUT TO BECOME UNDONE.
READY, SET...

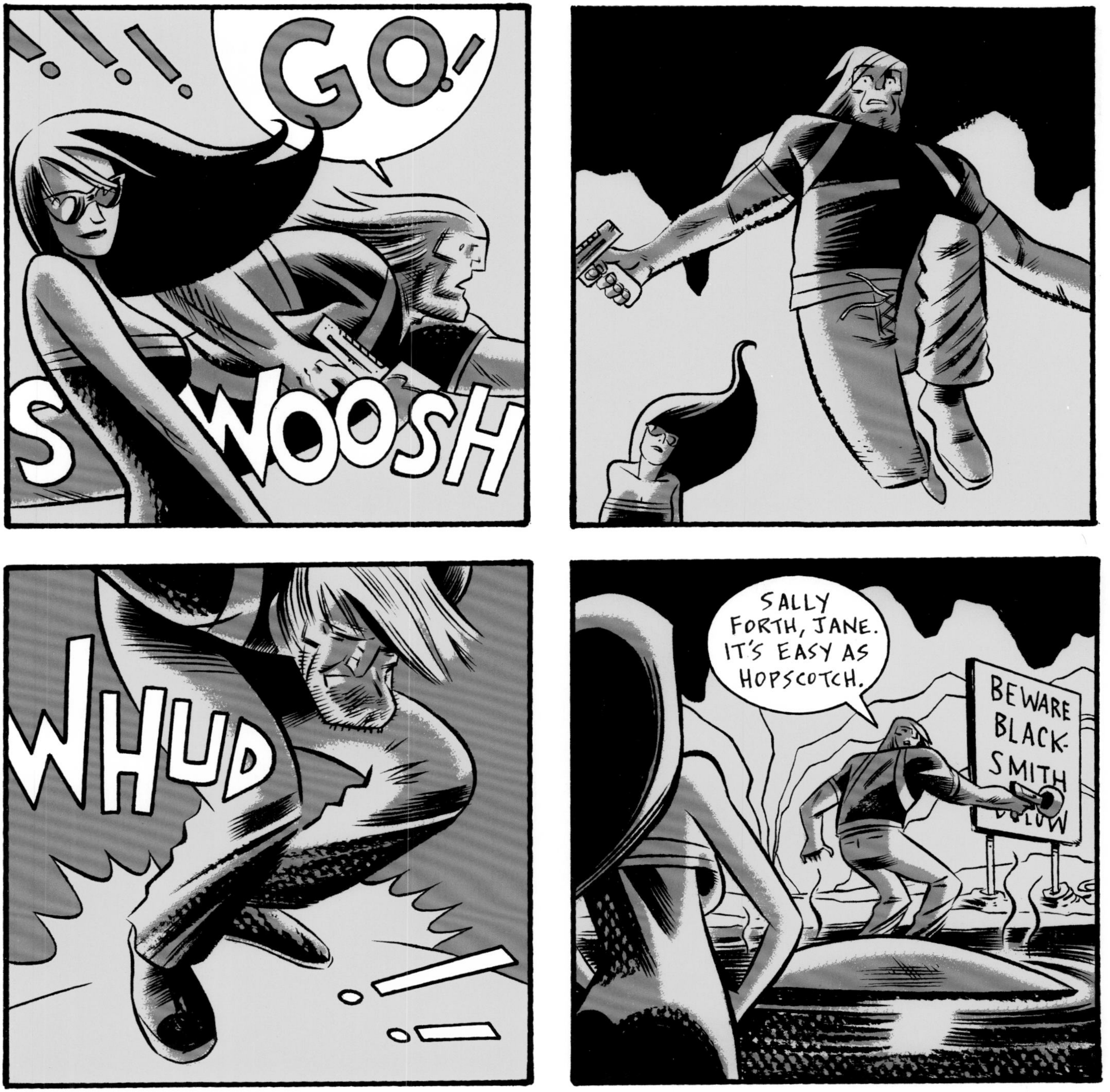
GO!
SWOOSH
WHUD
SALLY FORTH, JANE. IT'S EASY AS HOPSCOTCH.
BEWARE BLACK- SMITH

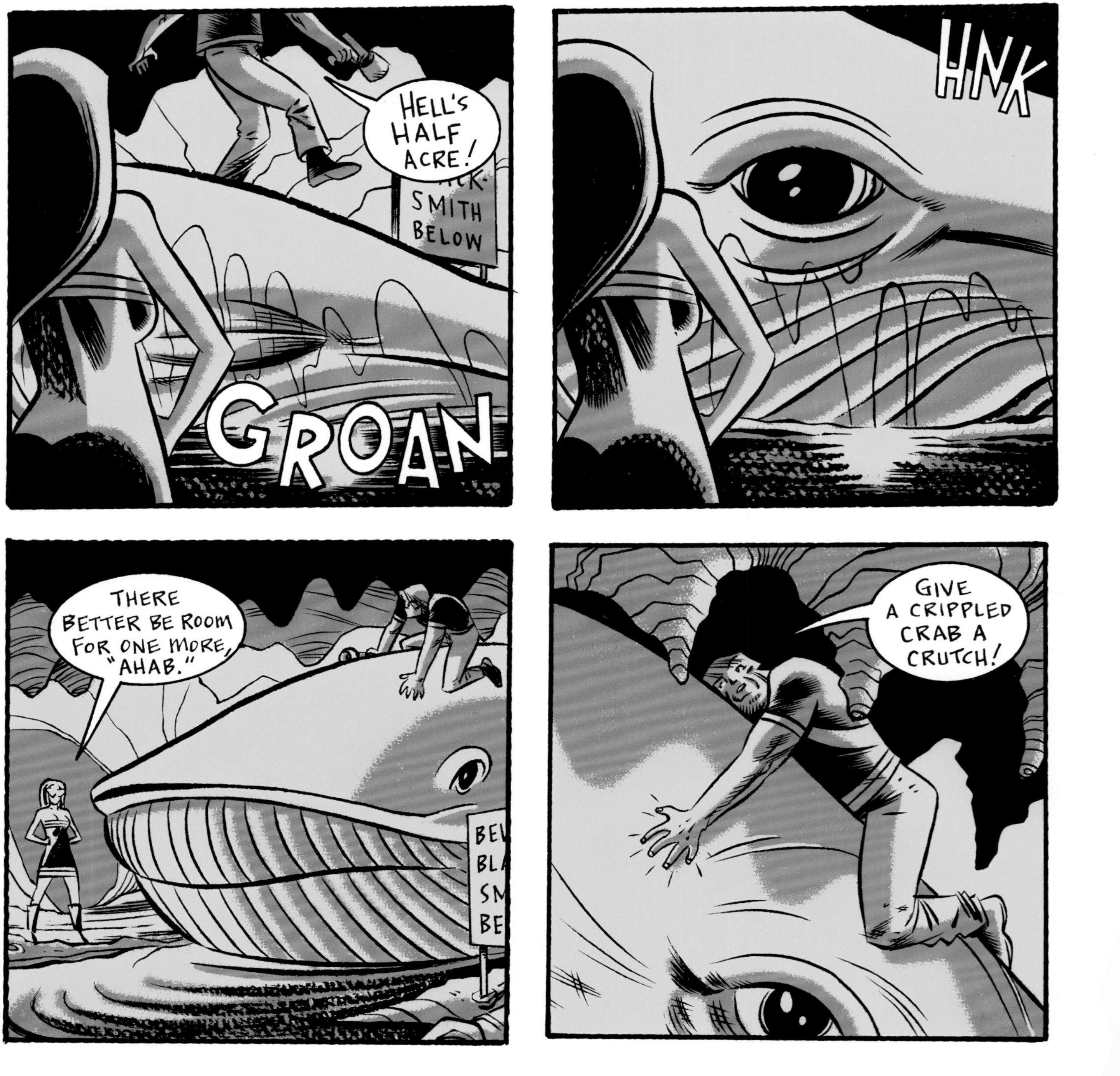

HELL'S HALF ACRE!
SMITH BELOW
GROAN
HNK
THERE BETTER BE ROOM FOR ONE MORE, "AHAB."
GIVE A CRIPPLED CRAB A CRUTCH!

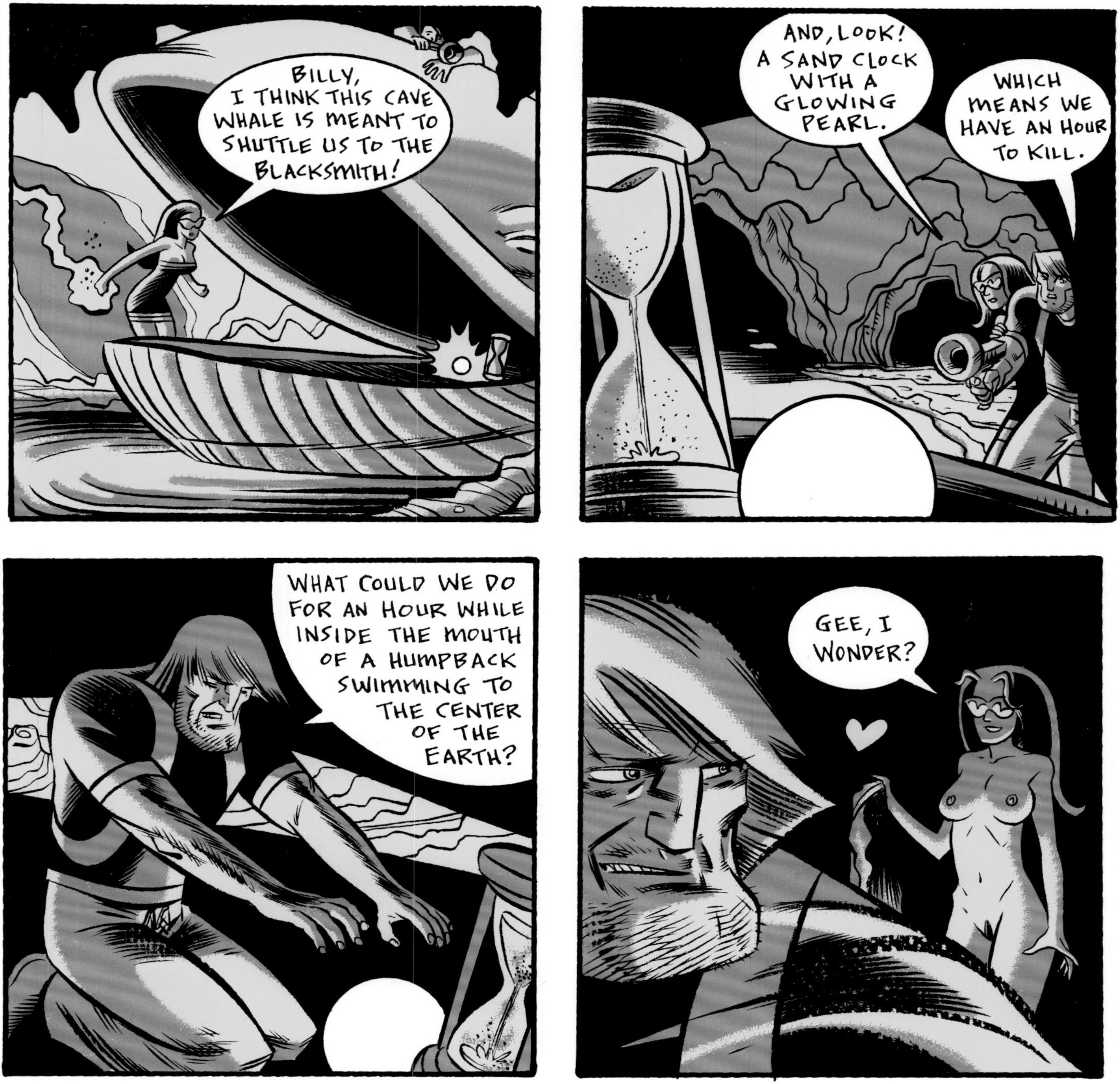
BILLY, I THINK THIS CAVE WHALE IS MEANT TO SHUTTLE US TO THE BLACKSMITH!
AND, LOOK! A SAND CLOCK WITH A GLOWING PEARL.
WHICH MEANS WE HAVE AN HOUR TO KILL.
WHAT COULD WE DO FOR AN HOUR WHILE INSIDE THE MOUTH OF A HUMPBACK SWIMMING TO THE CENTER OF THE EARTH?
GEE, I WONDER?

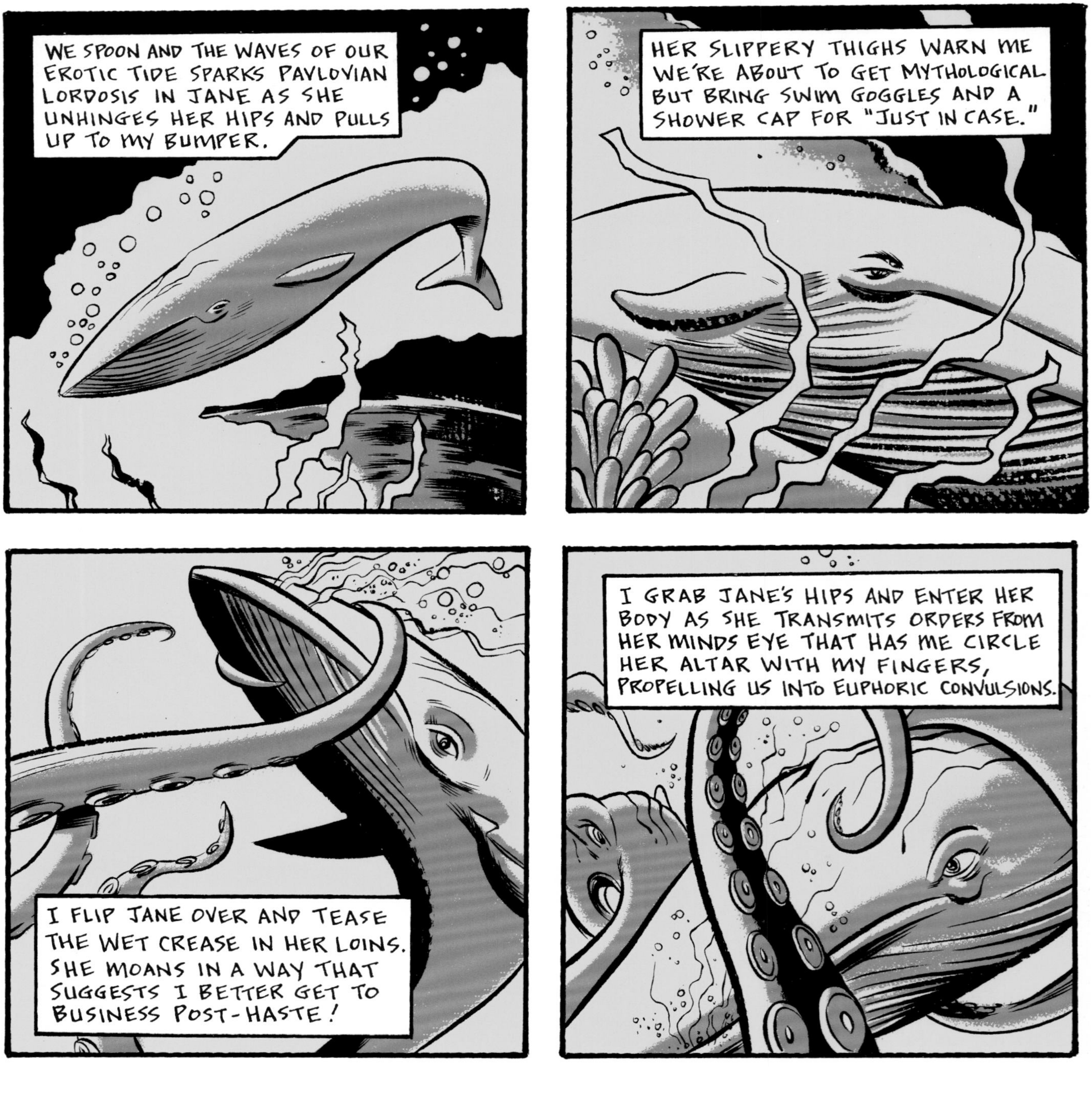
WE SPOON AND THE WAVES OF OUR EROTIC TIDE SPARKS PAVLOVIAN LORDOSIS IN JANE AS SHE UNHINGES HER HIPS AND PULLS UP TO MY BUMPER.
HER SLIPPERY THIGHS WARN ME WE'RE ABOUT TO GET MYTHOLOGICAL BUT BRING SWIM GOGGLES AND A SHOWER CAP FOR "JUST IN CASE."
I FLIP JANE OVER AND TEASE THE WET CREASE IN HER LOINS. SHE MOANS IN A WAY THAT SUGGESTS I BETTER GET TO BUSINESS POST-HASTE!
I GRAB JANE'S HIPS AND ENTER HER BODY AS SHE TRANSMITS ORDERS FROM HER MINDS EYE THAT HAS ME CIRCLE HER ALTAR WITH MY FINGERS, PROPELLING US INTO EUPHORIC CONVULSIONS.

JANE SLIDES BACK AND FORTH CLUTCHING ME FROM DEEP WITHIN WHILE MOANS TURN INTO SCREAMS AND SHE SHAKES AND SHUDDERS AND DIES A MILLION TIMES.

A PHOENIX GOES SUPER NOVA AND I GIVE JANE A MINUTE TO RECOVER BEFORE I DO THE REST OF WHAT NEEDS TO BE DONE.

I WON'T BE CHECKING EMAIL TONIGHT.

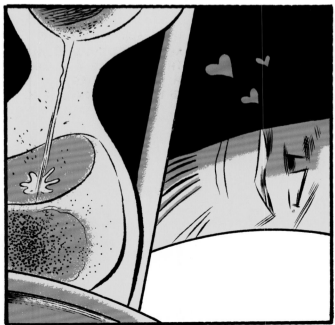

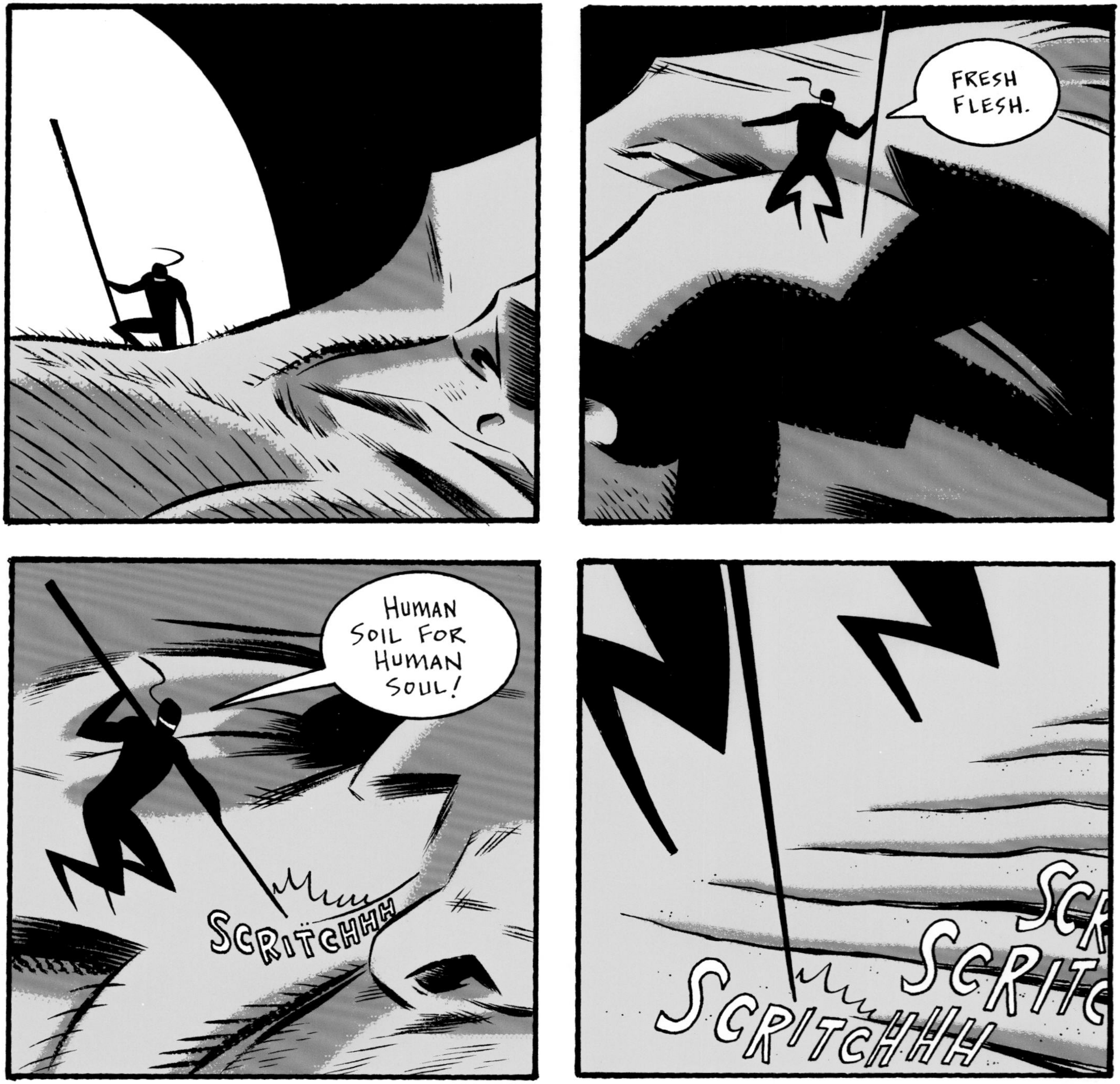
FRESH FLESH.
HUMAN SOIL FOR HUMAN SOUL!
SCRITCHHH
SCRITCHHH
SCRITC
SCR

BILLY! BARNACLE MITES ARE TRYING TO HARVEST YOUR SOUL!
!
?
!!! JANE!!! I'M GOING TO RICOCHET OFF YOUR IRON PALM WITH MY EYE BEAMS AND FRY THIS NINJA-COOTIE, PRONTO!
BET.
BZT

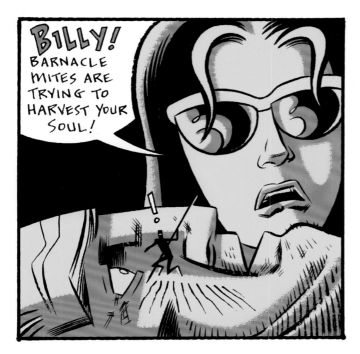

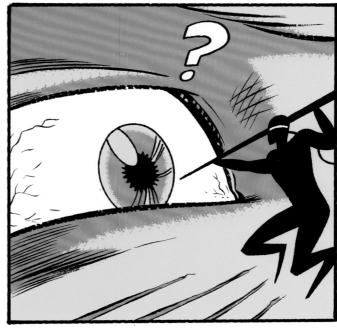

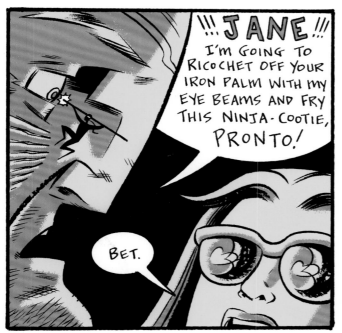

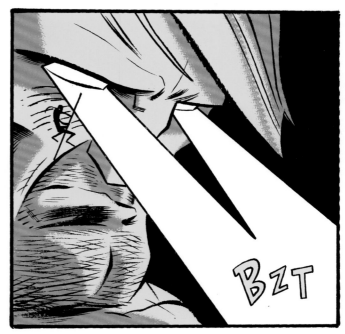

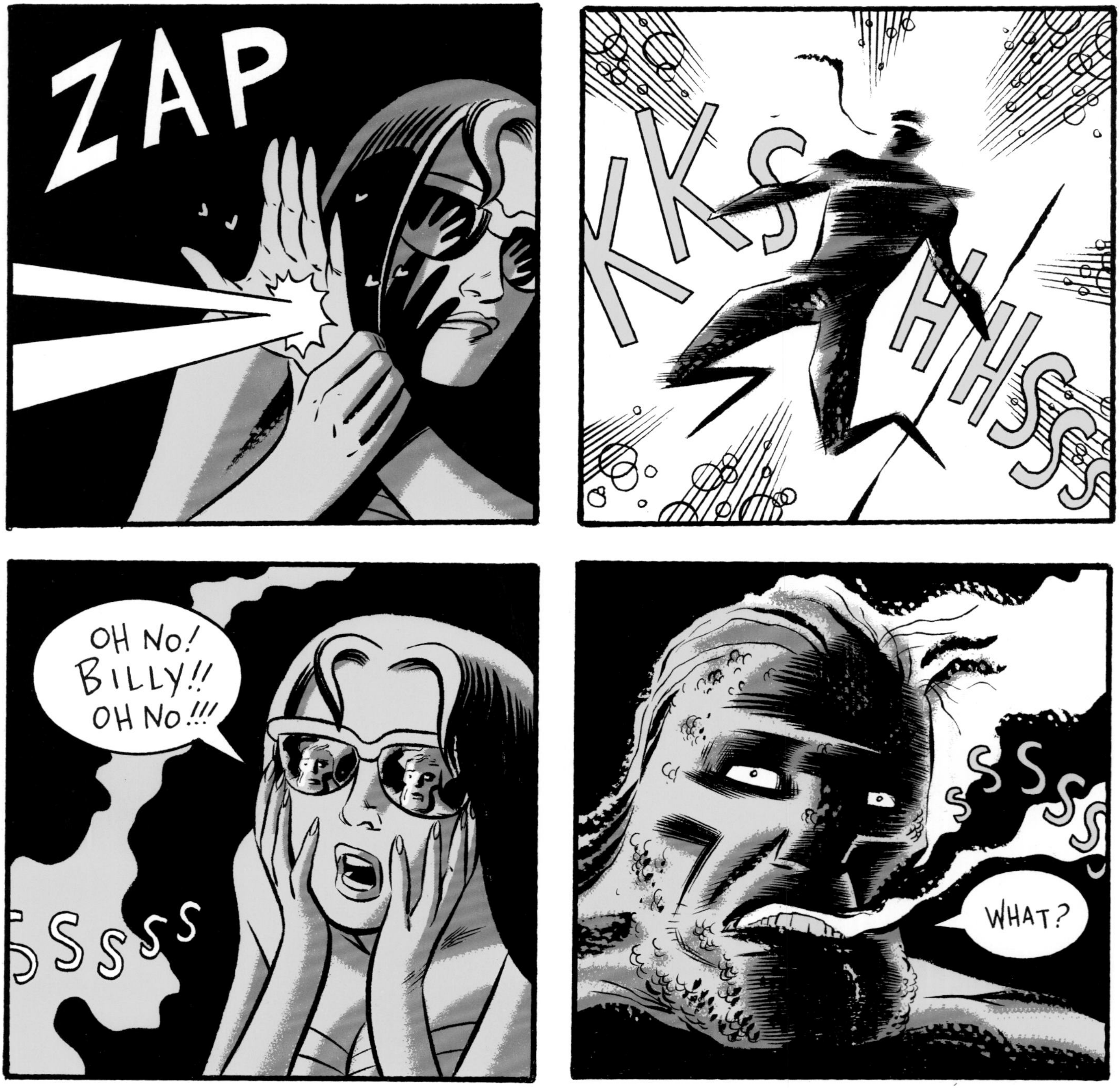
ZAP
KKSHHSSS
OH NO! BILLY!! OH NO!!!
SSSSSS
SSSSS
WHAT?

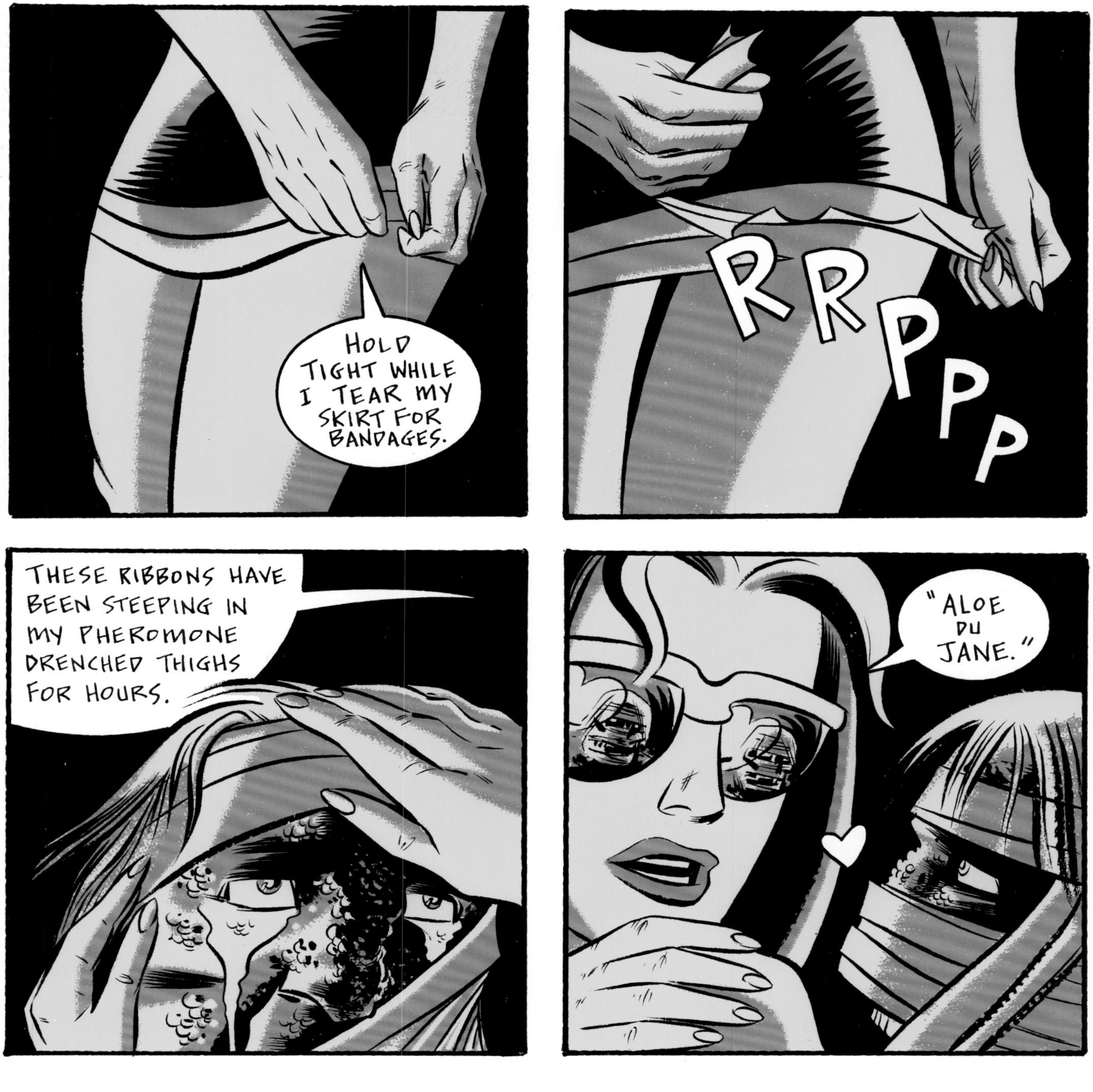
HOLD TIGHT WHILE I TEAR MY SKIRT FOR BANDAGES.
RRPPPP
THESE RIBBONS HAVE BEEN STEEPING IN MY PHEROMONE DRENCHED THIGHS FOR HOURS.
"ALOE DU JANE."

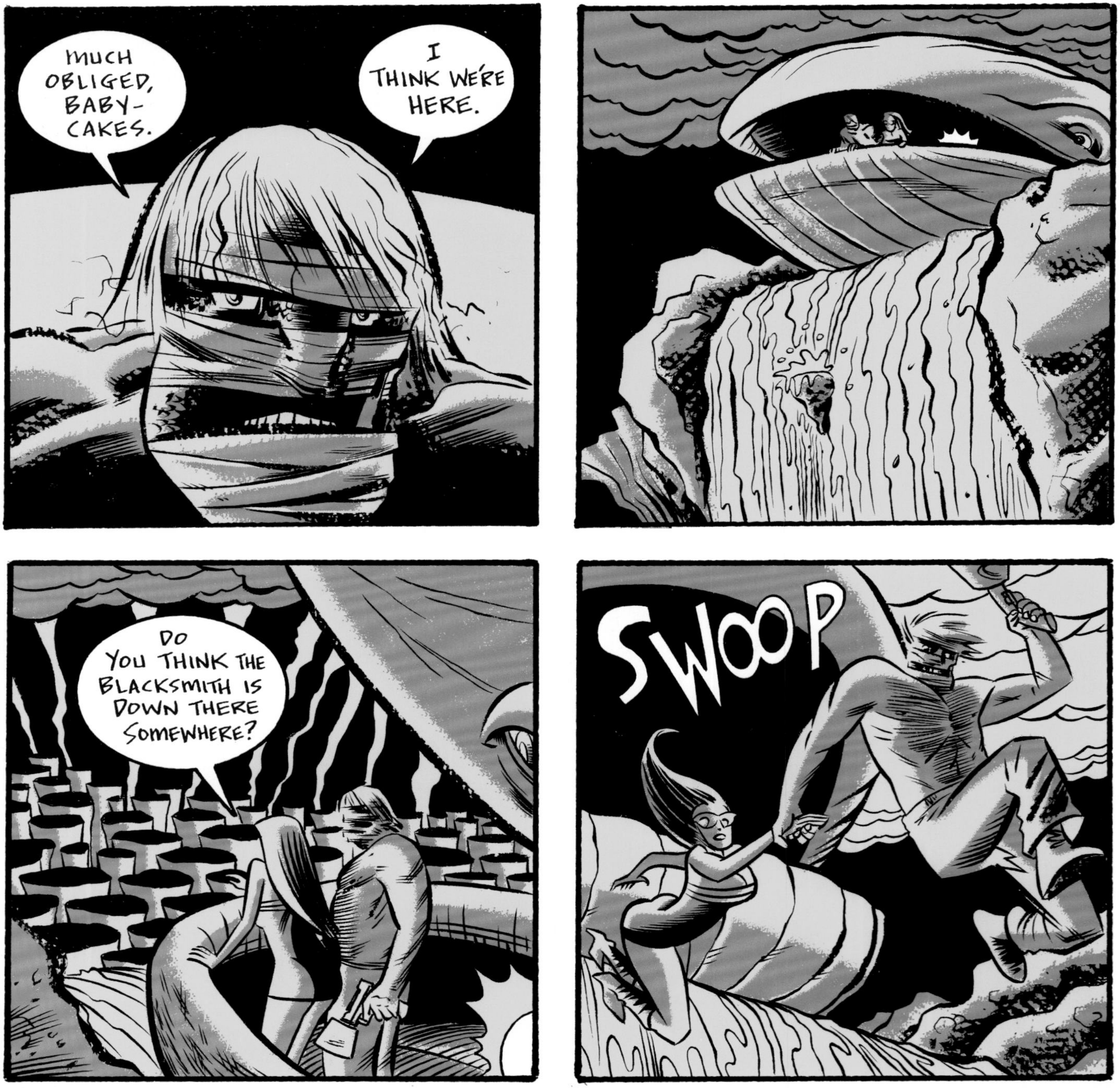
MUCH OBLIGED, BABY-CAKES.
I THINK WE'RE HERE.
DO YOU THINK THE BLACKSMITH IS DOWN THERE SOMEWHERE?
SWOOP

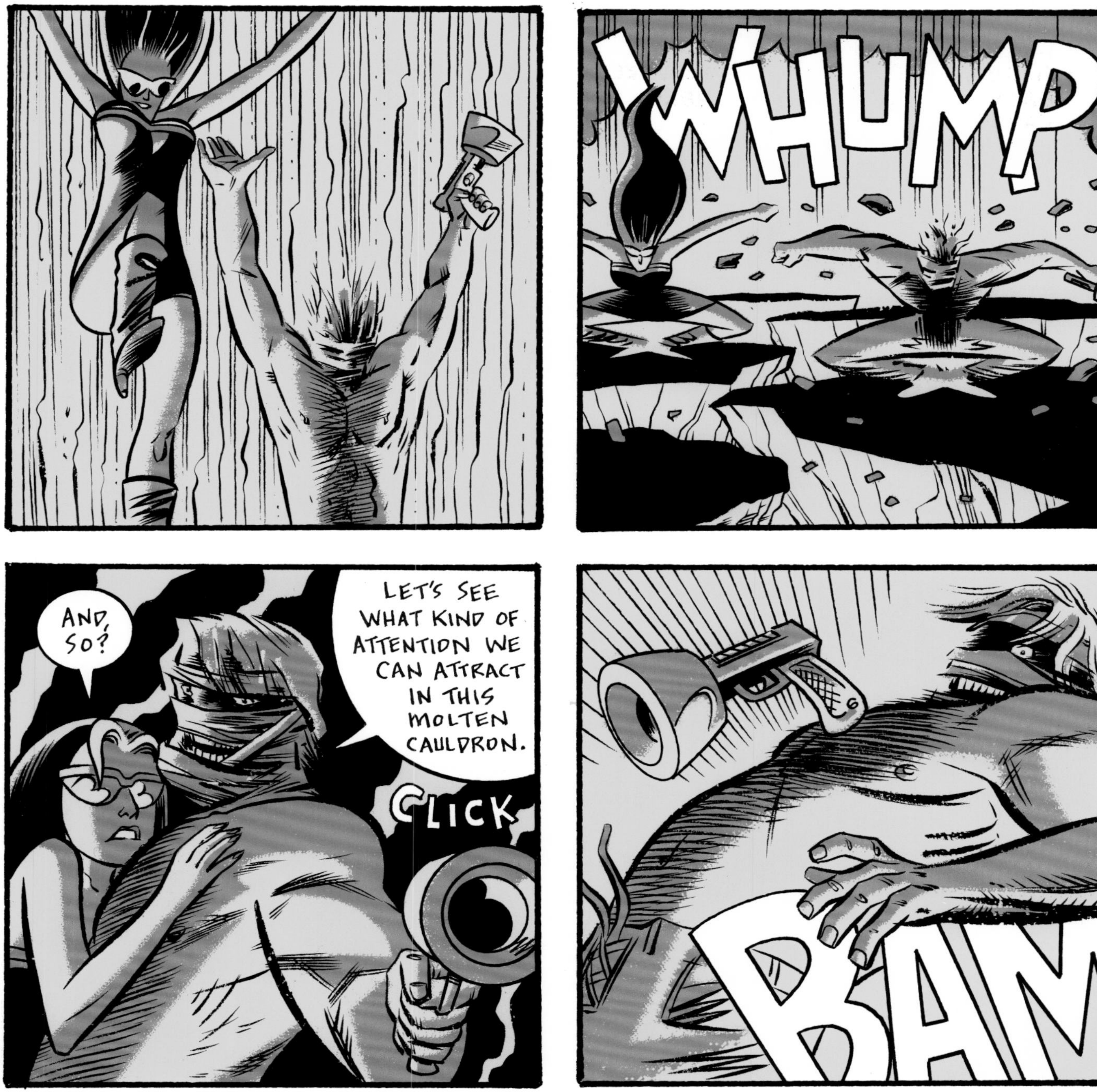
WHUMP
AND, SO?
LET'S SEE WHAT KIND OF ATTENTION WE CAN ATTRACT IN THIS MOLTEN CAULDRON.
CLICK
BAM

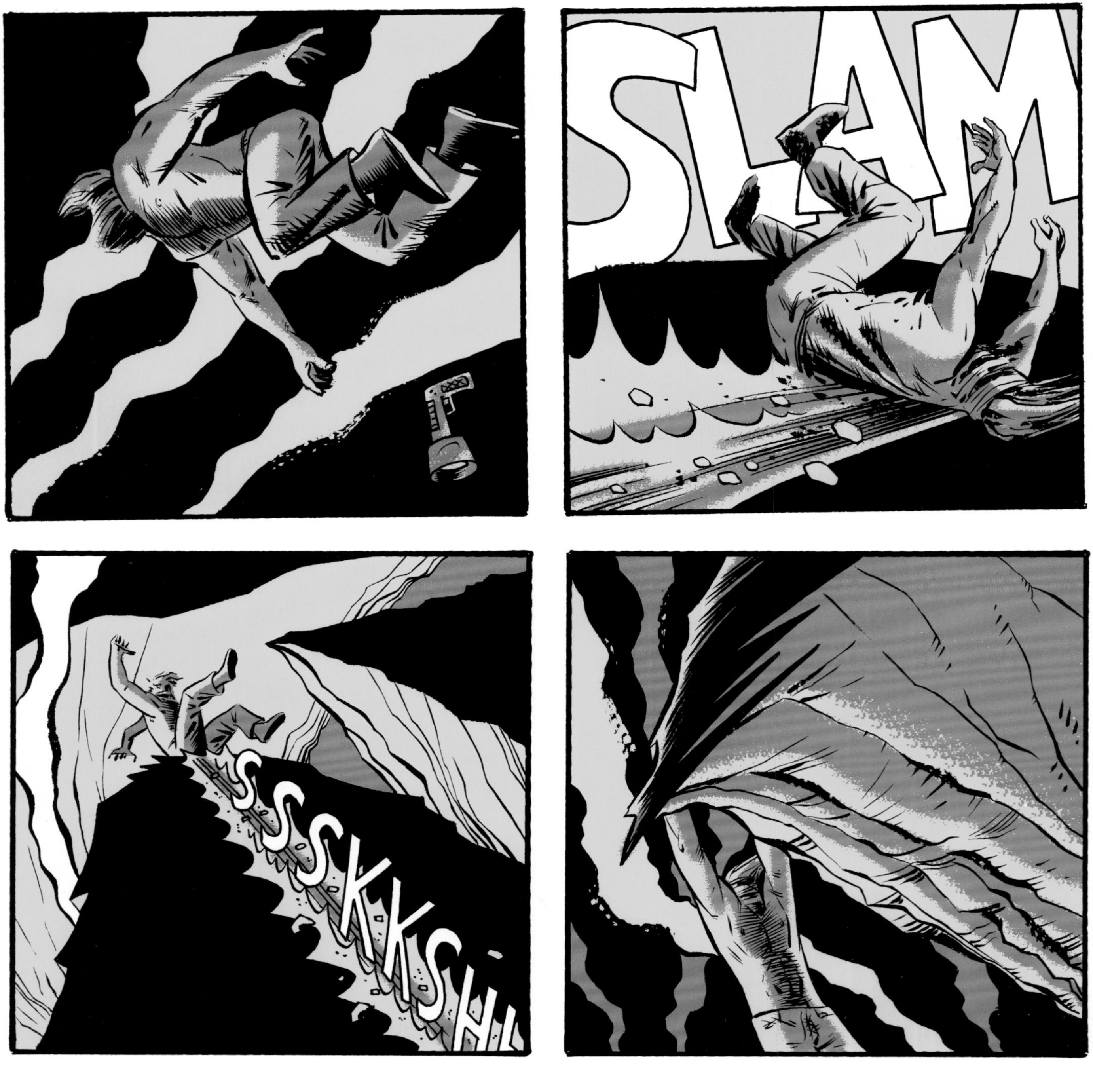
SLAM
SSSKKSH

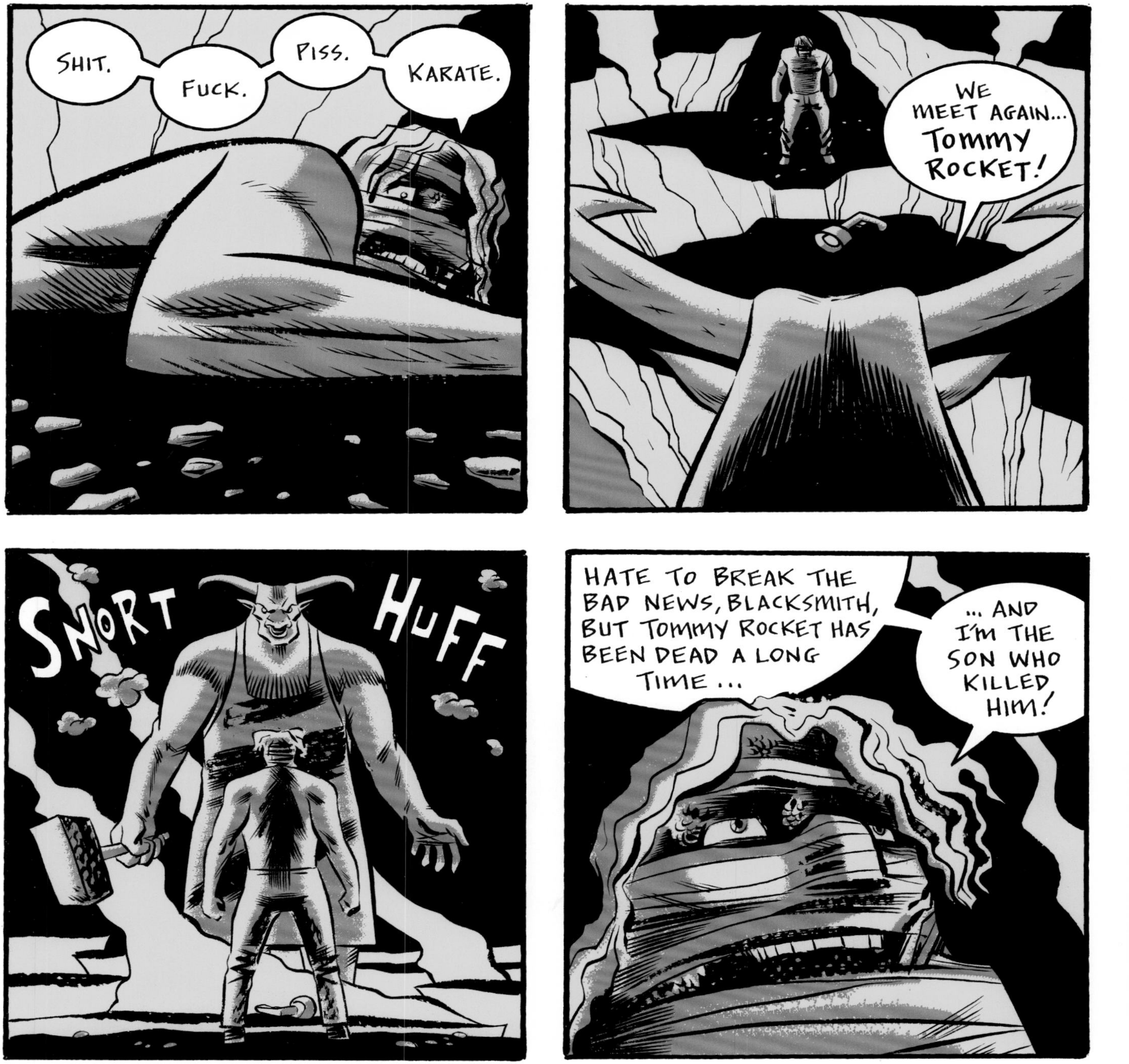
SHIT.
FUCK.
PISS.
KARATE.
WE MEET AGAIN... TOMMY ROCKET!
SNORT
HUFF
HATE TO BREAK THE BAD NEWS, BLACKSMITH, BUT TOMMY ROCKET HAS BEEN DEAD A LONG TIME...
... AND I'M THE SON WHO KILLED HIM!

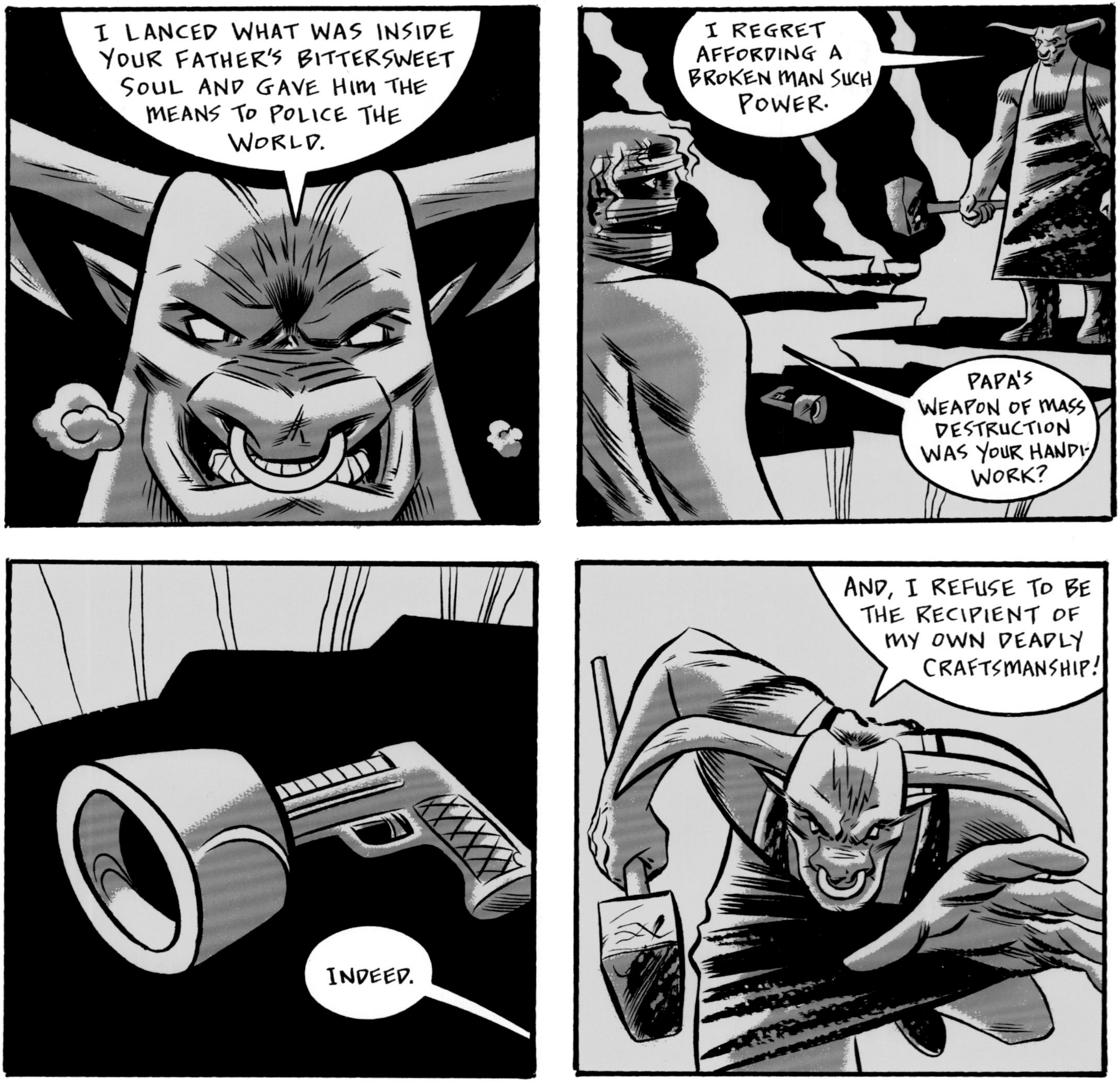
I LANCED WHAT WAS INSIDE YOUR FATHER'S BITTERSWEET SOUL AND GAVE HIM THE MEANS TO POLICE THE WORLD.
I REGRET AFFORDING A BROKEN MAN SUCH POWER.
PAPA'S WEAPON OF MASS DESTRUCTION WAS YOUR HANDIWORK?
INDEED.
AND, I REFUSE TO BE THE RECIPIENT OF MY OWN DEADLY CRAFTSMANSHIP!

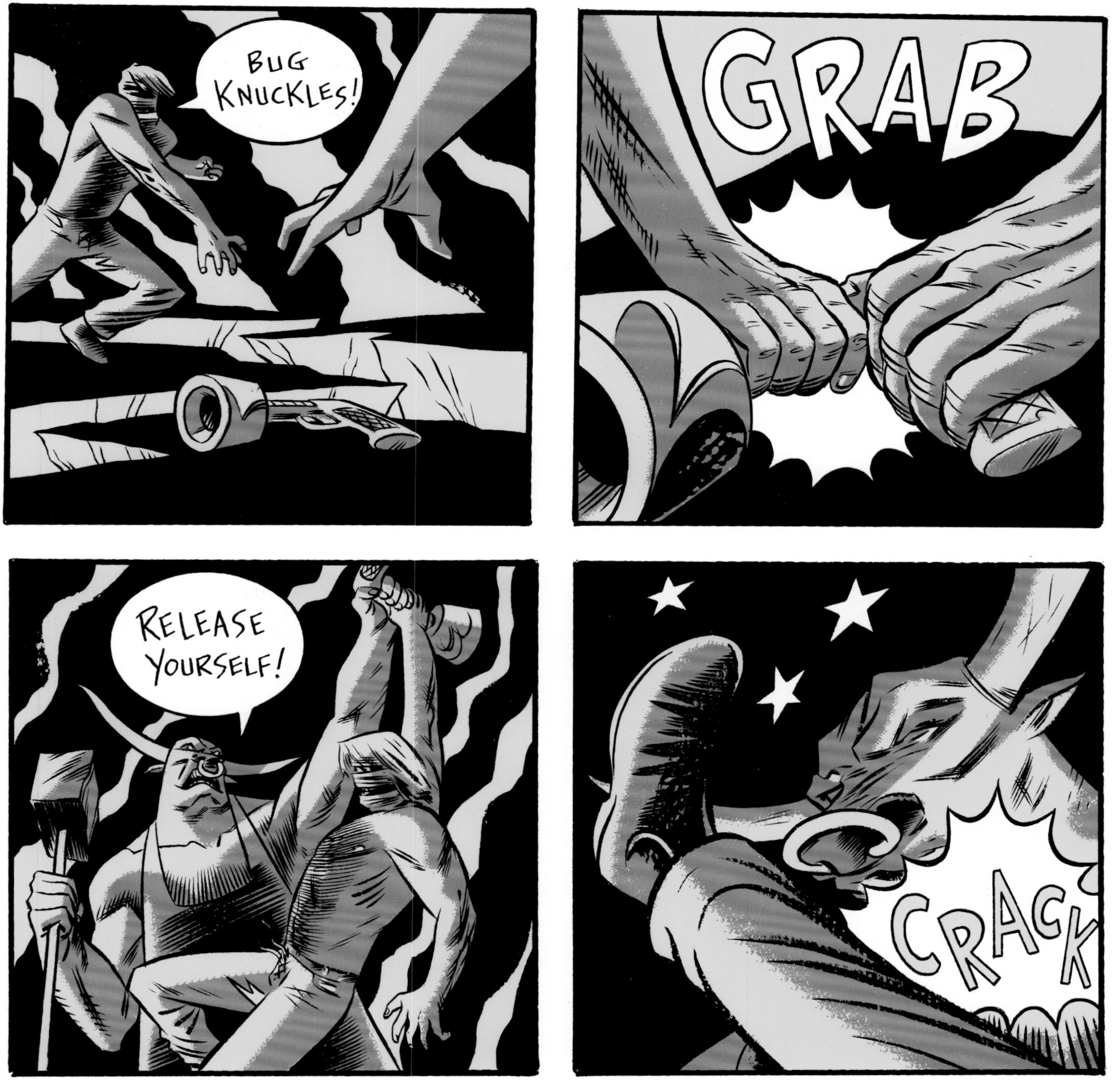
BUG KNUCKLES!
GRAB
RELEASE YOURSELF!
CRACK

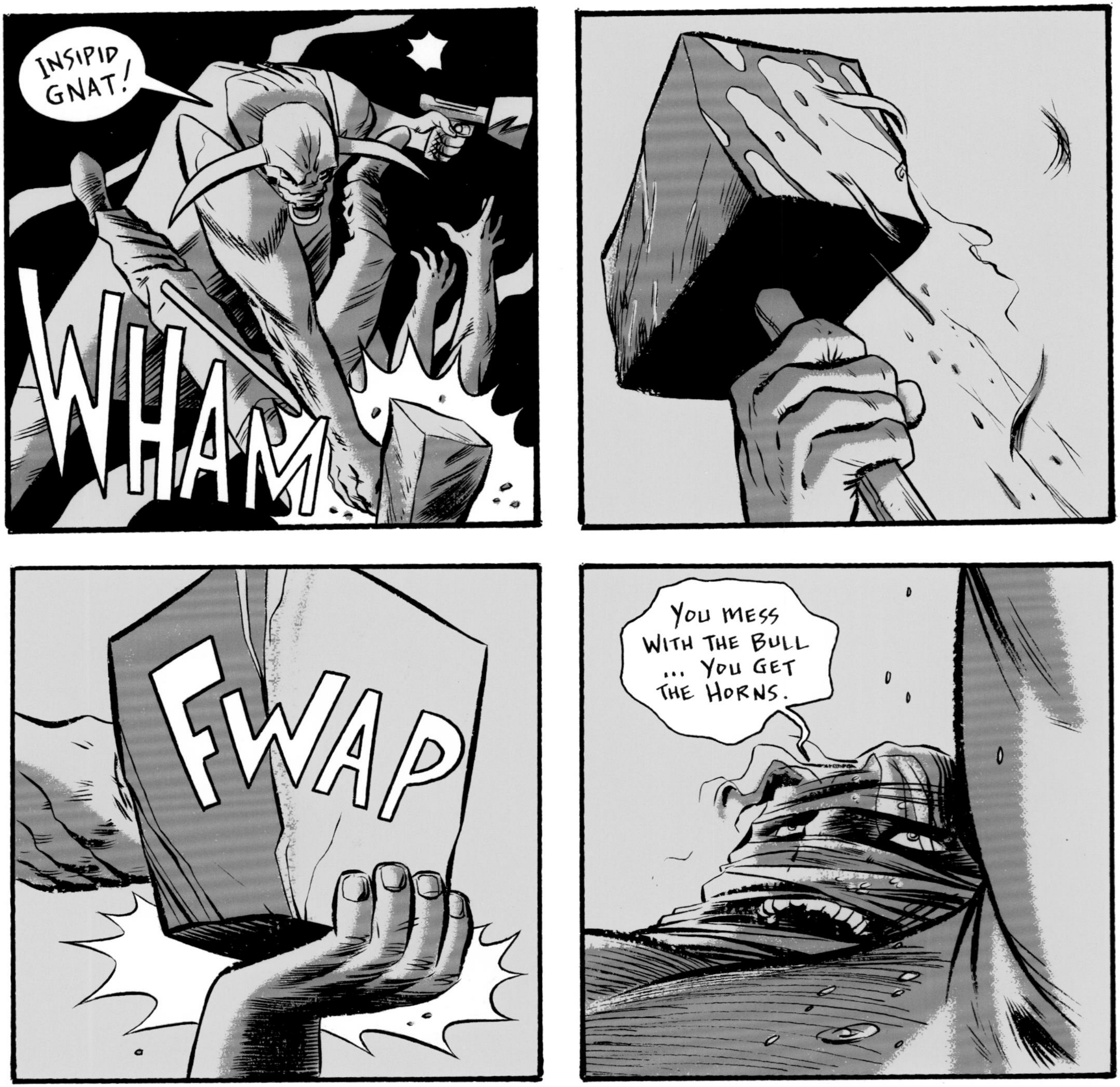
INSIPID GNAT!
WHAM
FWAP
YOU MESS WITH THE BULL ... YOU GET THE HORNS.

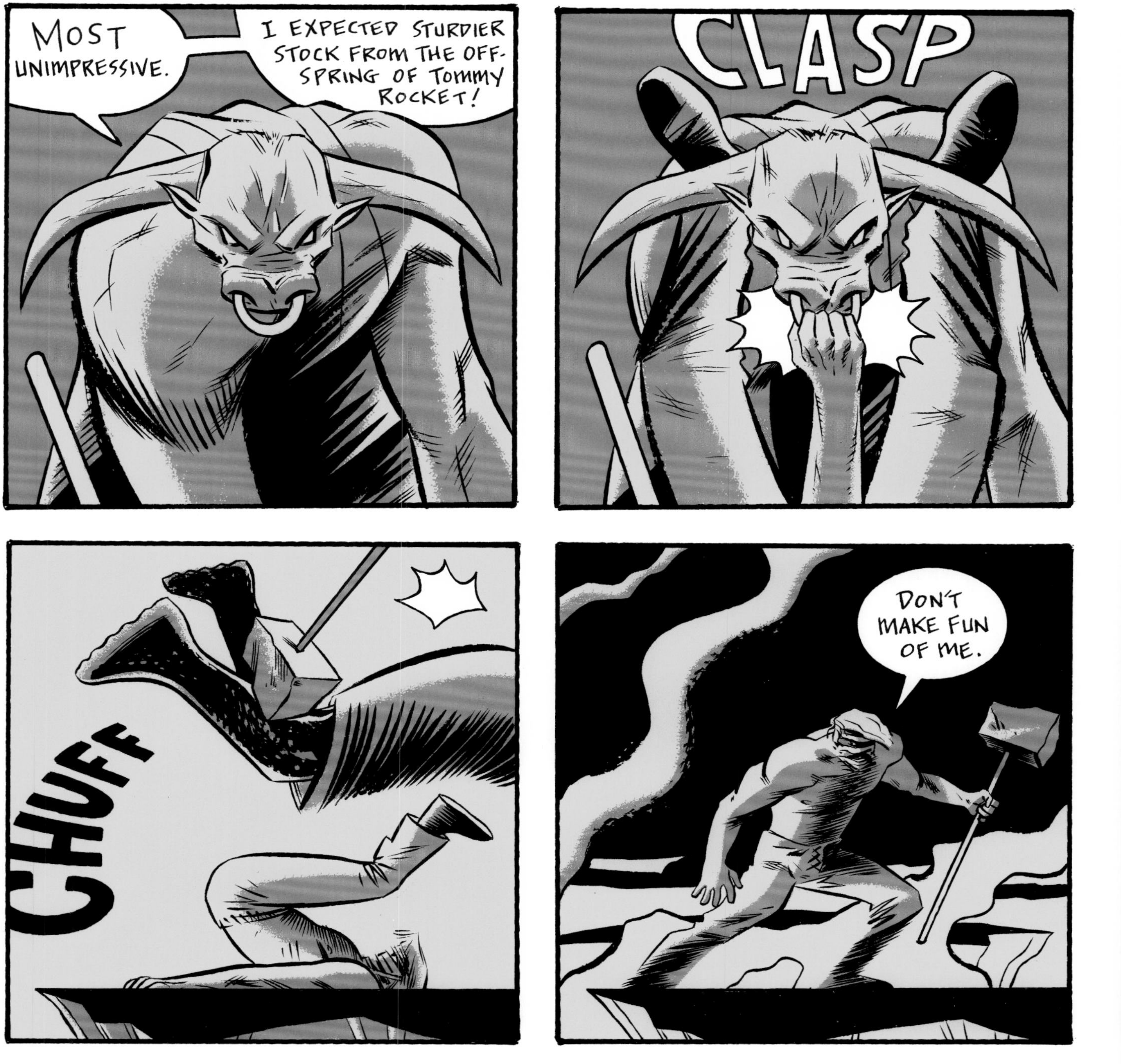
MOST UNIMPRESSIVE.
I EXPECTED STURDIER STOCK FROM THE OFF-SPRING OF TOMMY ROCKET!
CLASP
CHUFF
DON'T MAKE FUN OF ME.

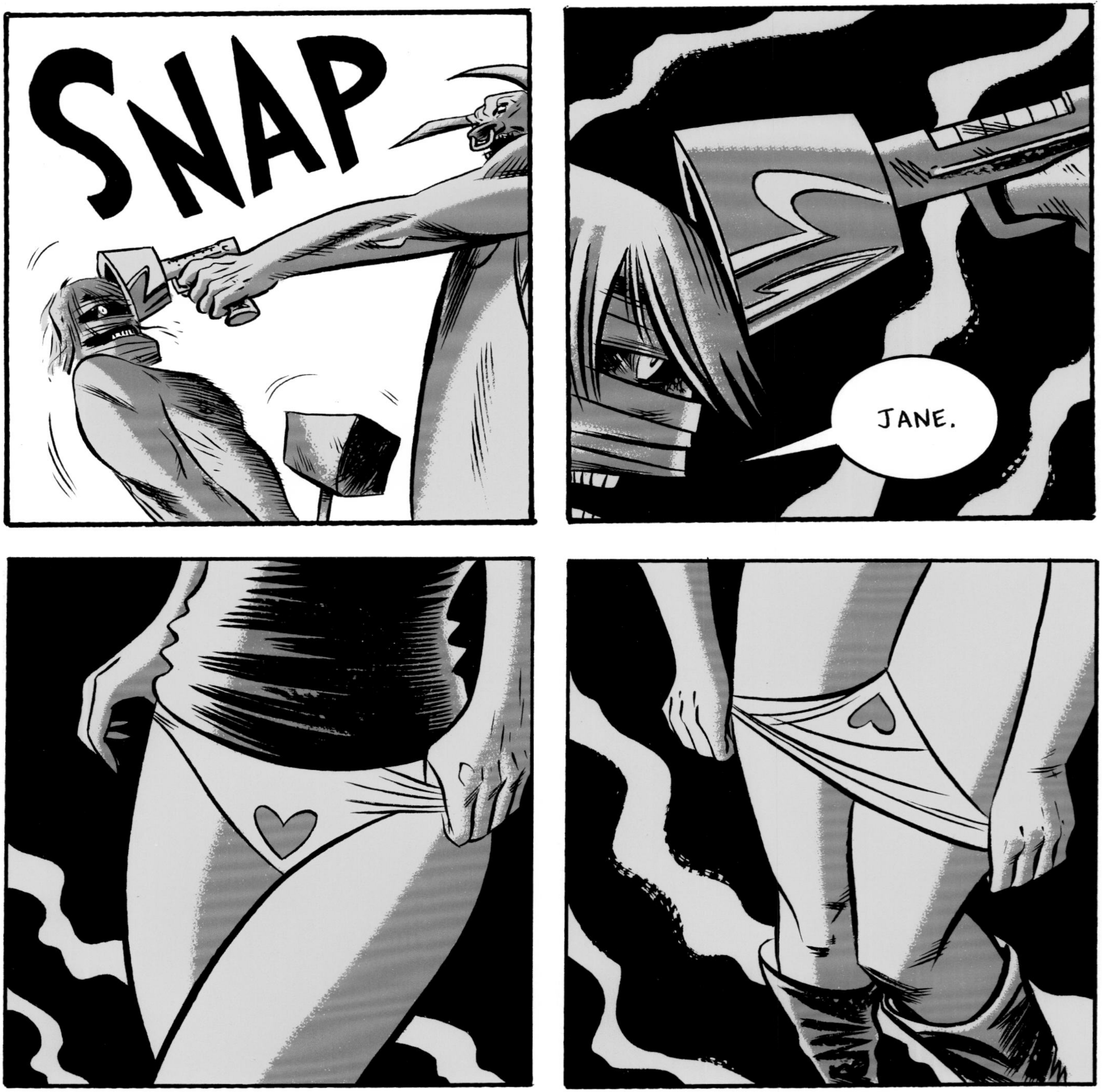
SNAP
JANE.

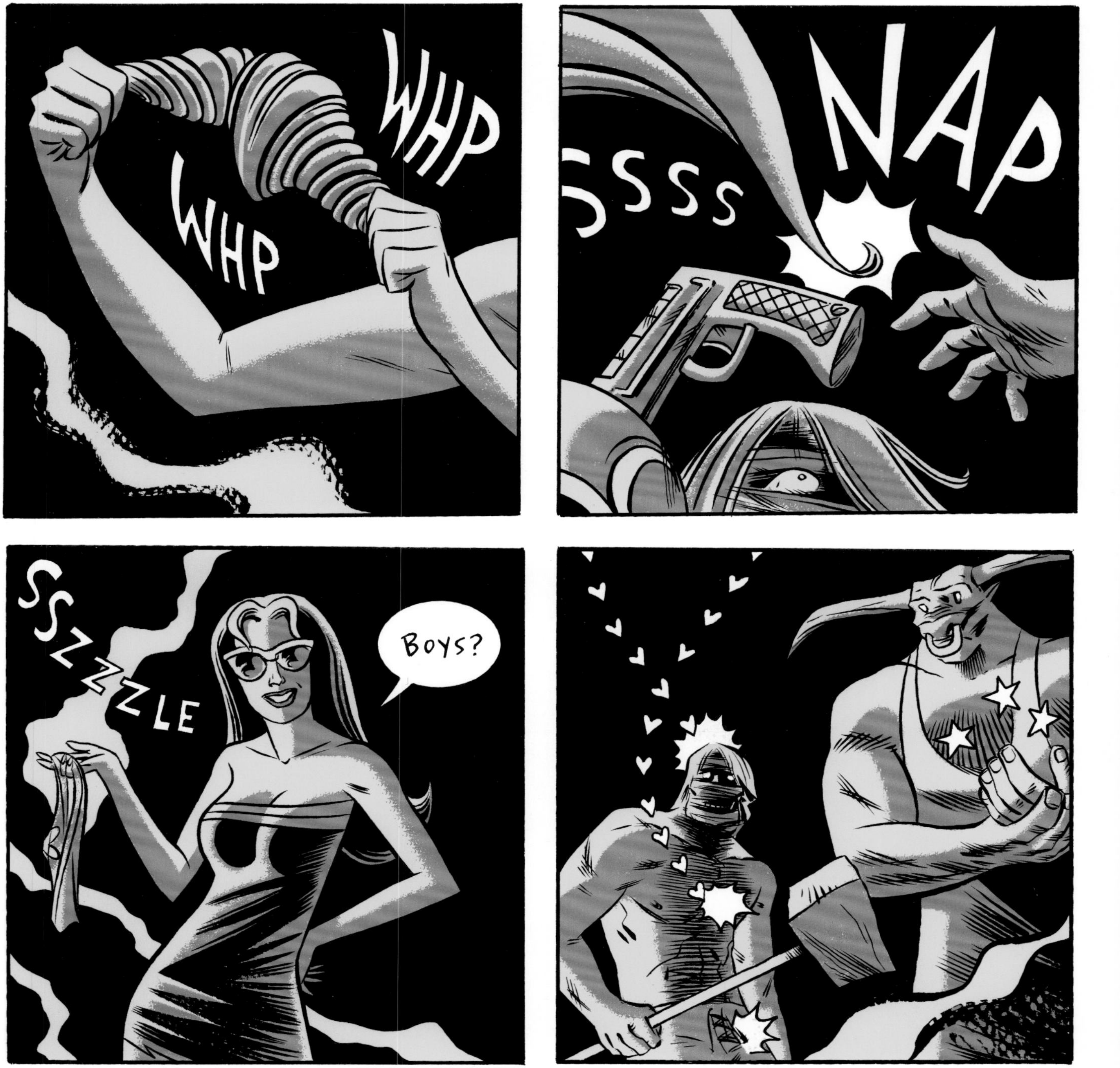
WHP
WHP
SSSS
NAP
SSZZZLE
Boys?

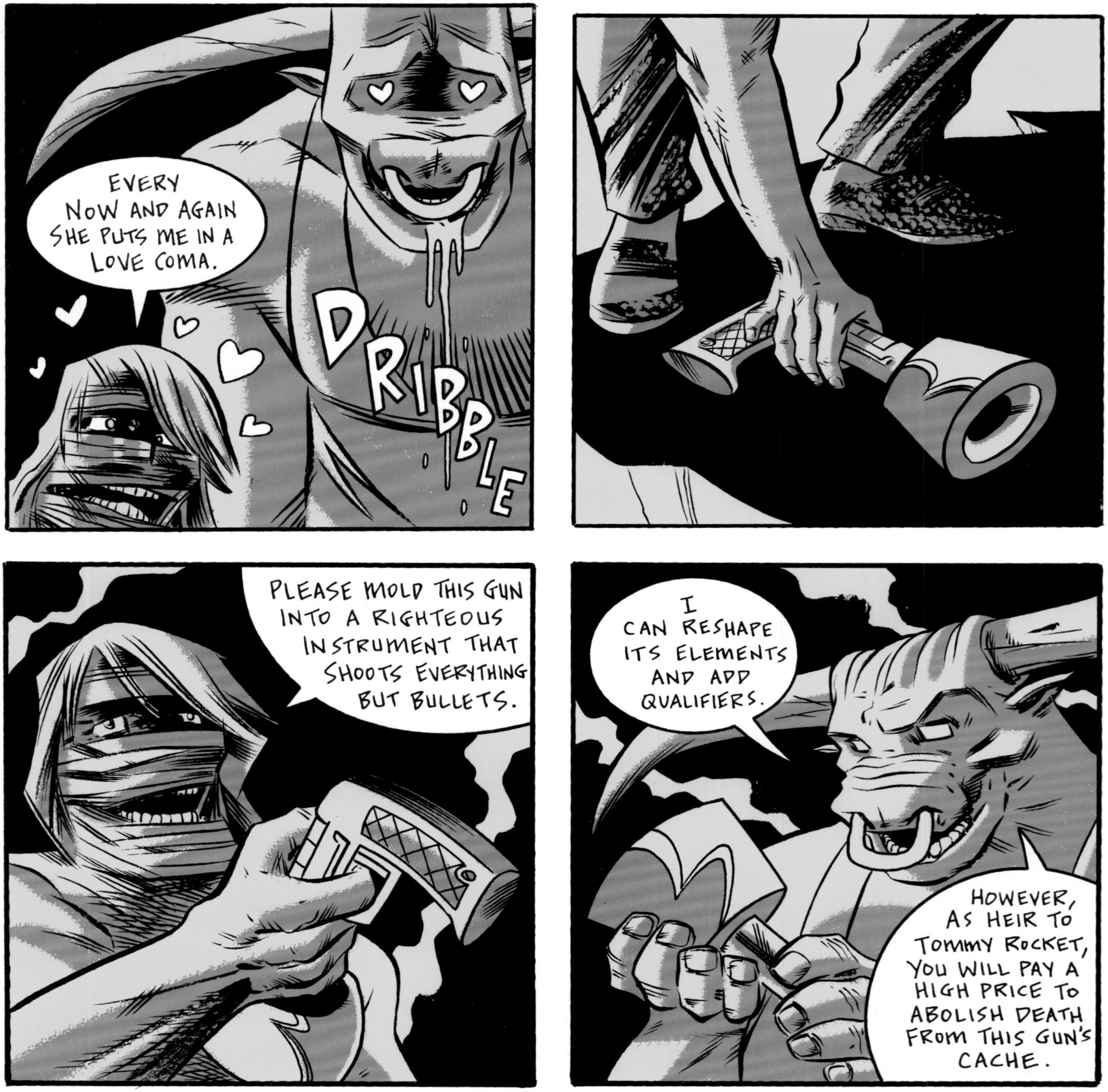
EVERY NOW AND AGAIN SHE PUTS ME IN A LOVE COMA.
DRIBBLE
PLEASE MOLD THIS GUN INTO A RIGHTEOUS INSTRUMENT THAT SHOOTS EVERYTHING BUT BULLETS.
I CAN RESHAPE ITS ELEMENTS AND ADD QUALIFIERS.
HOWEVER, AS HEIR TO TOMMY ROCKET, YOU WILL PAY A HIGH PRICE TO ABOLISH DEATH FROM THIS GUN'S CACHE.

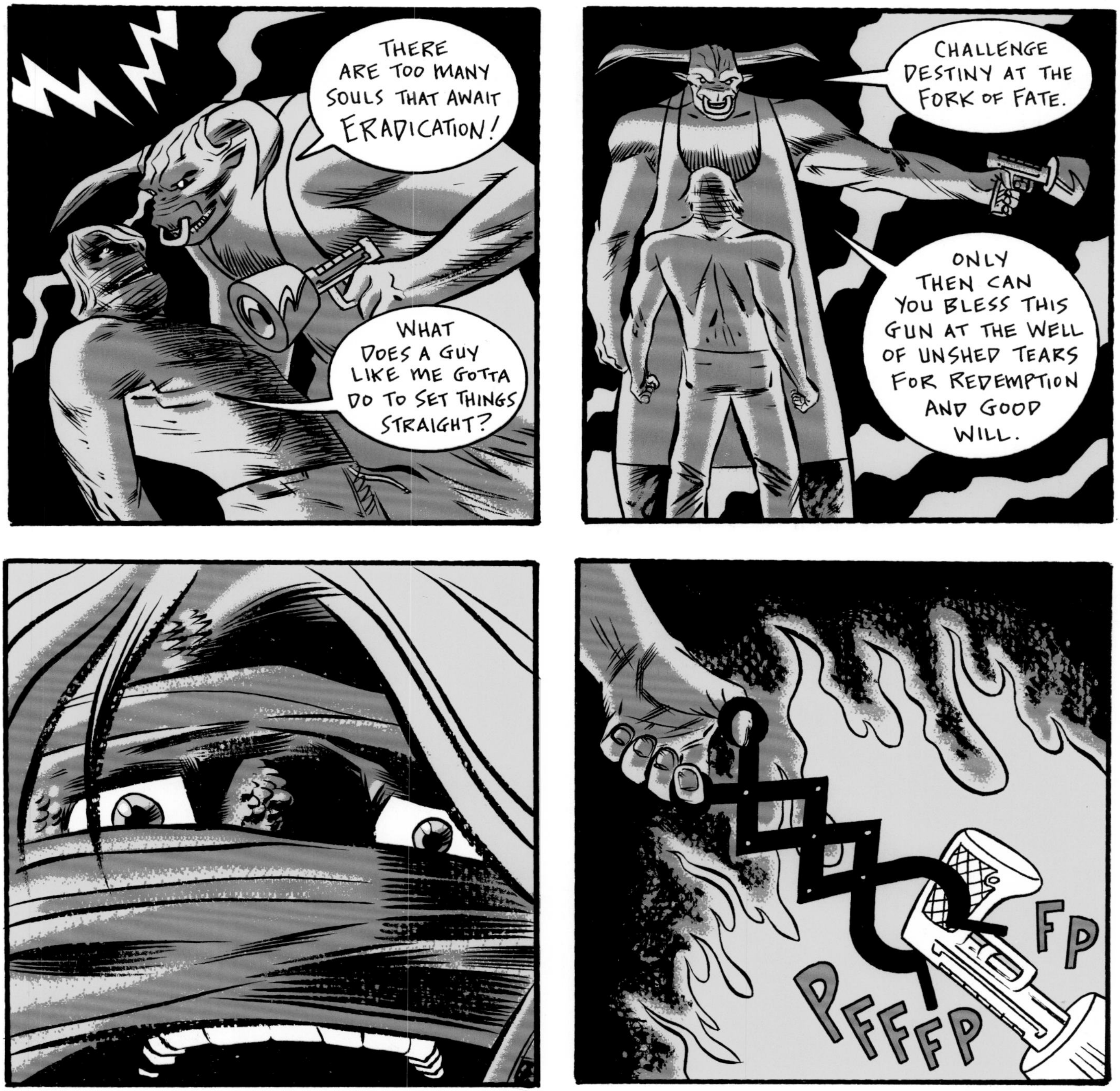
THERE ARE TOO MANY SOULS THAT AWAIT ERADICATION!
WHAT DOES A GUY LIKE ME GOTTA DO TO SET THINGS STRAIGHT?
CHALLENGE DESTINY AT THE FORK OF FATE.
ONLY THEN CAN YOU BLESS THIS GUN AT THE WELL OF UNSHED TEARS FOR REDEMPTION AND GOOD WILL.
FP
PFFFFP

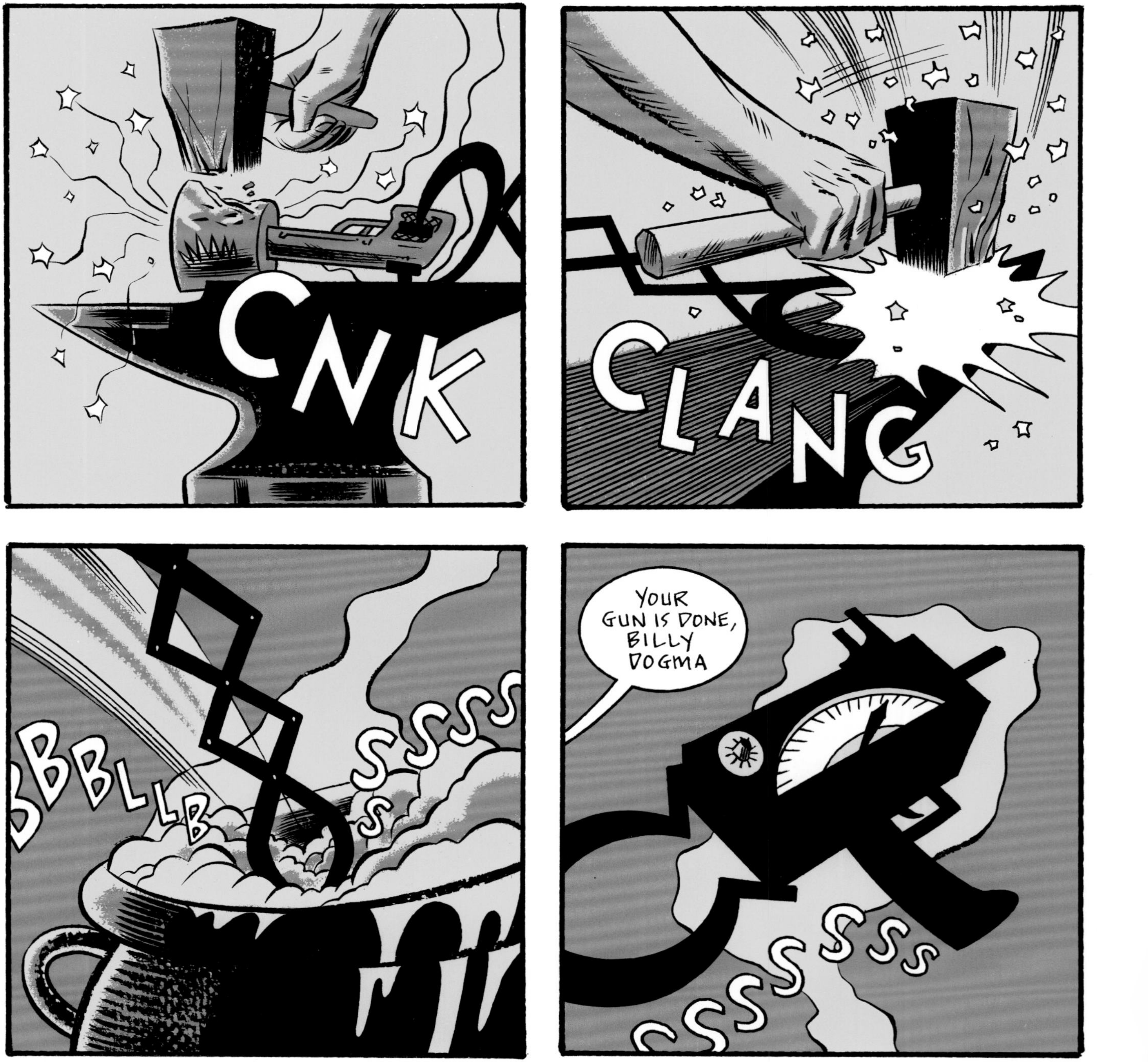
CNK
CLANG
BBBLLLB
SSSSS
YOUR GUN IS DONE, BILLY DOGMA
SSSSSSS

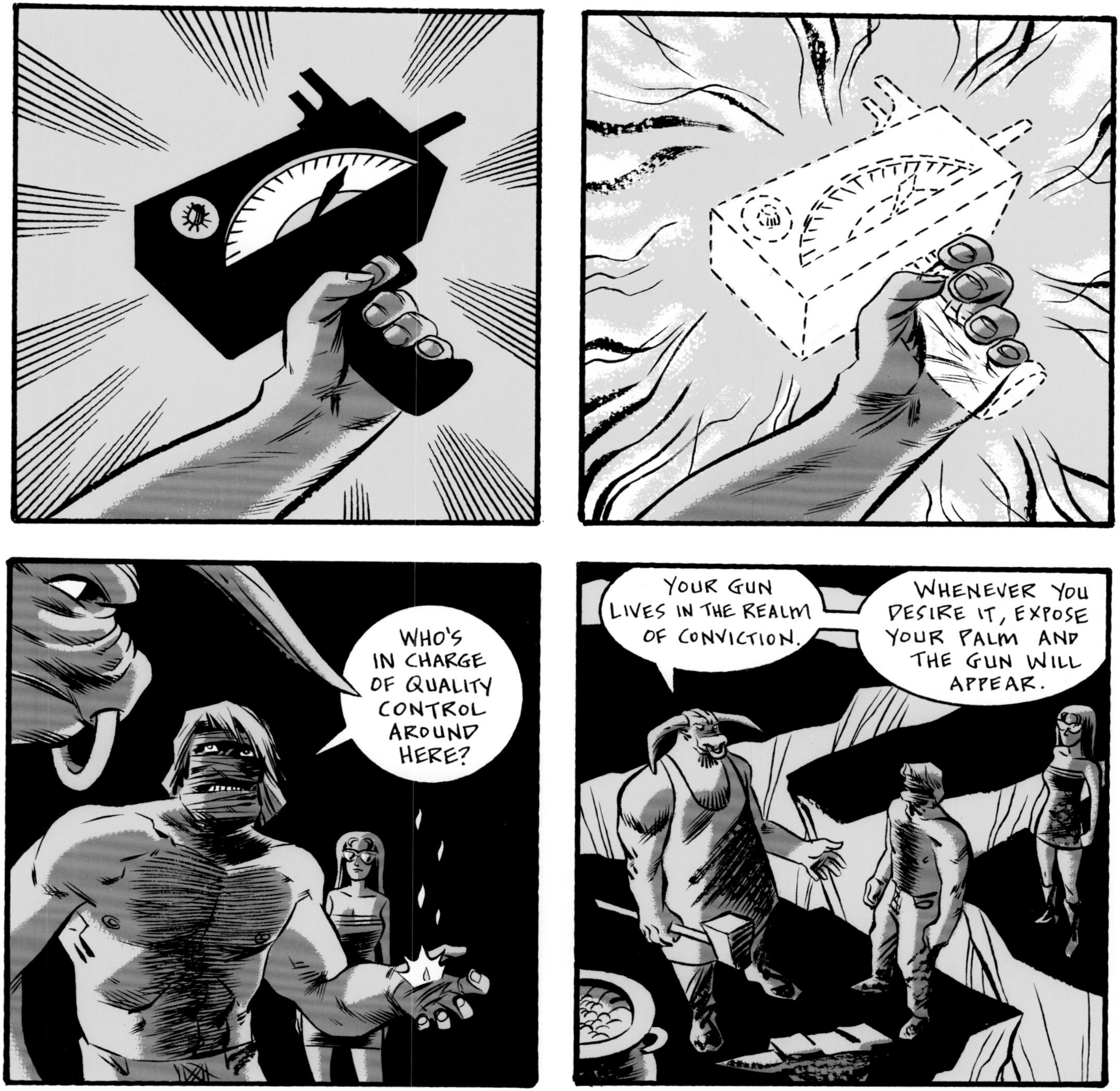
WHO'S IN CHARGE OF QUALITY CONTROL AROUND HERE?
YOUR GUN LIVES IN THE REALM OF CONVICTION.
WHENEVER YOU DESIRE IT, EXPOSE YOUR PALM AND THE GUN WILL APPEAR.

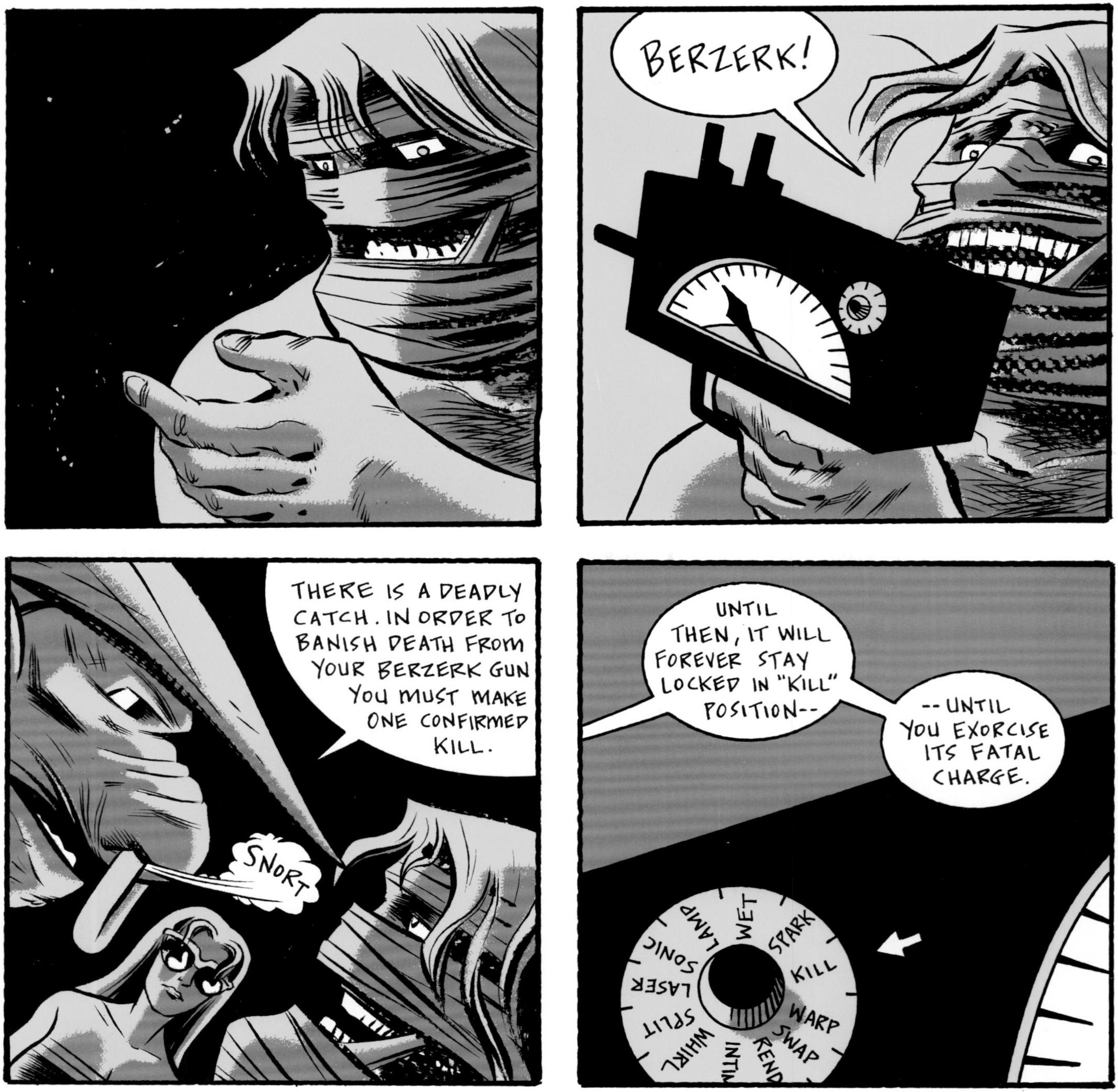
BERZERK!
THERE IS A DEADLY CATCH. IN ORDER TO BANISH DEATH FROM YOUR BERZERK GUN YOU MUST MAKE ONE CONFIRMED KILL.
SNORT
UNTIL THEN, IT WILL FOREVER STAY LOCKED IN "KILL" POSITION--
--UNTIL YOU EXORCISE ITS FATAL CHARGE.
WET
SPARK
KILL
WARP
SWAP
WHIRL
SPLIT
LASER
SONIC
LAMP

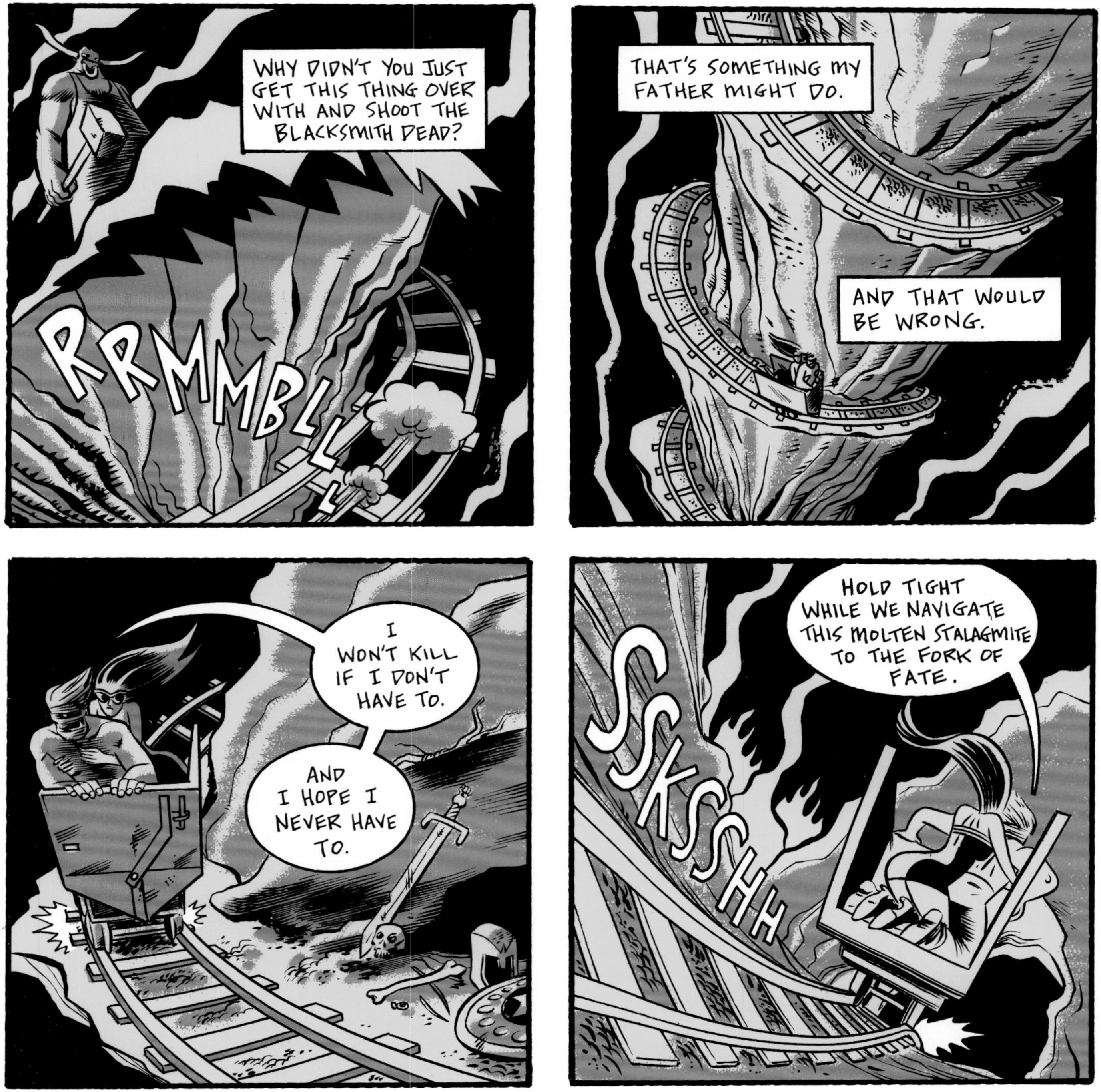

WHY DIDN'T YOU JUST GET THIS THING OVER WITH AND SHOOT THE BLACKSMITH DEAD?
RRMMBLLL
THAT'S SOMETHING MY FATHER MIGHT DO.
AND THAT WOULD BE WRONG.
I WON'T KILL IF I DON'T HAVE TO.
AND I HOPE I NEVER HAVE TO.
SSKSSHH
HOLD TIGHT WHILE WE NAVIGATE THIS MOLTEN STALAGMITE TO THE FORK OF FATE.

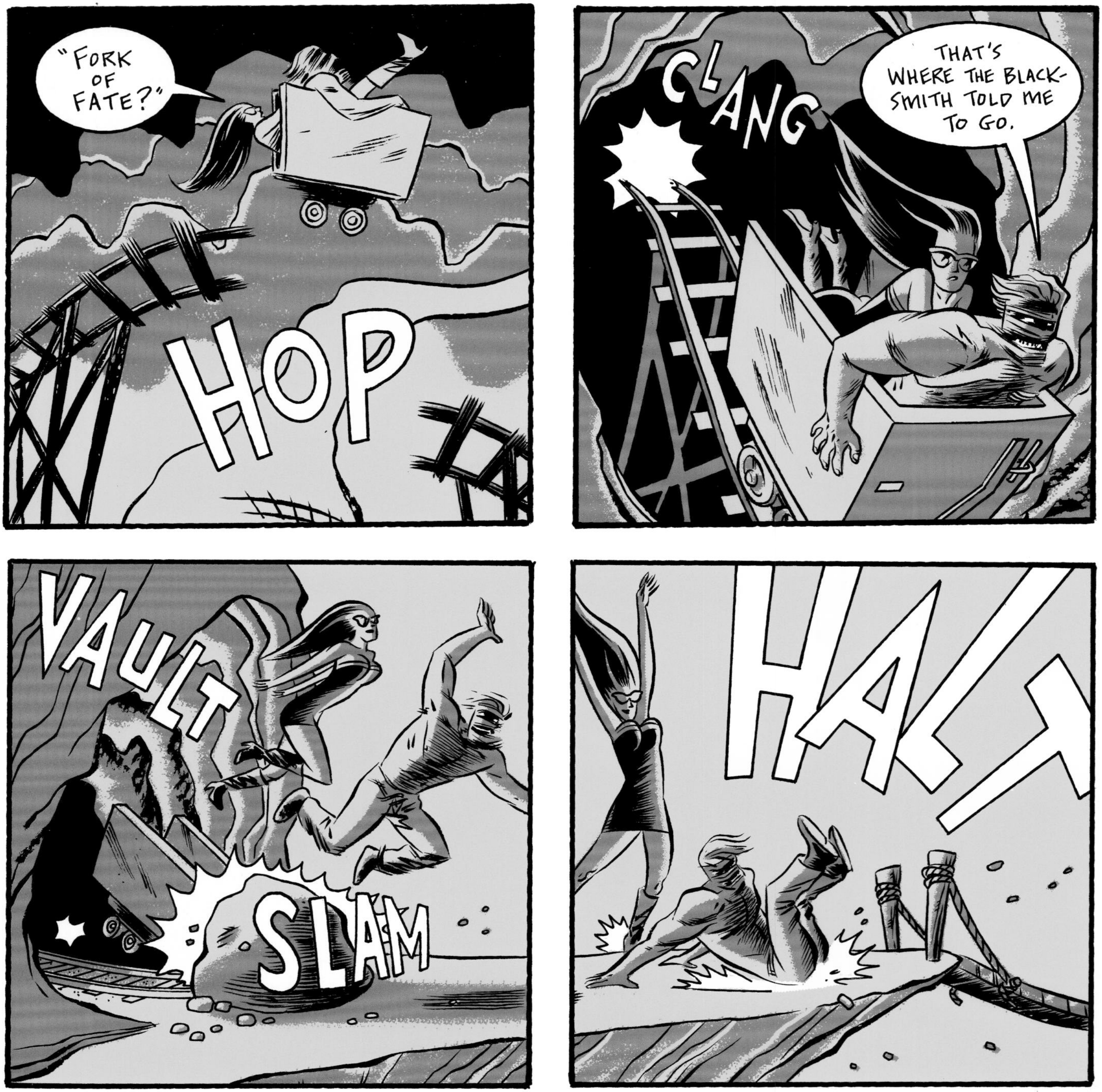
"FORK OF FATE?"
HOP
CLANG
THAT'S WHERE THE BLACK-SMITH TOLD ME TO GO.
VAULT
SLAM
HALT

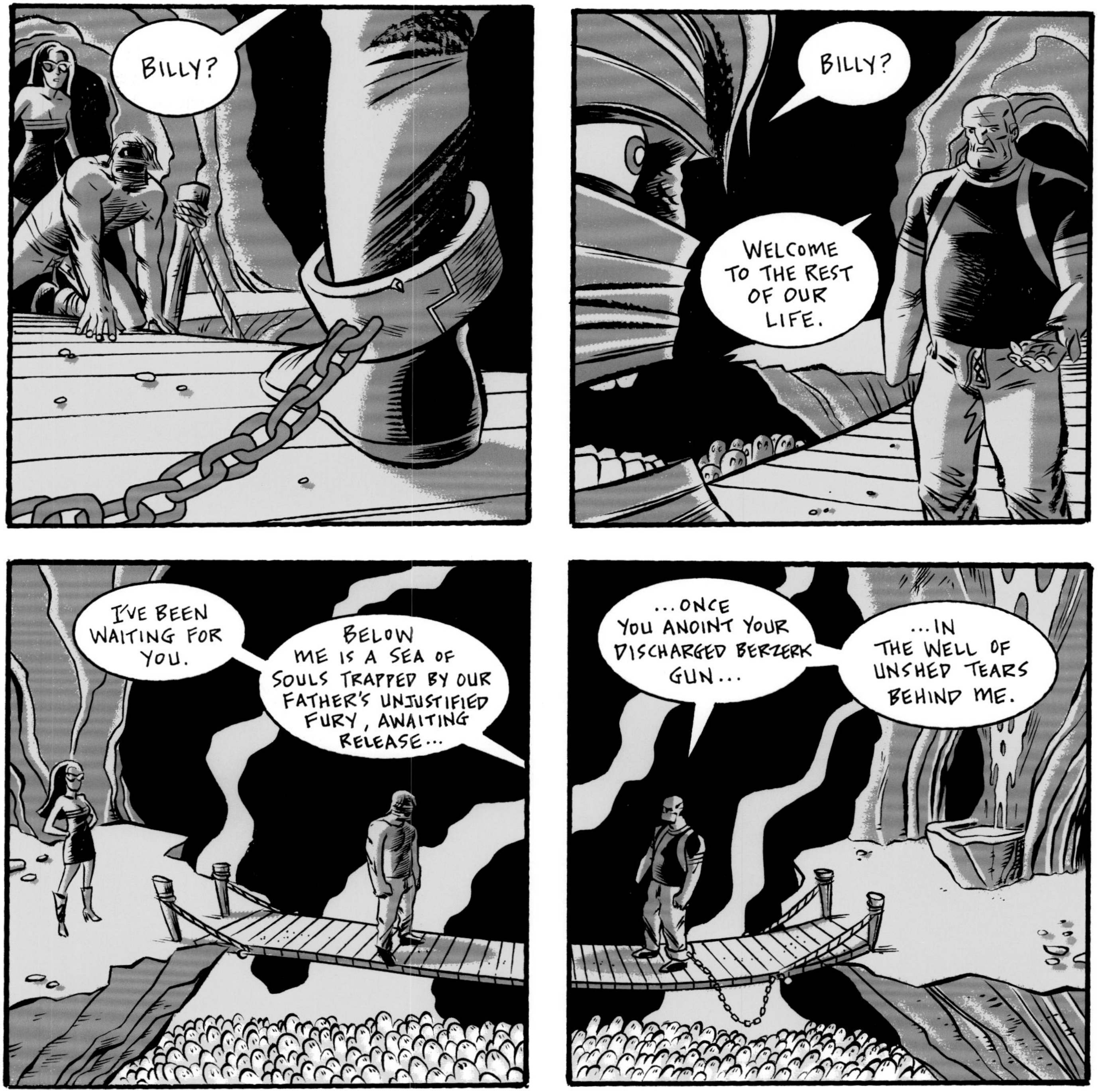
BILLY?
BILLY?
WELCOME TO THE REST OF OUR LIFE.
I'VE BEEN WAITING FOR YOU.
BELOW ME IS A SEA OF SOULS TRAPPED BY OUR FATHER'S UNJUSTIFIED FURY, AWAITING RELEASE...
...ONCE YOU ANOINT YOUR DISCHARGED BERZERK GUN...
...IN THE WELL OF UNSHED TEARS BEHIND ME.

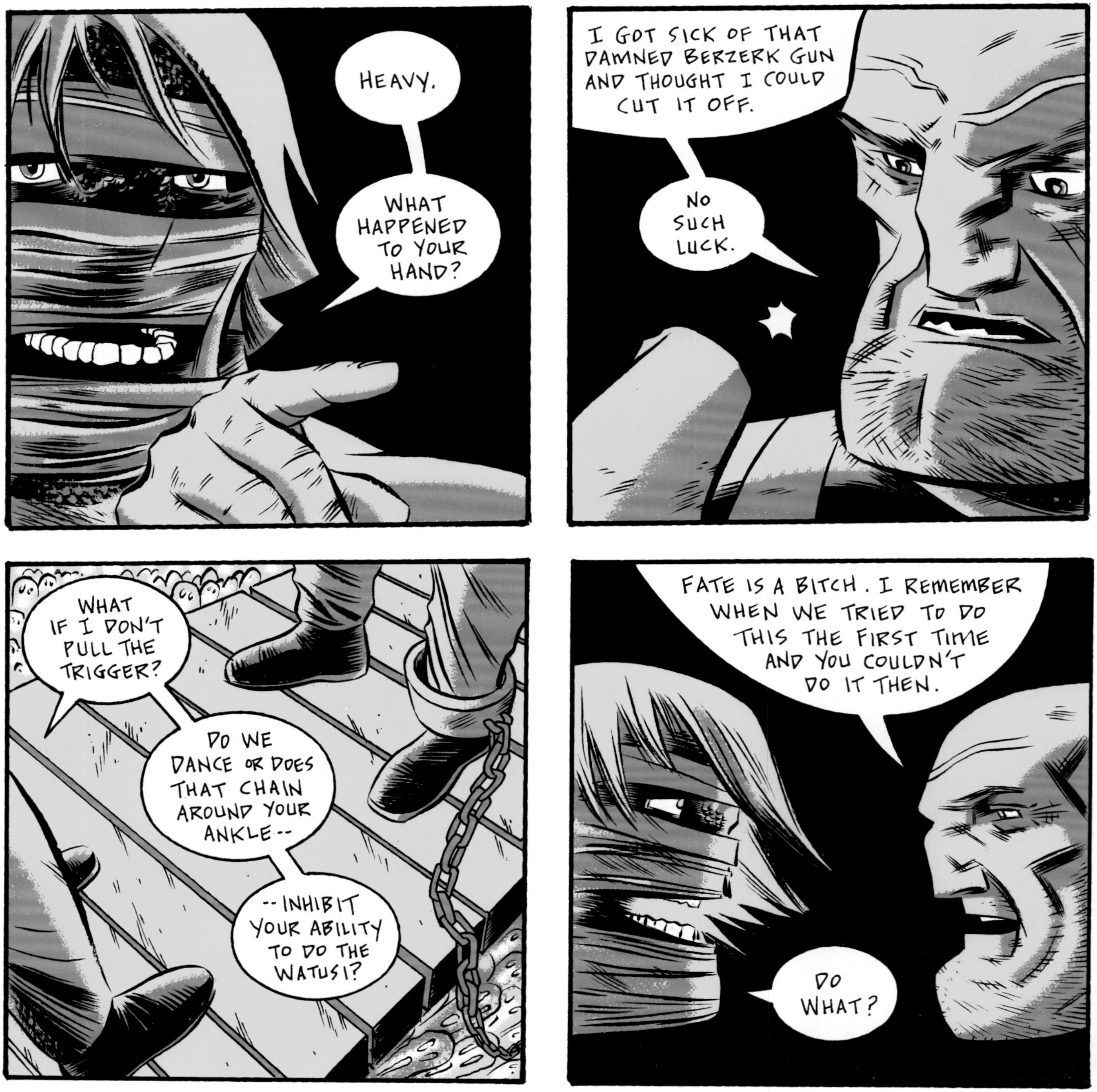
HEAVY.
WHAT HAPPENED TO YOUR HAND?
I GOT SICK OF THAT DAMNED BERZERK GUN AND THOUGHT I COULD CUT IT OFF.
NO SUCH LUCK.
WHAT IF I DON'T PULL THE TRIGGER?
DO WE DANCE OR DOES THAT CHAIN AROUND YOUR ANKLE--
--INHIBIT YOUR ABILITY TO DO THE WATUSI?
FATE IS A BITCH. I REMEMBER WHEN WE TRIED TO DO THIS THE FIRST TIME AND YOU COULDN'T DO IT THEN.
DO WHAT?

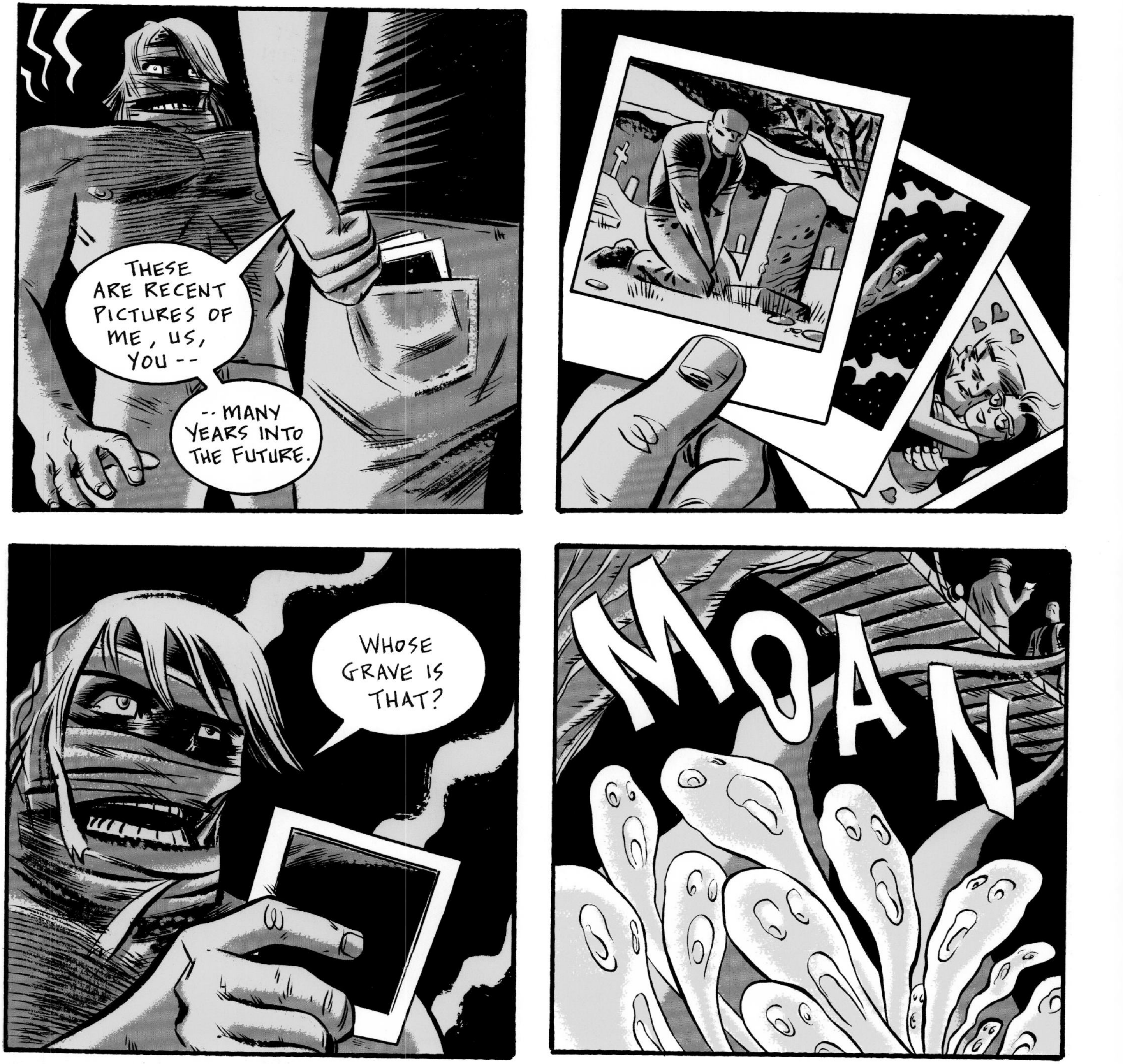
THESE ARE RECENT PICTURES OF ME, US, YOU --
-- MANY YEARS INTO THE FUTURE.
WHOSE GRAVE IS THAT?
MOAN

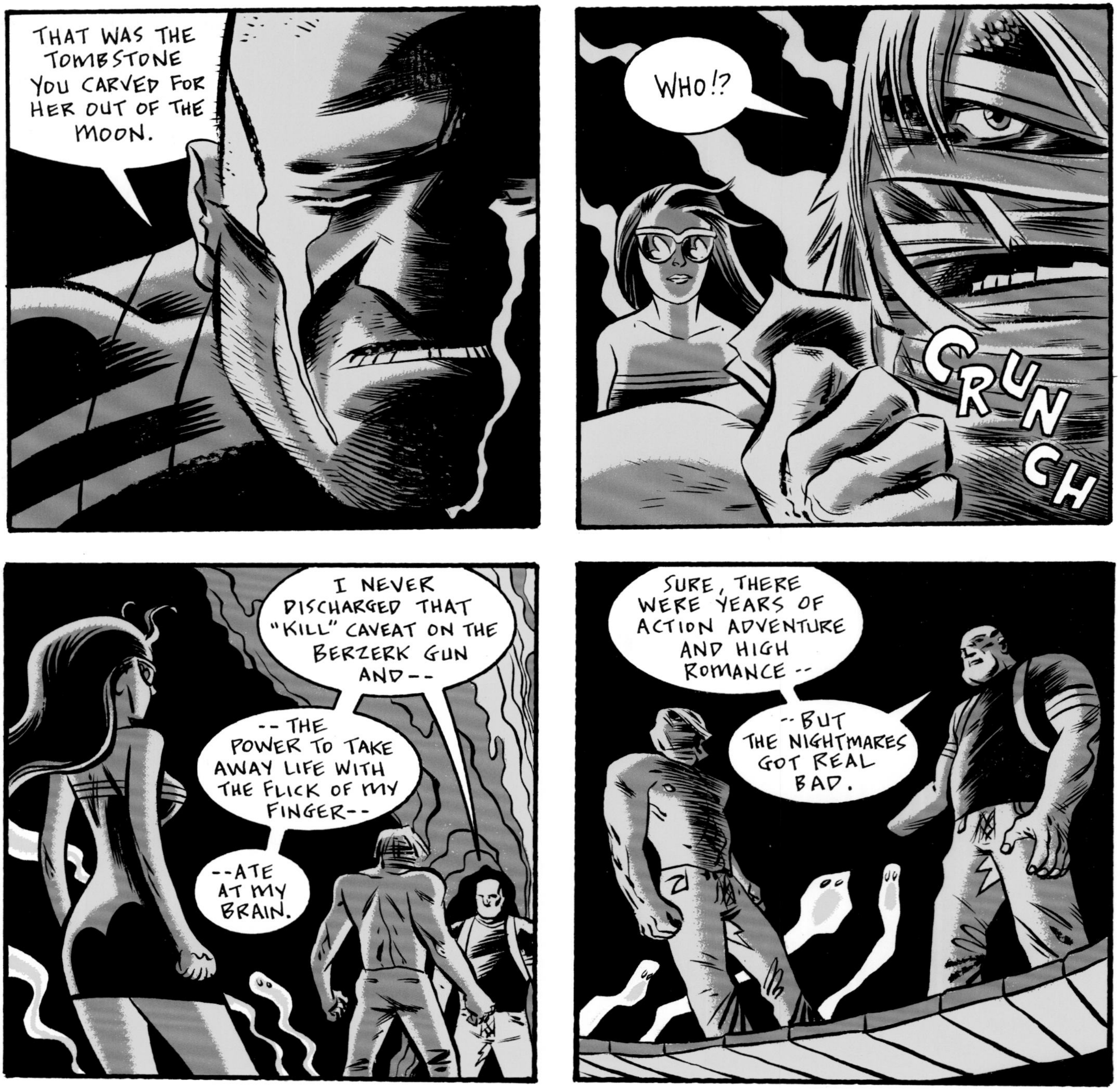
THAT WAS THE TOMBSTONE YOU CARVED FOR HER OUT OF THE MOON.
WHO!?
CRUNCH
I NEVER DISCHARGED THAT "KILL" CAVEAT ON THE BERZERK GUN AND--
-- THE POWER TO TAKE AWAY LIFE WITH THE FLICK OF MY FINGER--
--ATE AT MY BRAIN.
SURE, THERE WERE YEARS OF ACTION ADVENTURE AND HIGH ROMANCE --
-- BUT THE NIGHTMARES GOT REAL BAD.

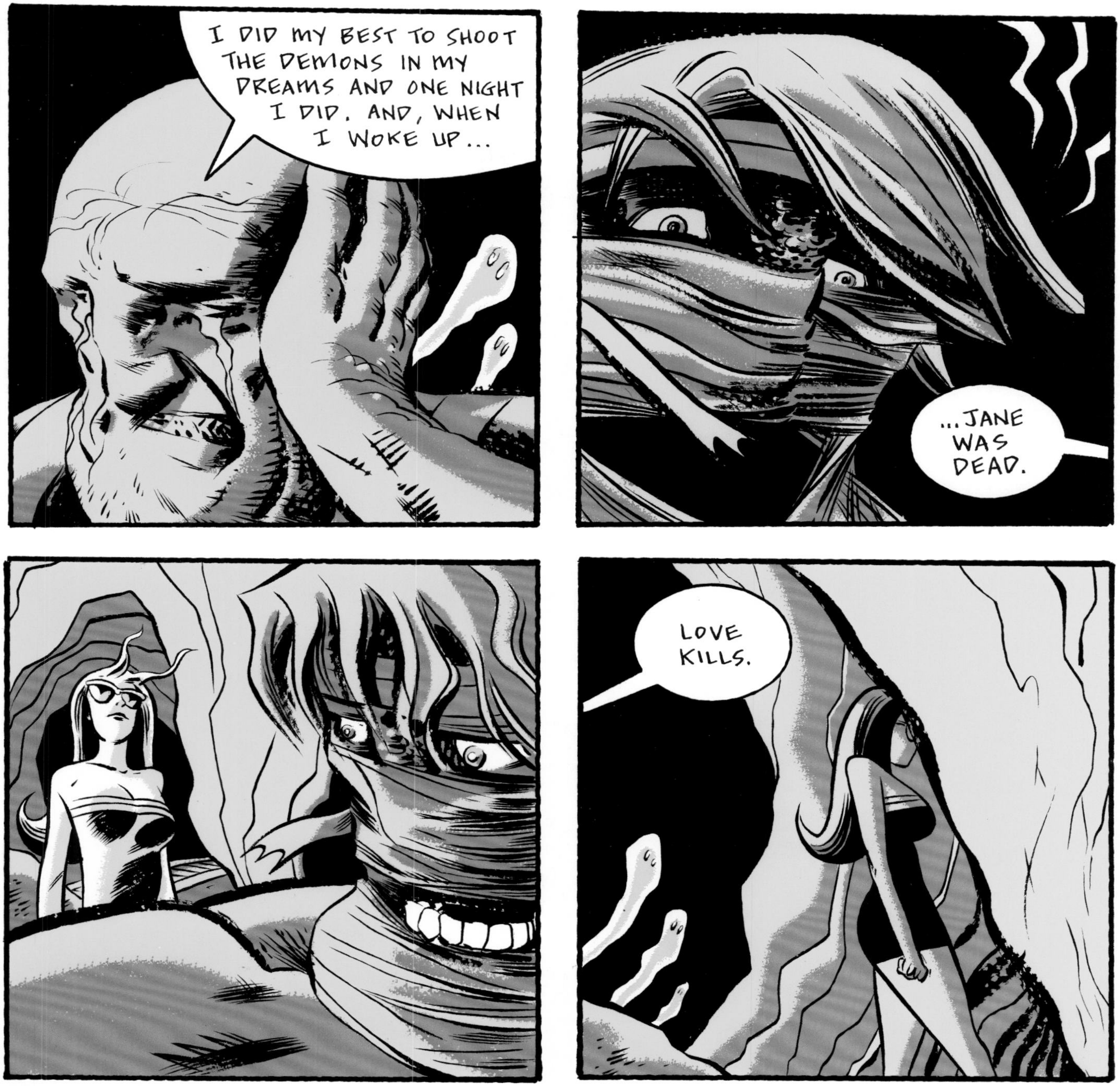
I DID MY BEST TO SHOOT THE DEMONS IN MY DREAMS AND ONE NIGHT I DID. AND, WHEN I WOKE UP...
...JANE WAS DEAD.
LOVE KILLS.

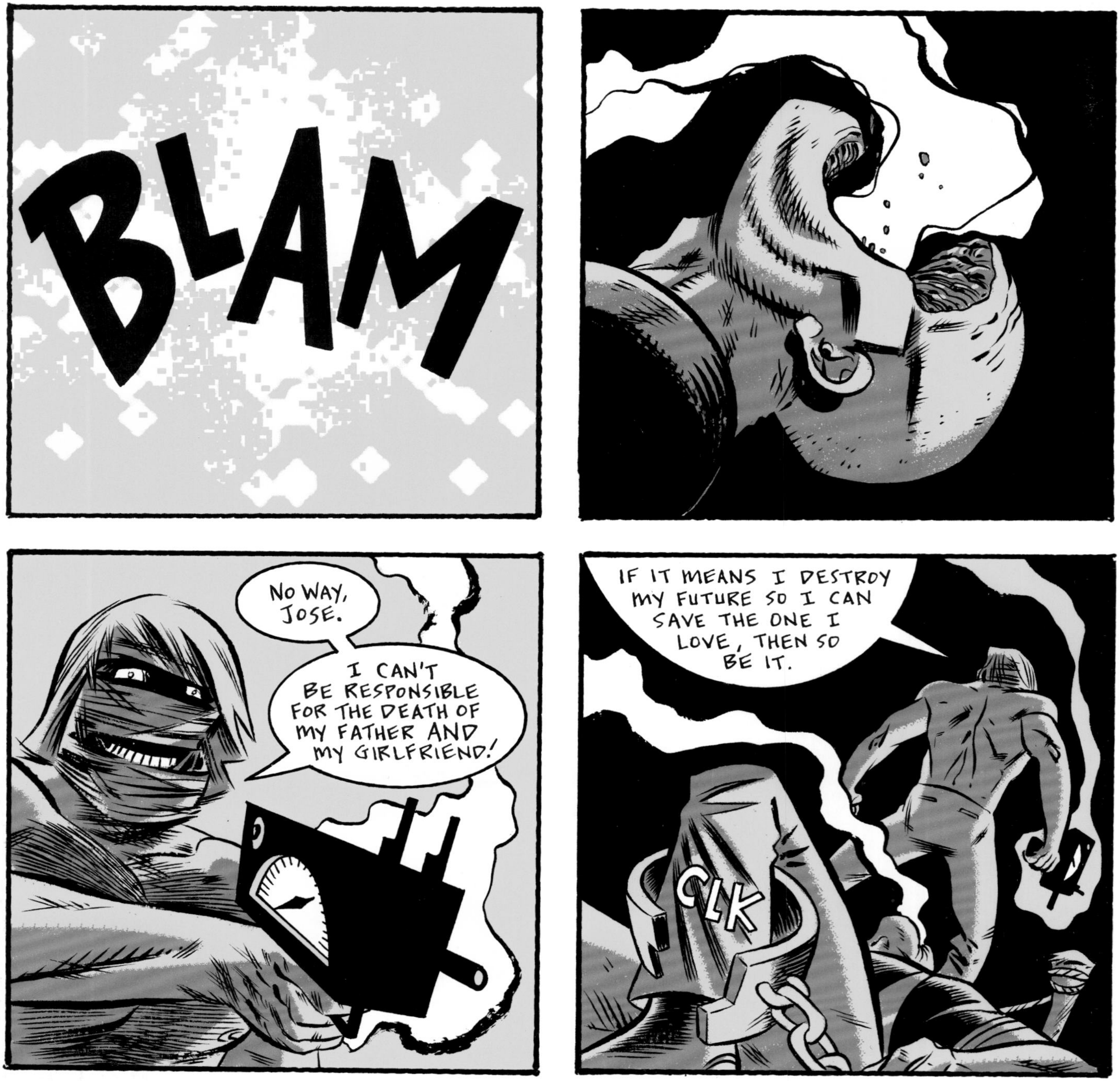
BLAM
NO WAY, JOSE.
I CAN'T BE RESPONSIBLE FOR THE DEATH OF MY FATHER AND MY GIRLFRIEND!
IF IT MEANS I DESTROY MY FUTURE SO I CAN SAVE THE ONE I LOVE, THEN SO BE IT.
CLK

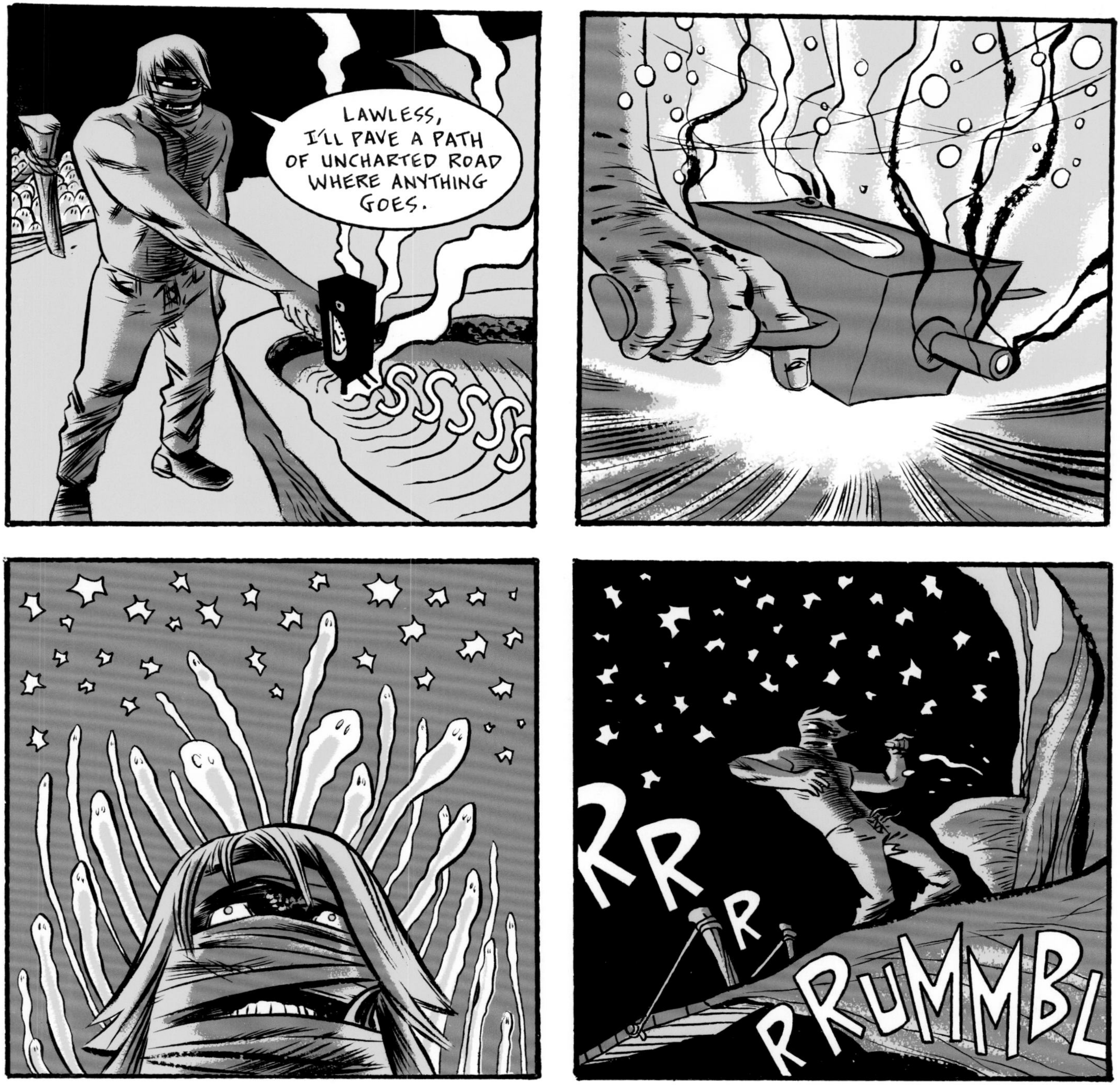
LAWLESS, I'LL PAVE A PATH OF UNCHARTED ROAD WHERE ANYTHING GOES.
SSSSS
RRR
RRUMMBL

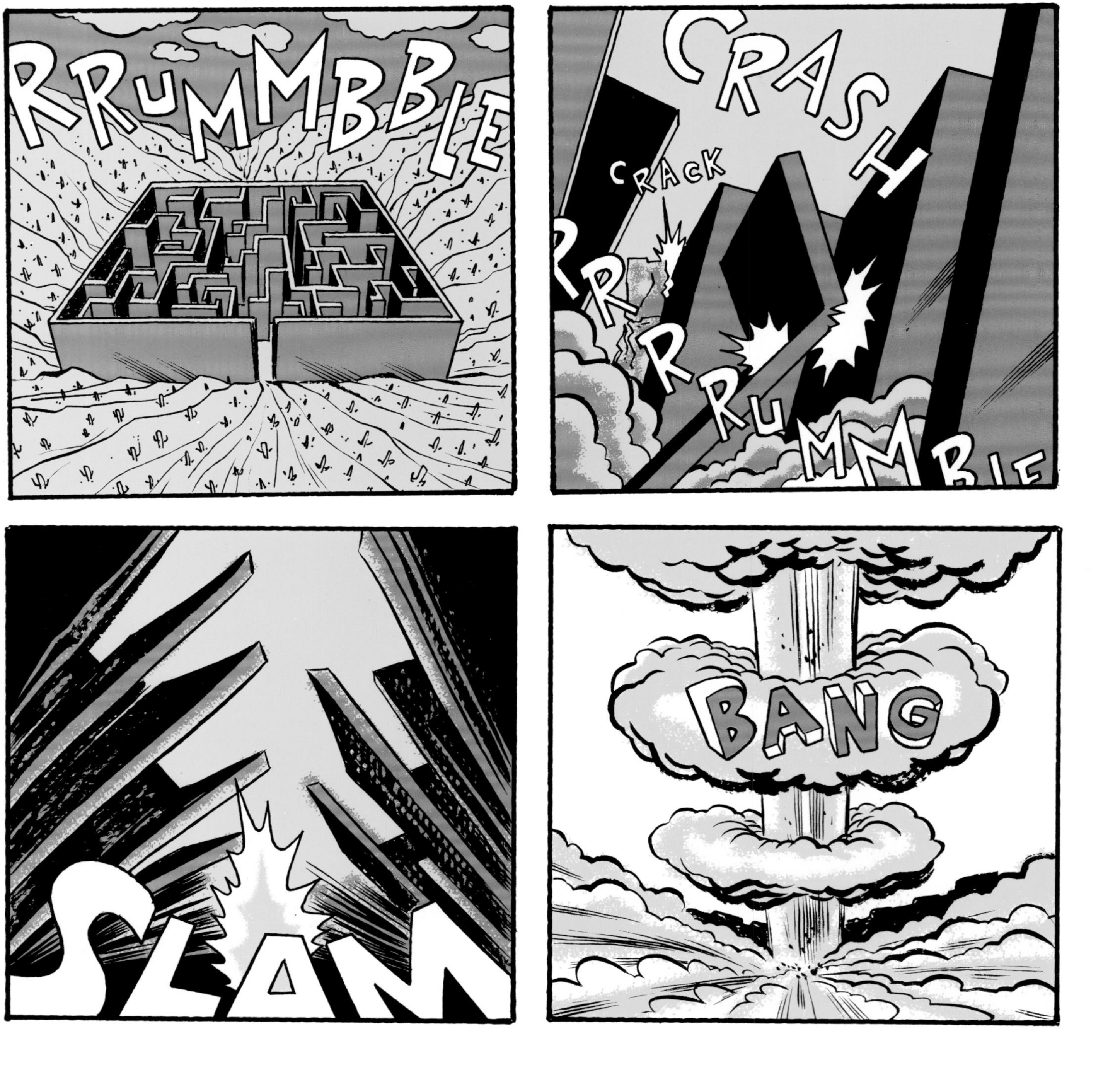
RRUMMBBLE
CRASH
CRACK
RRRRUMMBLE
SLAM
BANG

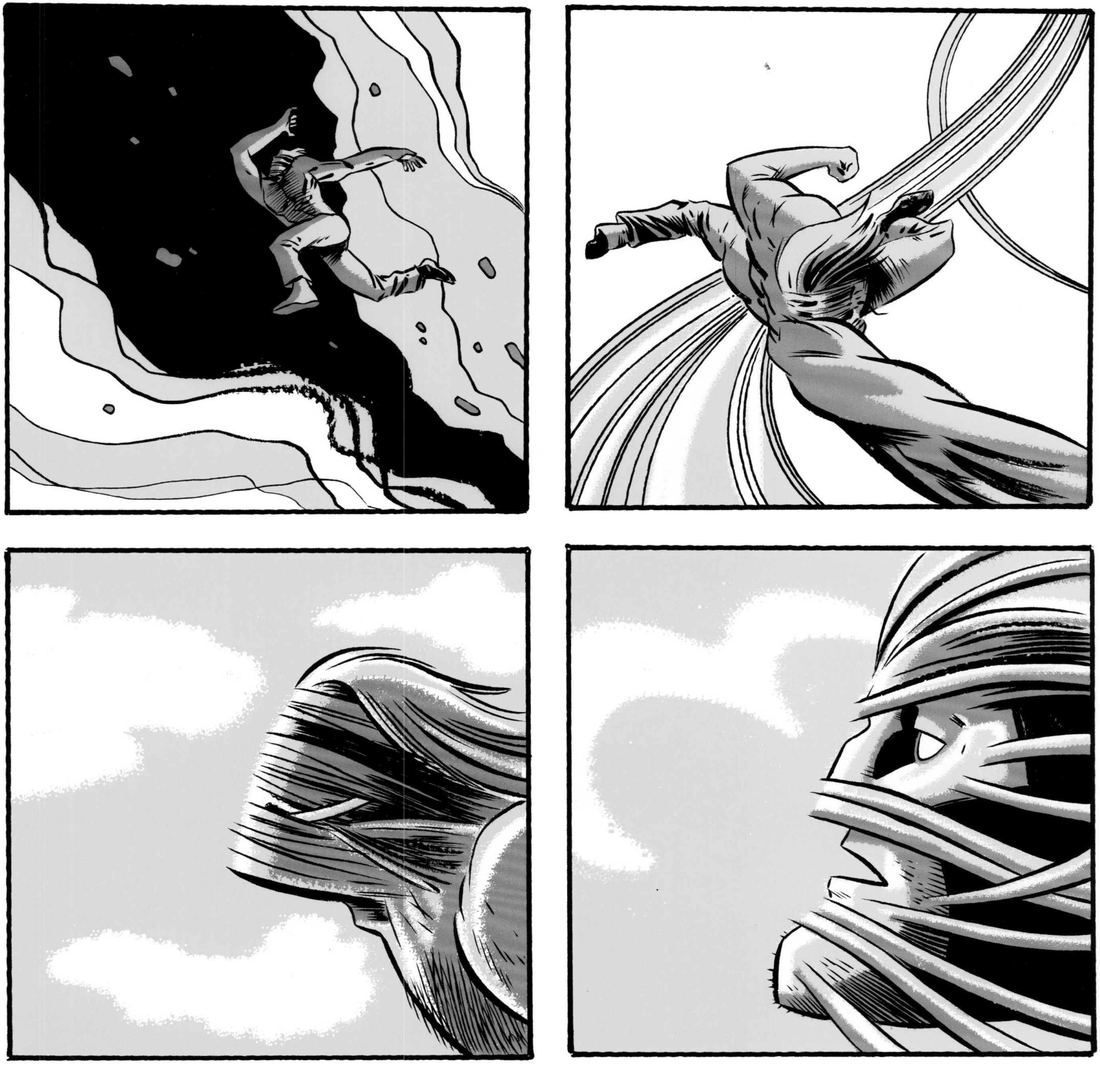

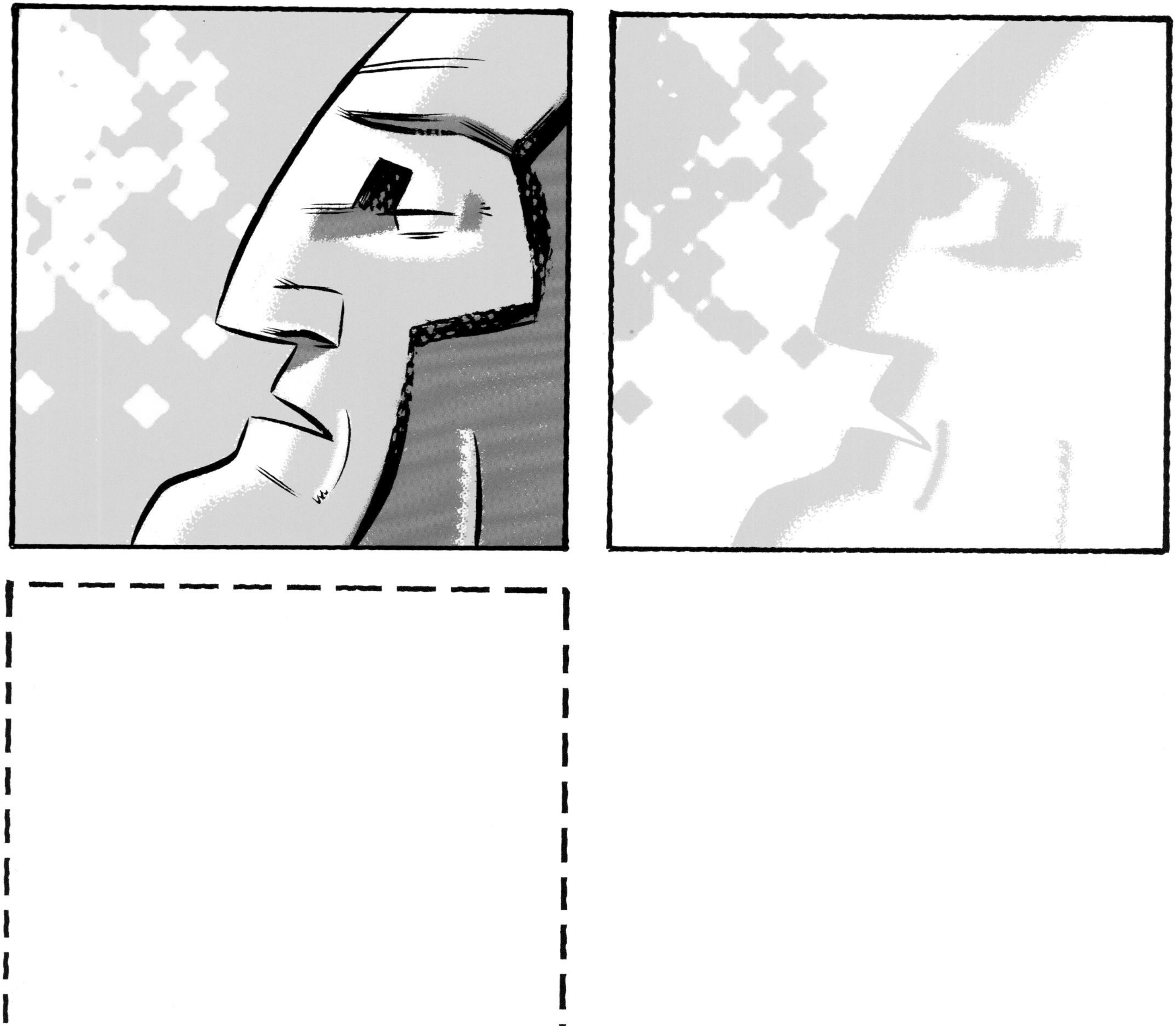

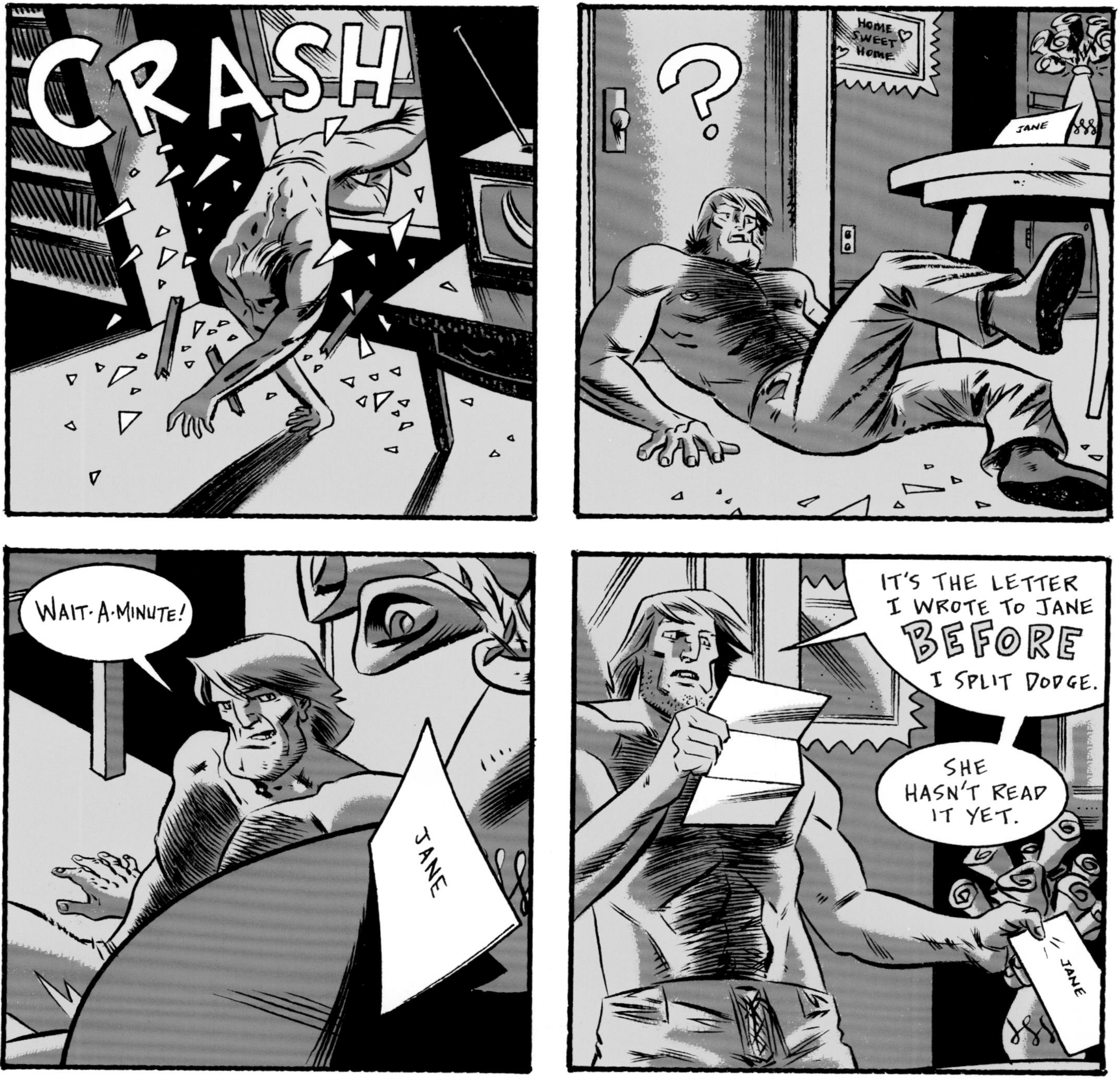
CRASH
HOME SWEET HOME
JANE
?
WAIT-A-MINUTE!
JANE
IT'S THE LETTER I WROTE TO JANE BEFORE I SPLIT DODGE.
SHE HASN'T READ IT YET.
JANE

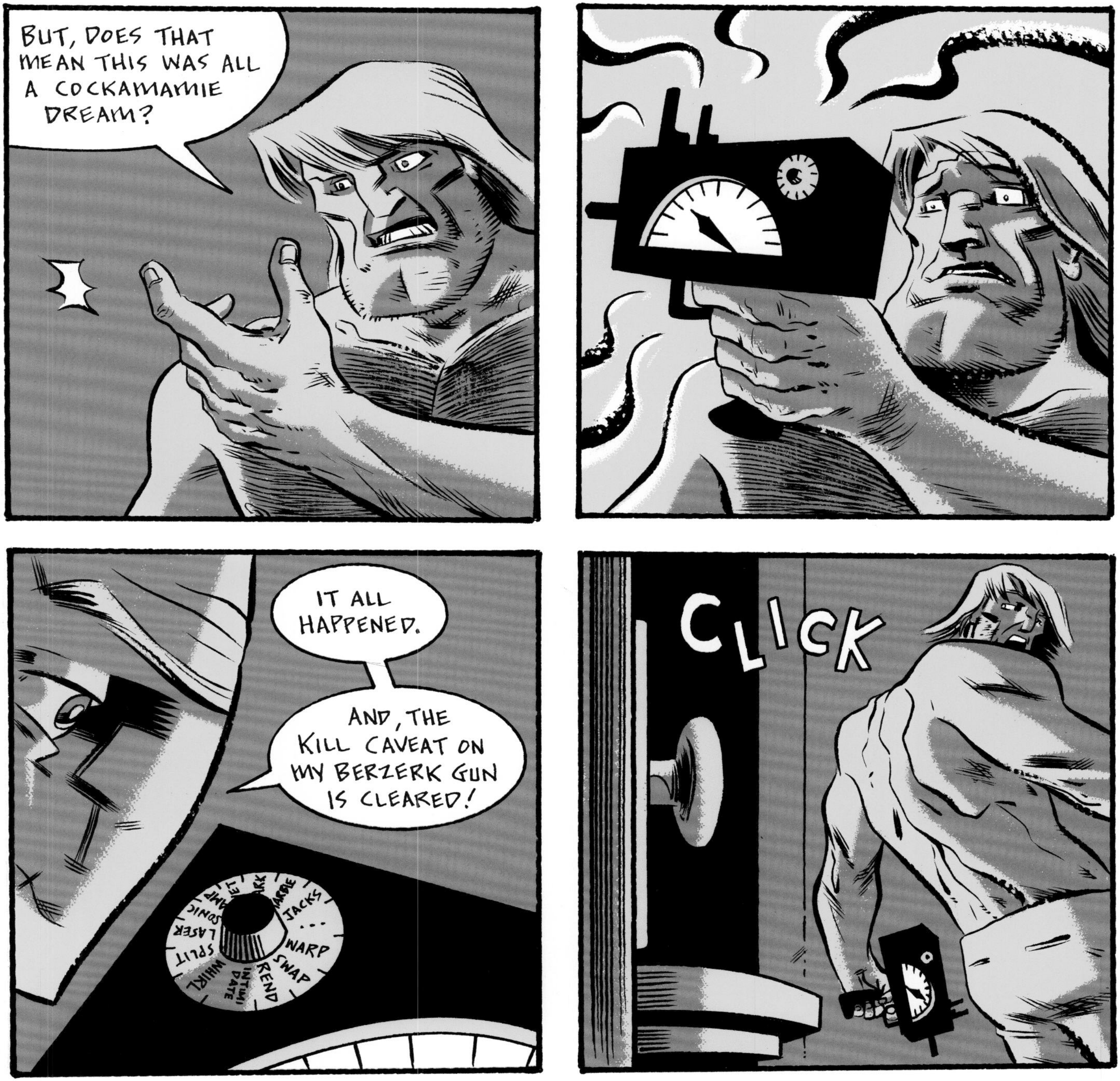
BUT, DOES THAT MEAN THIS WAS ALL A COCKAMAMIE DREAM?
IT ALL HAPPENED.
AND, THE KILL CAVEAT ON MY BERZERK GUN IS CLEARED!
JACKS
WARP
SWAP
REND
INTIMI DATE
WHIRL
SPLIT
LASER
SONIC
CLICK

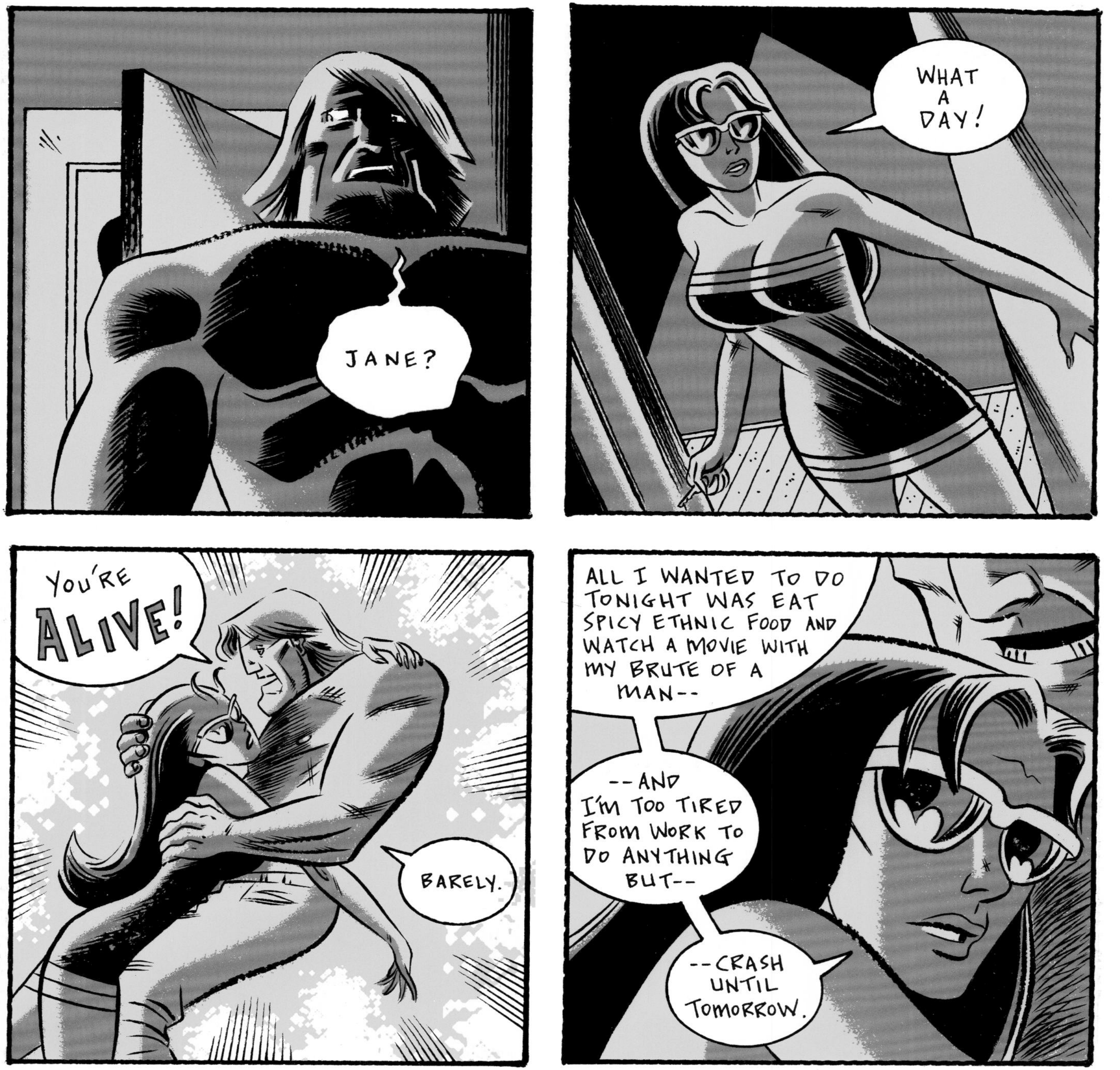
JANE?
WHAT A DAY!
YOU'RE ALIVE!
BARELY.
ALL I WANTED TO DO TONIGHT WAS EAT SPICY ETHNIC FOOD AND WATCH A MOVIE WITH MY BRUTE OF A MAN--
--AND I'M TOO TIRED FROM WORK TO DO ANYTHING BUT--
--CRASH UNTIL TOMORROW.

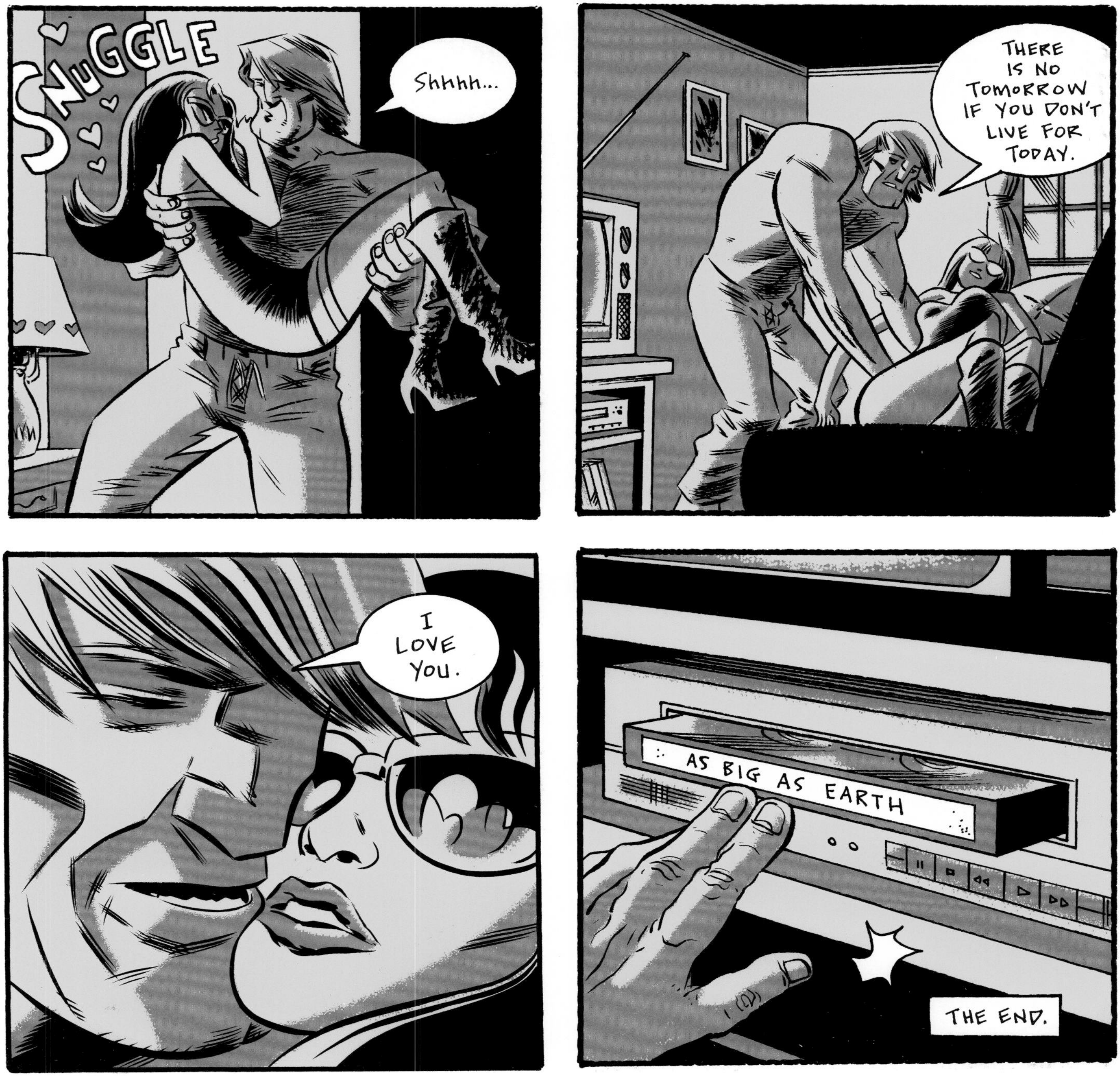
SNUGGLE
Shhhh...
THERE IS NO TOMORROW IF YOU DON'T LIVE FOR TODAY.
I LOVE YOU.
AS BIG AS EARTH
THE END.